S0-BSX-109

COMMUNITY POLICING

To
Mike Farrell

Colleague, Tutor, Friend,
and
Master Problem Solver

COMMUNITY POLICING
The CPOP in New York

Jerome E. McElroy
Colleen A. Cosgrove
Susan Sadd

Supported under award #87-IJ-CX-0006 from the National Institute of Justice, Office of Justice Programs, U.S. Department of Justice. Points of view in this document are those of the authors and do not necessarily represent the official position of the U.S. Department of Justice.

SAGE Publications
International Educational and Professional Publisher
Newbury Park   London   New Delhi

363.23
M14c

Copyright © 1993 by Sage Publications, Inc.

All rights reserved. No part of this book may be reproduced or utilized in any form or by any means, electronic or mechanical, including photocopying, recording, or by any information storage and retrieval system, without permission in writing from the publisher.

For information address:

 SAGE Publications, Inc.
2455 Teller Road
Newbury Park, California 91320

SAGE Publications Ltd.
6 Bonhill Street
London EC2A 4PU
United Kingdom

SAGE Publications India Pvt. Ltd.
M-32 Market
Greater Kailash I
New Delhi 110 048 India

Printed in the United States of America

Library of Congress Cataloging-in-Publication Data

McElroy, Jerome E.
   Community policing: the CPOP in New York / Jerome E. McElroy,
Colleen A. Cosgrove, Susan Sadd.
      p.   cm.
   Includes bibliographical references (pp. 246-250) and index.
   ISBN 0-8039-4789-5 (cl).—ISBN 0-8039-4790-9 (pb)
   1. Community policing—New York (N.Y.) I. Cosgrove, Colleen A.
II. Sadd, Susan. III. Title.
HV7936.C83M335 1993
363.2′3—dc20   92-29597

93 94 95 96 10 9 8 7 6 5 4 3 2 1

Sage Production Editor: Diane S. Foster

Contents

Acknowledgments

Expressing gratitude to those who have helped is usually a pleasure. But in the context of a project as long-running as this one, which required assistance from so many quarters, the pleasure is dulled some by the certainty that deserving friends will go unmentioned. We begin, then, with a grateful bow to those whose names do not appear, but who provided essential support nonetheless.

Benjamin Ward, as commissioner of the New York City Police Department, authorized the Community Patrol Officer Program (CPOP) as a pilot project, orchestrated its expansion throughout the department, and provided unstinting support inside and outside the department for both the program and the research. Thanks too to Robert Johnston, the chief of department, and to the various commanding officers and their staffs in the Patrol Services Bureau and the Office of Management Analysis and Planning for facilitating our execution of the demanding research design.

We owe particular thanks and respect to the police officers, CPOP sergeants, and commanding officers of the six precincts in which the research was conducted. If they saw us as threats or just as pests, they never let on, and they were always generous with their time and their frank appraisals of the program and of our efforts to assess it.

To James "Chips" Stewart and his staff at the National Institute of Justice, to William Betjemann and his staff at the New York State Division of Criminal Justice Services, to David Nee, formerly of the Florence Burden Foundation, to Craig Howard, formerly of the Ford

Foundation, to Oscar Straus of the Daniel and Florence Guggenheim Foundation, to Jody Weisbrod, formerly of the Norman Foundation, to Francine Lynch of Chase Manhattan Bank, and to Ann Dowling of the Philip Morris Companies, we say thank you for your capacities to couple financial support with the insight and encouragement researchers seek from professional colleagues.

Professors Jameson Doig of Princeton University, Herman Goldstein of the University of Wisconsin, and George Kelling of Northeastern and Harvard Universities served as members of the advisory committee from the very beginning of the project; Mark Moore of Harvard University joined the group toward the end, when we sought reactions to the draft of the final report. Their counsel in designing the research, their wisdom in helping us adjust to unanticipated turns in the road, and their help in identifying the concerns and findings of importance to the general professional audience were invaluable.

To conduct research of this sort at the Vera Institute of Justice is a particular pleasure. Even on the gloomiest midwinter day one finds colleagues willing to listen, advise, and encourage. But from among the many who gave of their time and expertise, several must be singled out.

Michael Farrell, whose understanding of policing and the NYPD is both comprehensive and detailed, and who was the principal architect and driving force behind CPOP, provided dispassionate advice on the research design, technical information about departmental and program operations, and sure guidance in securing access to offices and people in the department whose cooperation we needed. Mike was also the principal author of the two NYPD documents included here as appendixes.

Michael Smith, the director of Vera, inspired us with his enthusiasm for the project, empowered us with his fund-raising efforts on its behalf, and, through his sure grasp of the critical issues in American policing today, provided powerful substantive guidance in both the design of the research and the interpretation of the findings.

Sally Hillsman, longtime friend and colleague at Vera, performed wonderfully a role that few could manage at all. She was an unflagging source of support and encouragement, even as she put to us the hard questions about our research method and our substantive interpretations. She was surely born to the role of research director.

Although Michele Sviridoff was not a formal member of the project staff, she helped with its original design, generously shared her considerable knowledge of the literature on American policing, and inspired us with the sheer intellectual delight she projected when discussing what we were doing.

Professor David Weisburd of Rutgers University, whose reputation as a researcher on police is growing rapidly, actually found this interest when he came to work at Vera in 1984. David conducted Vera's exploratory research on the pilot CPOP project in the 72 Precinct and provided very important assistance in preparing the original design for this expanded research project. Although he left for the university before this project actually began, he remained an interested and helpful colleague throughout.

Lieutenant Thomas Madden, the police department's liaison officer to the Vera Institute, was always a ready source of information about the program's expansion and never failed to get us that piece of information about department regulations that we could not find anywhere else.

To those who served as the project's field researchers—Janet Weis, Tim Haft, Penny Shtull, and Anthony Petrosino—we are deeply grateful. These are the people who spent 6 months in each of the precincts—observing, conducting formal interviews, meticulously filling out other data collection forms, walking and riding patrol with the CPOs, sometimes at risk to their personal safety. In addition, they drafted memos describing their field observations and spent several hours each Friday briefing senior project staff on what was going on in the precincts and on the progress of their data collection efforts. They are truly the heroes of this research effort.

Finally, to Judy Woolcock, Delma McDonald, Scott Sparks, and Sarah Lyon, whose word-processing skills, limitless patience, and affable personalities served us so well, we thank you yet again.

Introduction

- The Why and the What of Community-Oriented Policing
- The Issues
- The Origins, Assumptions, and Essential Features of CPOP
- The Principal Concerns and General Design of the Research
- The Structure of the Book

The Why and the What of Community-Oriented Policing

Increasing numbers of street crimes, especially crimes of violence, a growing and openly competitive drug market, and the flight of small commercial establishments from the inner city provoked much concern and discussion during the 1980s about the crises of our cities and the role of the police in addressing them. The resulting literature reflects some consensus about the deficiencies of conventional urban policing, including:

- A recognition that reliance on the traditional tactics of preventive patrol, rapid response to citizen calls, and increasingly sophisticated investigative techniques offers little hope of improving crime-control performance (Kelling & Moore, 1988; Sparrow, Moore, & Kennedy 1990).
- A recognition that fear of crime is a serious matter in its own right, and that it is largely a product of perceived incivilities and signs of disorder on the neighborhood level (Skogan, 1990; Skogan, Lewis, Podelefsky, Dubow, & Gordon, 1982).
- A recognition that the police have not focused attention on such "quality of life" or "order maintenance" problems because of

1

their preoccupation with serious street crime and because their resources are largely consumed by mobile response to apparently disparate incidents. Whatever their merits, these tactics leave patrol officers relatively ignorant of the community's quality-of-life and order-maintenance concerns, and largely anonymous to community residents (Kelling & Moore, 1988; Skolnick & Bayley, 1986; Sparrow et al., 1990).

A strategy for correcting these deficiencies would appear to require, at least, the following elements: (a) an improved capacity to analyze crime and disorder problems in terms of the specific places, times, and situations in which they occur, as well as the people involved both as perpetrators and victims; (b) the deployment of police resources in accordance with a problem-solving plan based on these analyses (Goldstein, 1977, 1990; Eck & Spelman, 1989; Kelling & Moore, 1988); and (c) the design and implementation of these corrective strategies with input from and the cooperation of residents, merchants, and organizations immediately affected by them (Moore, Trojanowicz, & Kelling, 1988; Moore & Trojanowicz, 1988a, 1988b; Sparrow et al., 1990; Skogan, 1990).

The decade of the eighties has seen a number of police agencies implement projects and initiate departmental reorganization schemes embodying these elements. In addition, several research studies designed to describe the new programs and measure their effects on crime rates, fear levels, and the volume of calls-for-service have been carried out, many with the assistance of the National Institute of Justice (Eck & Spelman, 1989; Goldstein, 1990; Police Foundation, 1981; Skogan, 1990; Trojanowicz, 1983; Weisburd & McElroy, 1988; Farrell, 1988). The results of those studies and debates (often heated) over their meaning and implications began to appear in the literature during the latter part of the decade. This debate has been stimulated and fed by the series of papers emanating from the multiyear Executive Session on Policing sponsored by Harvard University's John F. Kennedy School of Government. Indeed, the products of those sessions have given much impetus to what is now perceived as the community policing movement and have helped to bring to the surface a wide range of issues related to it.

The police initiatives that are typically subsumed under the community policing rubric take many forms, but, according to David Bayley (1988), the four principal elements they appear to have in common are: "(1) community-based crime prevention, (2) proactive servicing as opposed to emergency response, (3) public participation in the planning and supervision of police operations, and (4) shifting of command responsibility to lower rank levels" (p. 226).

Kelling and Moore (1988), who see community policing as a newly evolved strategy of policing, describe the major elements of its character as follows:

> *Source of authority*—community support (political), law, professionalism
>
> *Function*—crime control, crime prevention, problem solving
>
> *Organizational design*—decentralized, task forces, matrices
>
> *Relationship to environment*—consultative, police defend values of law and professionalism, but listen to community concerns
>
> *Demand*—channeled through analysis of underlying problems
>
> *Tactics and technology*—foot patrol, problem solving, and so forth
>
> *Outcomes*—quality of life and citizen satisfaction (p. 13)

The Issues   The books, articles, and conference papers about community policing produced in the last few years reflect a large measure of agreement about the deficiencies of traditional police operations and organization, but they also surface a substantial number of reservations about community policing as remedy. Is community policing properly conceived as representing a radical break with the era of "professionalism" that has dominated American policing for the last 50 years, or is it merely a tactical refinement of that paradigm (Hartmann, 1988; Moore & Trojanowicz, 1988a; Kelling, 1988; Goldstein, 1990; Greene, 1989; Sparrow et al., 1990)? What has that evolutionary process meant to minority groups in the United States, and what stake do such groups have in the debate today (Williams & Murphy, 1990)? Does community policing actually portend a meaningful change in police operations and organization, or is it, in the words of Peter Manning, "a contrapuntal theme: harmony for the old melody. It now seeks control of the public by a reduction in social distance, a merging of communal and police interests, and a service and crime control isomorphism" (1988, p.28)?

Carl Klockars (1988), reflecting on the work of Egon Bittner (1967), describes community policing as the latest in a series of societal "circumlocutions" developed to help us live with the disquieting fact that the police are the institution with a "monopoly on a general right to use force." He says that the disturbing nature of that fact requires that society "wrap it in concealments and circumlocutions that sponsor the appearance that police are either something other than what they are or are principally engaged in doing something else" (p. 257). He suggests that in this regard, community policing may serve the same function as the rhetoric of legalization, militarization, and professionalization in earlier periods. While Klockars is sharp in critiquing many of community policing's underlying assumptions, it is not entirely clear whether he expects this rhetoric to have any real effects on the operations and organization of American police.

Virtually all commentators agree that the concept of "community" as used in the rhetoric of community policing is imprecise, perhaps interchangeable with the concepts of neighborhood, district, or beat, and largely uninformed by a century of sociological usage and study. This lack of precision has implications not only for how operational boundaries are drawn by police agencies, but, more important, for the assumptions they make about order and consensus in the areas in which they work, the social processes and structures to which the police relate, the kinds of problems to which they give their attention, the objectives they establish, and the variables and methods used to measure accomplishments (Mastrofski, 1988; Klockars, 1988; Bayley, 1988; Greene & Taylor, 1988; Kelling & Stewart, 1989; Kelling & Moore, 1988; Hartmann, 1988; Greene, 1989; Williams & Murphy, 1990; Skogan, 1990).

The community policing strategy seeks to have an impact on the levels of reported crime, the extent and nature of public-disorder problems on the neighborhood level, the level of citizen fear of crime, and the volume of calls-for-service received by the police agency. These are ambitious goals. In the seminal article by Wilson and Kelling, "Broken Windows" (1982), a theoretical scheme is offered that links disorder both to fear and to crime. But empirical research on the impact of community policing is sparse, and the results so far are inconsistent and mixed at best (Trojanowicz, 1983; Moore & Trojanowicz, 1988b; Moore et al., 1988; Skogan, 1990).

Greene and Taylor (1988) subjected Wilson and Kelling's hypothesized linkages between disorder, fear, and crime to empirical tests using data from a variety of studies. They found no evidence to support the hypothesized link between incivilities and a weakening of informal social controls; they found some evidence that "confirms an independent linkage between incivilities and fear, but suggests that the linkage is conditional, obtaining only for particular types of neighborhoods"; and they found evidence indicating that the apparent linkage between incivilities and crime is "largely driven by the linkage of both concepts with social class and does not exist independently" (p. 202).

Skogan's research leads him to a somewhat different conclusion regarding the impact of disorder on crime and the viability of the Wilson-Kelling hypothesis. On the causative effects of disorder on crime, he summarizes his findings as follows:

> The evidence suggests that poverty, instability, and the racial composition of neighborhoods are strongly linked to area crime, but a substantial portion of that linkage is through disorder: Their link to area crime virtually disappears when disorder is brought into the picture. This too is consistent with Wilson and Kelling's original proposition, and further evidence that direct action against disorder could have substantial payoffs. (1990, p. 75)

Greene and Taylor also reviewed the results of research on community policing projects in Newark, Oakland, San Diego, Houston, Boston, and Baltimore County, and concluded that the results are inconsistent and marred by deficiencies in the research designs. More time and additional research are needed before the success of community policing projects can be properly assessed.

Commentators have expressed numerous reservations about the potential effects of community policing, which serve as useful cautionary notes at this stage. These include:

- The rhetoric of community policing's proponents will create expectations that are impossible to meet (Klockars, 1988; Manning, 1988).
- The crime control mission of the police could get lost in the context of community policing's multiple goals (Bayley, 1988; Klockars, 1988; Hartmann, 1988).
- Community organizing efforts of the police could produce nothing more than a political action group sustained and directed by the police themselves (Klockars, 1988; Bayley, 1988).
- The police could themselves be co-opted by the community and lose the will to maintain public order (Bayley, 1988).
- The police could extend their reach undesirably far into the social and cultural life of the community (Bayley, 1988).
- The interests of minorities in the neighborhoods could go unprotected by the police because of their desire to be responsive to the wishes of the majority (Bayley, 1988; Mastrofski, 1988; Manning, 1988; Williams & Murphy, 1990; Skogan, 1990).
- The shift in supervisory responsibilities and styles required by community policing might not be made effectively, with a consequent increase in police corruption or abusive behavior (Bayley, 1988; Wasserman & Moore, 1988).

Finally, the literature on community policing cries out for empirical answers to a wide range of questions regarding what police officers actually do in the name of community policing (Manning, 1988); whether the officers are especially resistive to, or notably unprepared for particular community-policing tasks; how they react to their new assignments and how they are perceived by other officers (Trojanowicz, 1983); whether the officers actually change their perceptions of and attitudes toward neighborhoods in which they work and, if so, how (Manning, 1988); the nature and extent of community involvement in problem-solving efforts of the police (Goldstein, 1990; Kelling & Stewart, 1989); how the supervision and management of community policing efforts is actually carried out (Wasserman & Moore, 1988; Kelling, Wasserman, & Williams, 1988; Bayley, 1988; Weisburd, McElroy, & Hardyman, 1988; Sparrow et al., 1990).

The research reported here provides empirical grist for the police administrators, policymakers, and academics who are milling these questions. The findings go principally to questions of implementation, role performance, perceptions and attitudes of police officers, the selection of problems and the development of problem-solving strategies, the efforts of the officers to involve elements of the community in the problem-solving process, and the nature of the supervisory changes required by the program and the negative consequences of ineffective supervision. In addition, the book reveals some of the difficulties involved in measuring the impact of problem-solving strategies. While the study does not address directly the global issues presented by community policing's candidacy as the grand design for reorganization of police services in America, it provides much useful information about the feasibility of implementing it.

The research described here is an effort by the Vera Institute of Justice to study and evaluate a community-oriented, problem-solving policing program launched by the New York City Police Department (NYPD) in July 1984 as a pilot project in a single precinct and expanded to all 75 city police precincts by the end of September 1988. The Community Patrol Officer Program (CPOP) was designed to reflect what was known about community-oriented patrol in the early and mid-1980s, and it presented an opportunity to explore some of the questions identified above.

The Origins, Assumptions, and Essential Features of CPOP

In the second half of the 1970s, the profound fiscal crisis experienced by New York City resulted in the police department's loss of almost 10,000 noncivilian positions. Yet, the volume of calls-for-service received over the 911 system rose throughout the period (now estimated in excess of eight million calls). In response, an ever-increasing proportion of the patrol force was assigned to answering these calls, the resources available to precinct commanders for flexible deployment against local problems were reduced sharply, and the police accorded less and less attention to the problems of disorder that troubled the people. These problems, referred to in New York as "precinct conditions" or "quality of life" conditions, tended to worsen for a variety of reasons, including official neglect.

During the same period, the problem of street-level drug dealing, both a crime and a quality-of-life problem, arose in neighborhoods where it had never existed before. As a matter of policy at the time, the NYPD did not attack street-level dealing aggressively, but rather focused its narcotics enforcement resources on the detection, apprehension, and prosecution of major traffickers and the disruption of their supply and distribution systems. Given the extraordinary personnel retrenchment the department experienced between 1975 and 1981, that policy became more compelling. In the meantime, however, the problem spread and, with the advent of "crack" in the mid-1980s, it emerged as the problem about which the people of the city were most intensely concerned.

In 1982, having turned the corner on the fiscal crisis, the department began to hire new officers in large numbers. The Vera Institute of Justice, a consultant to the department for many years, was invited to help determine how best to use the new resources becoming available to the Patrol Services Bureau. Toward that end, senior staff at Vera interviewed the department's senior managers, all of the borough commanders, and many of the precinct commanders to elicit their perceptions of the problems and needs faced by the patrol force and their views on how new resources might be deployed most effectively to address these problems. In addition, Vera circulated a questionnaire to all precinct commanders soliciting information about the organizational structure of the precinct, the number and characteristics of patrol officers assigned there, the methods used to allocate these resources across tours and sectors, and the nature of the special patrol programs or units operating in the precinct, if any. Finally, Vera staff conducted an extensive review of the research and policy literature dealing with the patrol function.

This planning exercise resulted in a proposal to create a demonstration project, called the Community Patrol Officer Program (CPOP), in the 72 Precinct in Brooklyn, to study and report on the pilot project and, if the results merited it, to begin expanding it to other precincts in the city. The project was seen as an effort by the NYPD to embody the major principles of community-oriented and problem-solving policing in a new role to be performed by patrol officers at the precinct level. In a document entitled *The Community Patrol Officer Program: Orientation Guide* (1987), the department spelled out its view of those principles as follows:

> Community policing might best be described as a philosophical position which holds that the goals of policing, the conditions which it addresses, the services it delivers, the means used to deliver them, and the assessment of its adequacy should be formulated and developed in recognition of the distinctive experience, needs and norms of local communities as well as the dictates of law and prudent procedural regulations. . . . Operation Pressure Point [is another] department initiative [that is] rooted in this philosophy as are a wide variety of programs now being implemented by major departments throughout the country. Although these efforts differ from each other in important respects, the following operational and organizational principles appear to be more or less common to all:
>
> - continuous assignment of police units to specific neighborhoods or beats
> - insistence that the unit develop and maintain a knowledge base regarding the problems, cultural characteristics, and resources of the neighborhood
> - emphasis on the importance of the unit's reaching out to neighborhood residents and business people to assure them of the presence and concern of the police

- use of formal and informal mechanisms to involve community people in identifying, analyzing, and establishing priorities among local problems and in developing and implementing action plans for ameliorating them
- delegation of responsibility to the community police unit for addressing both the crime and order-maintenance problems of the neighborhood and expansion of the unit's discretion in fashioning solutions to those problems
- emphasis on increasing information flow from the community to the police and on the use of that information by various elements of the police agency to make important arrests and to develop important intelligence on illegal enterprises in the community
- sharing with representatives of the community accurate information on local crime problems and the results of on-going efforts to address them (p. 4)

CPOP was designed to operate as a special unit within the precinct. Typically, the units consist of 10 police officers, called Community Patrol Officers (CPOs), and a supervising sergeant reporting directly to the precinct's Commanding Officer (CO), usually a captain. Although the members of the unit sometimes take action together in the community, the principal actor is the individual CPO taking responsibility for addressing crime and order-maintenance problems within the beat to which he or she is permanently assigned. The beats are geographical areas ranging in size from 16 to 60 square blocks, which are characterized by residential or mixed residential/commercial land use patterns. The starting and ending times for the CPO's tour are set by the officer, with the approval of the sergeant, ostensibly to coincide with the time periods in which the problems of the beat are most evident. To enhance the accessibility of the CPO to the people, the officer usually patrols the beat on foot.

The role CPOs are expected to perform differs considerably from the role of the conventional patrol officer in the NYPD, with respect to both the officer's responsibilities and the manner in which the department structures the officer's time. The CPO's new responsibilities are described and assessed in detail in the pages that follow. The differences in the structuring of patrol time must be understood from the beginning.

At the time that CPOP was introduced, regular patrol officers changed tours every week and were assigned different regular days off (RDOs). CPOs, on the other hand, were authorized to vary their working hours and RDOs, with the approval of their sergeant, in response to the particular problems of their beats. Such flexibility was considered highly desirable by most police officers. Furthermore, whereas the majority of regular patrol officers move about in radio cars answering calls-for-service at the direction of the 911 dispatcher, the CPOs were specifically removed from the dispatcher's queue. This feature was considered necessary to ensure that the CPOs had sufficient time to carry out their additional responsibilities. Nevertheless, it was perceived as a major perquisite of the job.

The requirement that each CPO maintain a Beat Book was another perceived burden. The Beat Book contained the CPO's monthly work plan and imposed a "paperwork" demand on the officer. The task called for the recording of information on beat problems, priorities, corrective strategies, implementation progress, community organizations/community leaders, and commercial premises, among other items. The CPO's disdain for this dimension of the role never waned during the research period.

On the other hand, the fact that CPOs were expected to patrol alone, rather than with a partner; the fact that they were often assigned to very large beats, which they were to patrol on foot; and the fact that the value of the new role within the departmental "career path" was not well defined, represented structural differences that were widely perceived as undesirable.

The core of the program, then, is the CPO role, especially its problem-solving dimension. The role was designed to foster officer accountability for correcting problems at the neighborhood level, increase the officer's knowledge of and identification with the community to which he or she is assigned, and encourage the officer to take an active role in assisting the people of the community to identify and correct the quality-of-life problems that they find most disturbing.

The four major dimensions of the role have been described by Michael Farrell (1988), an associate director at the Vera Institute and the principal architect of the program, as follows:

Planner

The first responsibility of the CPOs would be to identify the principal crime and order-maintenance problems confronting the people within each beat area. Toward this end the CPOs would be expected to examine relevant statistical materials, record their own observations as they patrol their beats, and solicit and secure input from residents, merchants, and service delivery agents in the community. The problems identified would then be prioritized and analyzed and corrective strategies designed. These strategies would be reviewed with the Unit Supervisor and incorporated in the CPO's Monthly Work Plan, which would form the focus of the officer's patrol for the coming month.

Problem Solver

CPOs would be encouraged to see themselves as problem solvers for the community. This begins with the planning dimension of the role described above, and proceeds to the implementation of the action strategies. In the implementation phase, the officer would be encouraged to mobilize and guide four types of resources against beat area problems: the CPO acting as a law enforcement officer; other police resources on the precinct and borough levels that can be brought to bear through the CPO sergeant and the precinct commander; other public and private service agencies operating, or available to operate, in the beat area; and individual citizens or organizations in that community. The strategies developed by the CPO would call for the application of any or all of these resources, and the CPO's success in resolving the problems identified would turn in large part on his or her success in marshalling them and in coordinating their application.

Community Organizer

Community resources cannot be brought to bear on crime and quality-of-life problems unless the community is willing to commit them for that purpose. Increasing the consciousness of the community about its problems, involving community people and organizations in developing strategies to address the problems, motivating the people to help in implementing the strategies, and coordinating their action so that they may contribute maximally to the solution are all aspects of the community organizing dimension of the CPO role. The CPOs would be required to identify potential resources and, where they are not adequate, to help in organizing and motivating the citizenry.

Information Exchange Link

Through his or her links to the community, the CPO would be in a position to provide the department with information about problem conditions and locations, active criminals, developing gangs, illicit networks for trafficking in drugs and stolen property, information about citizen's fears, and insights into their perceptions of police tactics. In turn, the CPO could provide citizens with information pertinent to their fears and problems, technical information and advice for preventing crimes and reducing the vulnerability of particular groups of citizens, information about the police view of conditions in the neighborhood and strategies for addressing them, and information about police operations in the community. This information exchange aspect of the CPO role was expected to result in arrests that might not occur otherwise, greater cooperation between the police and citizens in addressing crime and order maintenance problems, and a heightened sense in the citizenry that the police are a concerned and powerful resource for improving the quality of life in the community.

The CPOP pilot project began in the 72 Precinct in Brooklyn in July 1984. After only a few months of operation, the department decided to expand the program to other precincts. Expansion began in January of 1985 and continued, slowed occasionally by budget concerns in the city, until late September 1988, when the program became operational in the last of the city's 75 precincts. Thus, as of this writing, CPOP is operating throughout the city and, on a given day, involves approximately 750 police officers and 75 sergeants.[1]

The Principal Concerns and General Design of the Research

Members of the Vera Institute's Research Department spent a year in an exploratory study of the pilot project in the 72 Precinct (Weisburd et al., 1988). The department's decision to expand the program to other precincts was made long before this study was completed; nevertheless, the experience and insights gained in studying the pilot enabled Vera research staff to design a more comprehensive piece of research that could be carried on in several precincts simultaneously. The design was completed, financial support for it was secured,[2] and the additional staff needed to plan and implement it were hired in July 1986. The formal data collection period began in December 1986 and ran through February 1988.

The research was guided both by practical and by theoretical interests. The department hoped this research would provide information that would enable the program managers to improve CPOP operations even before the research was completed. The staff at Vera hoped that it would also shed some light on some of the questions that police scholars had raised concerning community-oriented and problem-solving policing. It was thought that addressing the principal questions set forth below would enable the research staff to satisfy both of those objectives.

1. Can regular police officers implement all four dimensions of the CPO role? What are the major obstacles to implementation, and how do the officers adjust to them?
2. How do they react to the role in terms of their job satisfaction and their image of themselves as police officers? What features of the role do they like or dislike especially?
3. How do CPOs attempt to establish relationships with the community and involve community representatives in the problem-solving process? How effective are they at this aspect of the role?
4. How well do the officers implement the problem-solving process? Are particular aspects of that process more difficult for the officers to master than others, and, if so, why? Are there characteristics of background and experience that appear to prepare them well for effective performance?

5. What kinds of neighborhood problems are identified using this process? What kinds of strategies are developed by the CPOs, and what strategies appear most effective in dealing with particular problems?

6. To what extent does the content and effectiveness of the problem-solving process vary by the organizational characteristics of the beat?

7. What sort of challenges to conventional models of supervision are posed by the community-oriented, problem-solving aspects of the CPO role? How are these challenges met, if at all?

8. What is the impact of CPOP, if any, on the volume of calls-for-service and robbery and burglary complaints?

9. What is the nature of community reaction to the program?

10. What steps did the department take to institutionalize the program and to spread its influence throughout the Patrol Bureau?

To address these questions, the research staff developed a strategy that focused detailed attention on 6 of the 37 precincts in which the CPO program was operating in August 1986.[3] One precinct was selected from each borough command, except Staten Island, on the assumption that the specific procedures of the CPOP units might differ somewhat under the different borough commanders. In making the selections, the research staff were looking for precincts that were experiencing at least moderate levels of calls-for-service and crimes reported; that, when considered together, offered a reasonable degree of racial, ethnic, and socioeconomic heterogeneity; and that, on the basis of a necessarily superficial initial assessment, appeared to have reasonably well-functioning CPOP units at the time of the selection.

All the beats within each of the six precincts were included in the research, so that the CPOP unit dimension of the program could be studied as well as the activities of individual CPOs. In fact, no other feasible strategy would have permitted the staff to study CPOP supervision. Thus at the start of the data collection, the sample included 54 beats, an equal number of CPOs, and six supervising sergeants.

A full-time research assistant, called the field researcher, was assigned to each research precinct for 6 months to observe the activities of each of the unit members, problematic conditions in the community, strategy implementation efforts of the officers (and the effects of those efforts on the targeted problems), and interactions between the CPOs and other police personnel in the precinct. The time period was thought sufficient to permit the field researchers to discuss these matters informally with the officers and to talk with members of the community about community problems and program activities.

Structured interviews with each of the officers were conducted at the beginning and at the end of the data collection period. The initial interviews focused on: the officer's experiences in the department prior to joining CPOP; the reasons for deciding to join the program; his or her knowledge of and expectations about the program prior to joining; the officer's perceptions of and attitudes toward the community prior to becoming a CPO; the features of the program that the officer liked and those he or she disliked especially; those aspects of the role with which the officer had most difficulty, and why he or she believed them to be difficult; and what the officer wanted to be doing and the rank he or she hoped to hold in the department 5 years in the future.

At the end of the 6-month data collection period, another structured interview was conducted with each CPO. This interview sought some similar perceptual and attitudinal data in the hopes of determining whether any measurable change had occurred over that period. This Time-2 interview also solicited information regarding how the officer distributed his or her time across a number of tasks associated with the role, whether the role was preferred to that of the regular Radio Motor Patrol (RMP) officer and why, whether the officer thought that the program produced benefits for the community and/or for the department, and the steps the officer would like to see taken to improve the program.

The field researchers were instructed to identify three to five crime or quality-of-life problems that each CPO considered as priority concerns in his or her beat. For that purpose, the field researchers reviewed the officer's Beat Book and then asked the officer directly to designate such problems. A structured data collection instrument, called the "Problem Process Record" (PPR) was completed by the field researcher on the priority problems that each officer identified and worked on within his or her beat over the course of the 6-month data collection period. The PPR called for the collection of information about the nature of the problem identified and the process by which it was identified; the nature of the analytic process that the officer carried out with respect to the problem, and the major findings that it produced; the nature of the strategy that the officer designed to correct the problem, and the extent to which representatives of the community were involved in design and implementation; the extent to which the components of the strategy were implemented and what, if anything, the officer did when others were failing to carry out their responsibilities within the strategy; the apparent impact of the strategy on the problem identified.

The research staff attempted to use five indicators of impact on the problem: (a) the officer's assessment of impact, (b) the sergeant's assessment, (c) the researcher's assessment, (d) the assessments provided by a small sample of residents and merchants who lived and/or operated in immediate proximity to the problem, and (e) statistical or archival data where pertinent.

Using the PPRs as data sources, a scale was constructed for assessing the problem-solving performance of each of the officers on each of the problems with which he or she dealt. The scale uses subscales for different dimensions of the task: (a) problem identification and analysis, (b) strategy development, (c) strategy implementation, and (d) community involvement.

In-depth interviews were conducted with the sergeants and the commanding officers toward the end of the research period in each precinct. The sergeants were also asked to assess the overall performance of their officers on a questionnaire that the research staff had prepared for that purpose.

These data are used here principally to describe and assess the efforts of police officers attempting to carry out a problem-solving process on the neighborhood level. The aim of the material presented in Chapters 3 and 4 is to describe what happens when a department attempts to implement community policing on a broad scale. We expected to encounter notable individual successes and failures, but our research sought to describe the median performance level for the 750 officers who were serving as CPOs at the time the research was being done. We wished to estimate the level of productivity that the department could expect from the average unit, from the average CPO. This required a focus on those elements of the problem-solving process that were performed well and those that were performed poorly, in order to identify modifications that could produce higher levels of performance generally.

Some very good work has been done (see Eck & Spelman, 1989) in describing models of effective problem-solving police activities. Indeed, the nine case studies presented in Appendix A ("CPOP: Community Policing in Practice") perform that service ably, but that is not the intent in the main body of this document.

Nor was it our intention to describe and assess various strategies for addressing particular problems. That would have required considerably more time and resources than we had available, as well as a considerably larger pool of problems to study. In fact, one of the recommendations emerging from our study is that the department undertake the preparation of problem-specific manuals, each of which would describe and evaluate various strategies and tactics used to address a specific problem such as street drug trafficking.

Data describing some of the demographic characteristics of patrol officers in the department were collected from the Personnel Division to determine how and to what extent the officers in the research sample differed from their patrol colleagues in general. Data concerning civilian complaints made against the sample members were collected from the Civilian Complaint Review Board (CCRB), and data about corruption complaints against the officers were collected from the Internal Affairs Division.

Finally, members of the research staff, especially the research director, had frequent opportunities to interact with CPOs, supervising sergeants, and precinct commanders from many other precincts in which the program operated. These contacts, though largely informal, provided another source of information on the program. In some cases, they provided insights into program-related concerns that never arose in the research precincts. In other instances, the contacts in the non-research precincts were helpful in estimating whether patterns observed in the research precincts were generally true elsewhere.

Program Effects on Reported Robberies, Burglaries, and Calls-for-Service

While the CPO program was designed to identify and ameliorate quality-of-life problems in neighborhoods, the program design also recognized that these activities might have an impact, as well, on the volume of conventional street crimes in the neighborhood. This could occur directly, if the problem-solving process focused on such a crime as a priority concern of the residents, and if its corrective strategies were effective. Or, as suggested by Wilson and Kelling (1982), it could occur as an indirect effect of the program's success in addressing a neighborhood's quality-of-life problems.

The program designers also recognized the possibility that CPOP might affect the volume and nature of calls-for-service emanating from the beats in which the program operated. There were several reasons for seeing this as a conceivable program effect. First, the CPOs were instructed to encourage community residents to contact them directly, rather than using the 911 system, for concerns and problems that were not of an emergency nature. To receive such calls, each CPOP unit was given its own phone, covered during the day by the program's administrative aide, and an answering machine on which a caller could leave a message for any CPO when no one in the unit was available to take the call. Second, research findings published by Trojanowicz (1983) reported that the Foot Patrol Program in Flint, Michigan had produced a sizable reduction in calls-for-service coming from the neighborhoods in which the program operated.

Although no one seriously expected the program to show significant effects on the volume and nature of conventional street crime complaints and calls-for-service for at least a few years after implementation began, everyone wished to see whether there was any evidence of such a change. Toward that end, data on robberies, burglaries, and calls-for-service were assembled and analyzed.

The precinct was used as the unit of analysis, rather than the beat, both because the number of incidents at the beat level tend to be small and because the resources required to do an effective analysis on the beat level would have been prohibitive. Instead, the analysis compared all 37 of the precincts in which CPOP was operating at the time the research began with the 38 in which it had not begun by then. In addition, before-and-after comparisons were carried out for both CPOP and non-CPOP precincts.

The methods used to construct this analysis and the results of the various statistical tests applied are described by the authors in a separate paper, which is available upon request (Sadd, 1989). However, because the conditions were not right for formal hypothesis testing, and because this document is principally concerned with issues of implementation in the department and in the community, the details of those analyses are not presented here. It suffices here to say that these analyses failed to produce evidence that the CPO program reduced reported burglaries or calls-for-service on the precinct level during either the first or second year of the program's operation. Evidence indicated a weak effect on the level of reported robberies during the first year, but none continuing into the second year.

In the opinion of the authors, these findings are neither surprising nor discouraging. As will be seen in subsequent chapters, CPOs in the research precincts rarely identified robberies or burglaries as priority problems in their beats, so they were rarely the object of concerted problem-solving efforts. In a few instances, attention was given to the concentration of burglaries in a small portion of a beat, and some evidence suggested that the volume of that crime dropped in those areas while the strategy was being carried out. Nevertheless, unless the beats covered a very large proportion of the precinct, and all of the CPOs focused their problem-solving efforts on the burglary problem in their respective beats, a significant precinctwide reduction in the volume of burglary would be unlikely to occur. The same is true for the robbery problem.

Some evidence in the research precincts showed that the incidence of burglaries and robberies could be reduced by effective efforts to combat the drug problem in selected locations. Specifically, in a few instances, where an officer's anti-narcotics strategies were widely perceived to be effective, the number of robberies, burglaries, assaults, and larcenies committed in the immediate vicinity of that location went down noticeably. Again, however, these efforts are not likely to have an effect on the annual volume of such crime reports unless they extend to many locations throughout the precinct and continue for extended time periods.

With regard to calls-for-service, it is possible that the CPO program has two effects that cancel each other out. On the one hand, CPOs may encourage community residents and merchants to call the CPOP office concerning nonemergency problems and, thereby, reduce somewhat the volume of calls made to 911. On the other hand, the implementation of CPOP may also increase the residents' expectations regarding the willingness of the police to take action on crime and quality-of-life problems, thereby increasing the volume of calls-for-service.

As previously indicated, the hoped-for effect on calls-for-service in New York was provoked by Trojanowicz's 1983 report that calls-for-service in the experimental foot patrol areas of Flint fell by 43.4% over the 3 years of program operation. After careful investigation, it appears that the meaning of the term *calls-for-service* in Flint is dramatically different from what the indicator means in New York City. In New York, the term refers to all calls made to the police over the 911 emergency system. In 1988, approximately eight million such calls were received, with police units dispatched on half that number. The volume has been climbing every year since the system went into effect. In the Flint study, the term appears to apply only to those conditions that result in citizens completing a formal complaint report.

Finally, it is worth repeating the caution that the failure to find precinct-level impacts on robberies and burglaries does not mean that the CPO program does not or cannot affect such conditions. Evidence suggests that such effects can be achieved in limited areas when CPOs focus the problem-solving process on those problems. Of course, such effects will be welcomed by the residents of those areas, but they will not be reflected in precinctwide statistics without a comparable focus in other high-incidence areas within the precinct. That could happen as CPOs become more adept at problem solving and precinct commanders become more adept at using other precinct resources to implement effective problem-solving strategies more widely.

The Uniqueness of Vera's Role   The Vera Institute of Justice has been intimately involved with CPOP from the beginning. Vera program staff were responsible, solely or in part, for the following developments: the planning research that generated the idea for CPOP, converting that idea into a program model and a set of program operations that they believed might work in the NYPD, securing the support of department officials for the conduct of a pilot project, and overseeing operations of the pilot project in the 72 Precinct. They also collaborated with department officials in preparing and implementing the plan by which CPOP was expanded to all precincts, designing and organizing the 80-hour orientation and training program used to initiate the program in each precinct, delivering many of the training lectures, and designing and delivering much of the 4-hour training and orientation program provided to all command level personnel in the Patrol Services Bureau. Vera program staff were responsible for an important audit of CPOP operations in the first 21 precincts to which it was expanded, and prepared a report and recommendations for strengthening the program, to which the police commissioner and senior officials of the department responded by adopting major revisions to the CPOP model and the citywide structure supporting it. Finally, Vera program staff designed and carried out a supplemental program of training in community policing for supervisors; they designed and secured outside financial support for a program of intensive training in the problem-solving process for CPOs; and they delivered that training to CPOP units throughout the city.

Vera's Associate Director for Police Planning, Michael Farrell, was responsible for the program development tasks outlined above. But he collaborated in that work with staff on the research side of the institute. The principal author of this report, and the person responsible for directing this research, was Vera's Associate Director for Research. While it is customary to emphasize an arm's-length distance between the personnel studying a program and those with significant responsibilities for its development and operation, that ordinarily desirable condition could not be achieved in this case. We did not strive for rigid separation between the program and the research staff. Rather, throughout this research, Vera's associate directors for police planning and for research met regularly with each other and with policymakers in the department, including the commissioner, in order to bring interim research findings to bear on the continuing evolution of the CPOP program itself.[4]

This blurring of the lines separating program from research, despite the probable gains in program development efficacy, may give rise to reservations about the neutrality and objectivity of the research. Those reservations are legitimate, in our view. They may be alleviated somewhat by a forthright exposition of how the conventional separations were shunned in this case. In the end, however, the reader must be satisfied that the researchers asked the right research questions; used data collection instruments that would provide them with the information needed to address those questions; used, within the limits of feasibility, the most appropriate logic for analyzing the data; and drew conclusions about the program that are supported by those analyses. We believe that a reader applying those criteria will be satisfied with the objectivity of this book.

It is generally true that the research staff for this study hoped to find clear and decisive evidence of the program's success. That sentiment flowed not only from the involvement of their colleagues in Vera's program staff in the design and management of CPOP, but also from these researchers' belief that the principles of community-oriented and problem-solving policing were commendable ones for an urban police department to pursue, and that the CPO program, in design at least, was an appropriate vehicle for those principles in the NYPD. Despite these hopes, loyalties, and beliefs, the research evidence reported here is not a clarion of CPOP's unambiguous successes. But it remains the case that our reports of shortcomings in program implementation, manifestations of inadequate understanding of, or skill in performing, various CPO tasks, and the need for more leadership and attention from command personnel are all made with an expectation that remedies will be found.

Although the tone of the book reflects the generally positive disposition of the research team toward at least the principles that underlie the CPOP program, it is clear that CPOP is not without flaws. But not one of those flaws, nor all of them in concert, suggests a fundamental inappropriateness or unworkability of the CPOP model in the context of the NYPD. If a bias exists here, it is our belief that shortcomings should be expected, that CPOP represents a reasonably successful effort to move the department in a desirable direction, and that the failings can and should be corrected with time, patience, and renewed effort.

***The Present
Status of
Community
Policing in
the NYPD***
The research described in this book was completed in 1989. Under Commissioner Benjamin Ward, the department had created CPOP, expanded it to all 75 precincts, and provided for a fair amount of training for command, supervisory, and field personnel in the Patrol Services Bureau. Commissioner Ward's personal contributions to the implementation of the program are detailed in Chapter 6. Ward left in mid-1989 and was eventually replaced by Lee Brown, who had introduced community policing and a number of related innovations in Houston, Texas. He immediately signaled his intention to expand the initiative from that of a special program operating in each precinct into a corporate strategy for focusing, organizing, delivering, and assessing police services throughout the NYPD.

Toward that end, Commissioner Brown has directed the preparation of a strategic plan that puts the principles of community policing at the core of the department's operations (Brown, 1991). He has also triggered a number of specific implementation efforts, including those intended to: increase the proportion of the force given patrol assignments; dramatically increase the number of patrol beats to be covered by permanently assigned beat officers; reduce the proportion of a tour during which the average radio car team is responding to centrally dispatched calls, so as to increase the time available for these officers to carry out community-oriented, problem-solving activities; reorganize precinct-based tactical units so that they can be deployed more flexibly in response to priority problems on the neighborhood level; enhance the capability of management information systems to assist precinct personnel in the identification and analysis of priority neighborhood problems; provide extensive training at all levels of the department in the principles, values, and operations of community policing; operate one precinct as an experimental "hothouse" in which the roles of all precinct personnel are to be redefined and assessed in terms of the principles of community policing; and create "Precinct Management Teams" to ensure that local citizens work directly with precinct command staff in the priority-setting, problem-solving process.

Thus the efforts to convert the NYPD to a community-policing philosophy and style continue and have advanced beyond the activities that were described and evaluated by the research reported on here. Nevertheless these findings helped to focus the department's plan and to give shape to some of the specific implementation efforts now under way. Moreover we believe these findings will be useful both to scholars exploring the substance and limits of community policing and to police administrators preparing to move their own departments in this direction.

**The Structure
of the Book**
The report of our findings begins with the presentation in Chapter 2 of data describing the CPOs in the research precincts in terms of standard demographic characteristics and prior experience in the

department. The officers' levels of understanding and expectations regarding the program at the time they volunteered for it are described, as are their perceptions and attitudes about the program and the community since they became CPOs.

Chapter 3 focuses on the dimensions of the CPO role, the kind of performance that was called for in the program design, the level of performance that was observed in the research, the nature of the difficulties encountered by the officers in mastering different aspects of the role, and the kinds of action that the department might take to improve the level of performance. A clearly related focus is evident in Chapter 4, in which the instruments created by the research staff to evaluate the performance of individual CPOs are described and the results of their application are reported.

The uniqueness of the CPO role creates a series of challenges to the CPOP supervisor, and these are the concerns of Chapter 5. The challenges are divided into those related to the supervisor as leader and guide for his or her subordinates in the unit and those related to the supervisor's responsibilities as the department's agent of control over the behavior of the unit members. The primary tasks of the supervisor within his leader and guide function (e.g., representing the program within the department, assisting in representing the program in the community, and assisting the CPOs in implementing their role) are examined closely. In addition, CPOP's experience of officers' abuse of patrol and administrative time, complaints about corruption, and complaints of abusive behavior toward civilians are considered in some detail. The monitoring and control of these deviations are considered specific responsibilities of the unit sergeant in his or her capacity as a control agent.

The relationships between CPOs and regular patrol officers in the research precincts is examined in Chapter 6, including the non-CPOP officers' perceptions of the content and legitimacy of the CPO role. In addition, this chapter considers the critical importance of the precinct commander to the effective performance of the CPOP unit and its integration with other patrol resources on the precinct level. The chapter also presents a description of the support given to CPOP by the police commissioner from the commencement of the pilot project through the expansion of the program to all precincts in the city.

Chapter 7 presents the findings of a series of interviews that the research staff conducted with community leaders within each of the six research precincts. These interviews shed light on the leaders' perceptions of crime, of drug and disorder problems in the community, on their understanding of CPOP's purpose in their respective precincts, and on their assessment of CPOP's present and potential effectiveness.

The book's concluding chapter (Chapter 8) first presents the recommendations that the research staff believed would strengthen the CPO program and the influence of the principles of community-oriented, problem-solving policing in the New York City Police Department. It presents, as well, some of the authors' reflections—on the extent and nature of internal change that must accompany a department's effort to enact the principles of community policing, on the difficulties that will be encountered in attempting to realize fully the community's contribution to the process, and on how the implementation and effects of community policing might be monitored by units of local government.

Notes   1. A more detailed description of the program design and its rationale, as well as the content and structure of the orientation and training program provided, is presented in the Farrell article (1988), "The Development of the Community Patrol Officer Program: Community-Oriented Policing in the New York City Police Department"; the *Orientation Guide* (September 1987); *Community Patrol Officer Program: Implementation Guide* (October 1985); and *Community Patrol Officer Program: Supervisory Guide* (May 1988).

2. Support for the research on CPOP was provided by the City of New York, by the National Institute of Justice within the U.S. Justice Department, by the New York State Division of Criminal Justice Services, and by the Burden Foundation, the Ford Foundation, the Daniel and Florence Guggenheim Foundation, the Norman Foundation, the Chase Manhattan Bank, and the Philip Morris Companies.

3. More detailed explanations of specific aspects of the research design appear in the chapters in which they are particularly relevant.

4. It should be noted, as well, that a substantial part of the funds supporting the research came from the technical assistance contract under which Vera has provided the city for many years with planning, program development, and research assistance on virtually all aspects of law enforcement and criminal justice. That contract, funded from the police department's budget, also financed virtually all of the program development and management assistance provided by Vera's program staff to the CPO program.

2

The Officer's Perception of the Role

- Introduction
- Methods
- Recruitment to CPOP
- Reasons for Volunteering for CPOP
- Positive and Negative Aspects of CPOP
- Ways to Improve CPOP
- Major Findings in Brief

Introduction   The CPO program sought to create a new role for patrol officers in the New York City Police Department. The research project detailed in this book was designed to describe and analyze how that role was implemented and the nature of its effects on the community, on the problems on which the officers focused their attention, and on the police officers themselves. This chapter addresses a series of questions about the characteristics of those who volunteered for the program, their reasons for so doing, and the understandings, expectations, and attitudes that they brought to it. Attention then focuses on the ways in which the officers allocated their time among a variety of activities that make up the role, and on their assessments of the relative importance of these activities. The effects of experience are considered next; that is, whether experience in the role brings about any change in the officers' perceptions of the role itself, their aspirations and expectations concerning their future careers, and their perceptions of and attitudes toward the community. Finally, the officers' views regarding desirable and undesirable features of the role and the program are considered, along with their suggestions for improving them.

Methods   To address these questions the research staff collected demographic data describing the program participants in the six research precincts and examined them against comparable demographic statistics for the department as a whole.

In addition, a rather extensive interview, lasting over an hour, was conducted with each research subject at the start of the research period in each precinct (the T-1 interview). Another interview, of similar length, was conducted at the end of the research period (the T-2 interview), which sought to identify perceptual and attitudinal changes in the CPOs concerning the program, the community, their aspirations, their career expectations, and the department itself. Questions in the T-2 interview were also directed at each officer's identification of the major types of activities in which he or she was involved as a CPO, evaluation of their relative importance, and estimation of how they distributed their time proportionally among those activities. Finally, the observational notes prepared by the research assistants, who were at the research sites at least four full days a week, were examined for what they contained concerning how the officers spent their time and what they may have said informally about their experiences in and attitudes toward the program.

These data do not permit an actual comparison of perceptions and attitudes before and after participating in CPOP. It must be remembered that the program was operational in each of the six precincts when the research periods began. Indeed, the officers had been serving as CPOs for an average of 12.9 months at the time they became research subjects. Thus the T-1 interview could not measure attitudes that were unaffected by program participation. To approximate such a measure, however, the officers were asked to recall certain motivations, knowledge, perceptions, and attitudes that they harbored at the time they were invited to volunteer for the program. They were asked to provide similar types of information to describe their states of mind at the times of the T-1 and T-2 interviews. The analyses presented here explore changes over these three points in time, while recognizing that the data regarding the first of those points are subject to the distortions of the respondents' memories.

The T-1 interviews were administered to 63 CPOs and 6 unit coordinators. Because some officers left during the research period, they were not reinterviewed; nor were replacement officers who served for less than three of the 6-month research period. Therefore, for most of the analyses of change presented in this chapter, the sample size is 51.

As previously indicated, all police officers in the CPOP, in both the research and the nonresearch precincts, volunteered for the assignment. Before considering the demographic profile of the research subjects, a brief description of how they were recruited to the program is provided.

Recruitment to CPOP

Union regulations within the NYPD require that any assignment that does not comply with one of the department's standard tour charts must be staffed with volunteers. CPOs are encouraged to set the beginning and ending times for their tours, subject to the approval of their sergeants, in response to the special needs of their beats, rather than rotating tours in accordance with one of the standard charts. Therefore all CPOs volunteer for their assignments. Nonetheless, when a new unit was begun in a precinct, the CPOP sergeant approached officers already assigned to the precinct and invited them to volunteer.

This invitation to volunteer was considered an important feature of the program both by its designers and by the CPOP supervisors. The obviously novel quality of the program, especially the increased discretion and freedom of movement it gave the officers, placed a premium on selecting the right people for the job. The sergeants and the precinct commanding officers looked for officers whom they thought they could trust to avoid corruption hazards and to put in a solid day's work without close supervision. In addition, they sought officers whom they believed were reasonably outgoing and capable of working amicably and effectively with residents, merchants, and community leaders on the neighborhood level. Finally, they tried to select officers whom they thought would work well together.

Once the sergeant had prepared a list of candidates and reviewed the list with the commanding officer, he approached each candidate individually. Typically, the sergeant would describe the program to the officer, based on what the sergeants had learned from orientation meetings with the designers of the program, describe what he or she perceived to be some of the benefits of the program for the officer, express his or her confidence in the officer's capacity to perform the role well, and ask him or her to think seriously of volunteering for the assignment. While not everyone who was approached accepted the sergeant's invitation, the sergeants in the research precincts were largely satisfied with the complement of officers they assembled.

In all cases, the officers assigned to a unit had been working in that precinct for some period of time prior to receiving their invitation. Most of them knew the CPOP sergeant before joining the unit, either indirectly by reputation or directly as a former member of his or her patrol squad. In most cases, the officer's knowledge of and respect for the sergeant was an important factor in his or her decision to volunteer. Shortly after each group was formed, the members participated with the sergeant in the program's formal training program. As will be seen in the pages that follow, the amount of information provided to the officers and the perceptions they formed prior to beginning that training were rather varied.

Demographic and Background Characteristics of the Officers

Sixty-nine officers, including the 6 unit coordinators and 63 beat officers completed the Time-1 interview. Eight (11.6%) were female and 61 (88.4%) were male. Fifty-five (79.7%) of the officers were white; 9 (13.0%) were Hispanic, and 5 (7.2%) were black. Department statistics as of July 1989 indicate that 85.6% of police officers (the number does not include personnel of other ranks) were males and 14.4% were females; 75.0% were white, 11.3% were black, 12.9% were Hispanic, and 0.8% were classified as "other."[1] Thus a slightly higher proportion of the CPOs in the research sample were males and white, while a somewhat lower proportion of the sample were black officers.

The age of the CPOs ranged from 24.3 years to 47.4 years with an average of 30.2 years old (sd = 4.7). The average age for police officers throughout the department was just over 32 years. Over two thirds of the CPOs (69.6%) lived in New York City, and few of the them had military experience (15.9%), although such military experience was slightly more common among the CPOs than among police officers in general (14.0%).

The CPOs in the research sample were somewhat better educated than police officers in general. Nearly a third of the CPOs had only a high school education (31.9%), compared with 42.2% of the officers in general; 55.0% of the CPOs compared with 47.0% of the police officers in general had some college education, and 13.0% of the CPOs compared with 10.9% of the officers were college graduates. Only three of the CPOs indicated that they were currently enrolled in school, and five officers indicated that they currently held a second job. Thus, in the research precincts at least, the abandonment of the rotating tours was not accompanied by large numbers of CPOs taking second jobs or enrolling in school.

Over half the CPOs in the research precincts were married (56.5%, plus an additional officer, representing 1.4% of the sample, cohabiting), 33.3% single, 7.2% divorced, and one officer was separated. Comparable figures for police officers throughout the department were: 42.5% married, 56.8% single, 0.1% widowed, 3.2% divorced, and 1.3% legally separated. The spouses of 28 of the 39 married CPOs (71.8%) were working outside the home, 20 of them full-time. One third of the CPOs indicated that they had no dependents, and one quarter of them had one dependent; the remaining 41% had between two and five dependents (generally two or three). Fourteen of the CPOs indicated that they spoke a second language: 10 of them Spanish, 2 French, and 2 spoke languages other than Spanish or French.

Reasons for Becoming a Police Officer and a CPO

During the initial research interview, the CPOs were asked a series of open-ended questions designed to probe why they had joined the force, which aspects of the police officer job they liked or disliked, and why they volunteered for CPOP. Up to five responses to the question, "Why did you become a cop?" were coded for each officer. The most frequent responses pertained to the pay and benefits, job security or steady employment, having family members who were

Reasons for Volunteering for CPOP

The length and type of prior police experience of the CPOs in the sample varied widely, with the number of years in the police department ranging from 1.6 years to 21.8 years (mean = 5.7 years, with a standard deviation of 4.3 years); the average amount of time in the precinct in which they served as a CPO was 3.3 years ($sd = 2.1$). For police officers in general, the average number of years on the job was 7.3 years in July 1989, while the average length of time in their commands was 3.4 years. In this connection, it is worth noting that, in the earliest planning meetings with department officials, the designers of the program suggested that the ideal candidate for the role would be an officer with between 6 and 9 years of experience in the job. It was felt that experience of that duration would provide some assurance that the candidates would be comfortable in their identity as police officers and with their ability to function on the street. Department officials agreed with that hypothesis, but pointed out that because the city's fiscal crisis had precluded hiring new police officers during the second half of the 1970s, very few patrol officers were available with that level of experience. Thus, in general, the CPOP officers tended to be fairly young, with a little less time on the job than was true for police officers in general.

To determine the nature of their prior experience, the CPOs were asked which of a list of types of patrol work they had done. Nearly all (95.7%) had been assigned to Radio Motor Patrol (RMP), and over half (58.0%) had been on conventional foot patrol posts. Seven officers (10.1%) had been in the TOPAC car (Total Patrol Concept), concentrating on quality-of-life conditions in the precinct, and 7 had been assigned to precinct clerical positions. Three officers had been in anti-crime units, 2 in Street Narcotics Enforcement Units (SNEU), and 11 in other units. None of the officers had been in Street Narcotics Apprehension Program (SNAP) or Robbery Investigation Program (RIP) units. Thus the officers had very little special unit training or experience before entering CPOP.

The main sources of information about CPOP for these officers prior to joining the unit had been other CPOP officers (44.9%) and the CPOP sergeant (36.2%); 13 (18.8%) learned about the program from other sources. Each CPO was asked an open-ended question concerning why he or she had volunteered for CPOP, and the responses were checked on a list.[2] The two most frequently cited factors were flexible hours, mentioned by 68.1% of the respondents, and fixed days off (56.5%). The distribution of responses is presented in Table 2.4.

To assess the knowledge base supporting the officer's decision to join the program, each was asked, as an open-ended question, "What did you know about CPOP before you volunteered?" After recording the officer's spontaneous responses on a checklist, the researcher called attention to each specific feature in the list by asking the respondent if he or she was aware of it at the time the decision was made. The responses to both of these questions are presented in Table 2.5.

TABLE 2.4   "Why Did You Volunteer?"

Reason	Percentage Mentioned (N = 69)
Flexible hours	68.1
Fixed days off	56.5
Community involvement	34.8
Something different	26.1
Walking the beat	18.8
Working conditions (e.g., steady post)	15.9
Ability to follow up	14.5
Independence	11.6
Not RMP	10.1
No midnights	5.8
Career advancement	1.4
Other	8.7

As expected, the officers generally knew more about the program than they indicated when the question was asked in an open-ended manner. Nevertheless, wide discrepancies occurred in the percentage of officers indicating an awareness of specific features in both lists, ranging from 98.6% to 41.2% when the list was read, and from 71.0% to 11.8% in response to the open-ended question.

In general, the working conditions offered by the program, including its reliance on foot patrol, the flexible hours and fixed days off it offered, and the fact that it involved working with the community, enjoyed high recognition percentages in both lists. On the other hand, some of the program's more specific community-oriented features, such as its focus on quality-of-life conditions and its requirement that officers work with community organizations, provide information to the public, and help form community groups were less well known at the time they decided to volunteer. Moreover, the relatively large differences between the percentage of officers who mentioned

TABLE 2.5   "What Did You Know Before You Volunteered?"

Feature	Percentage Mentioned (N = 69)		
	Open	List Read	Change
Foot patrol	71.0	98.6	27.6
Responsible for specific beat	46.4	94.2	47.8
Flexible hours	60.9	92.8	31.9
Fixed days off	58.0	91.3	33.3
Work with community	56.5	87.0	30.5
Focus on quality of life	11.6	76.8	65.2
Work with organizations	13.0	58.0	45.0
Serve as information source	5.8	51.5	45.7
Help form community groups	13.0	45.6	32.6
Beat Book	11.8	41.2	29.4

intended to stay in CPOP (86.4%), and for 16.9% of them, the assignment of choice in 5 years would be CPOP. The most popular single unit aspired to by these officers was OCCB (18.6%), followed by CPOP and the Detective Bureau (13.6%), with Anti-Crime a distant fourth (6.8%). No one wanted to be in RMP duty in 5 years; 5.1% wanted to be in a RIP unit, 33.9% in other specialized units, and 5.1% wanted to leave the police department within 5 years. Over half the officers aspired to the rank of sergeant (60.3%) within 5 years, 14.3% each to lieutenant and detective; 6.3% wanted to remain police officers and 4.8% responded "other."

In considering these findings regarding the perceptions and aspirations of the CPOs in this research, data provided to Vera by the NYPD provides some insight into the actual transfer and promotion patterns for officers assigned to CPOP throughout the city. The NYPD database consists of information on the 1,044 officers assigned to CPOP *at any point* between November 15, 1987 and January 15, 1989 (a period that was generally later than the period during which the research data were collected). Of these officers, 291 (27.9%) left the CPOP unit during this time span. Thirty-one (10.7%) of these officers left involuntarily; that is, they were asked leave because they were not adjusting well to the CPOP assignment, or, in a few cases, because they were charged with allegations involving serious misconduct.

Data regarding change in assignment for officers who left the program voluntarily were available for 245 of the 260 officers. Of these 245 officers, 67.3% transferred to assignments that are considered desirable, including Anti-Crime units (7.8%), OCCB (17.1%), other details (35.1%), or promotion to sergeant (7.3%). However, one out of five (19.7%) returned to RMP, and an additional 13.0% left because of retirement, resignation from the NYPD, on-the-job injuries, or other reasons. Thus the citywide data suggest that opportunities are available to the CPOP officers and that when officers leave the unit, it is, in most instances, to advance their careers.

Positive and Negative Aspects of CPOP

Each CPO was asked in open-ended questions to mention positive and negative aspects of CPOP. The results were consistent with the reasons given for joining the program: the most popular features were flexible hours (71.0%) and fixed days off (60.9%); the least popular feature was the Beat Book (disliked by 33.8%) (see Tables 2.6 and 2.7).

It is worth noting that a much higher percentage of respondents identified features that they liked about the CPO role than features they disliked. Moreover, it is not surprising that flexible hours and fixed days off were the most frequently identified features that the officers liked. Throughout the department, these are the most desirable perquisites of any assignment. The fact that almost half of the respondents identified community involvement as a positive feature of the program is more noteworthy. It seems unlikely that an equally large percentage of the general patrol force would identify community involvement as something they desired in their assignments. This

TABLE 2.6 "What Features of CPOP Do You Like?"

Job Feature	Percentage Mentioned (N = 69)
Flexible hours	71.0
Fixed days off	60.9
Community involvement	49.3
Independence	30.4
Ability to follow up	29.0
Walking the beat	17.4
Positive feedback	8.7
Like coworkers	7.2
Hours, chart days	5.8
Other	13.0

suggests that the sergeants were reasonably successful in recruiting people who were positively disposed to this dimension of police work.

The fact that almost a third of the officers identified independence and the ability to follow up as features of the CPO role that they liked also deserves comment. Officers assigned to RMP duties often express ambivalence about the assignment. On the one hand, they tend to see this type of work as the core of police work, which, although sometimes tedious or excessively demanding, does provide a certain level of excitement and busyness. On the other hand, at least as often they complain that they are tied to the radio, deprived of any discretion in choosing conditions on which to work, and prevented from having any significant impact on the conditions to which they respond, because they must get back on the radio for a new assignment within 20 to 30 minutes. Against this backdrop, the ability of the CPO to exercise discretion in identifying problems and developing strategies to correct them offers an attractive opportunity for independent action. In addition, the CPO's responsibility for implementing the problem-solving strategies provides a much-desired opportunity to follow through and have an observable effect on a condition in the community. Thus these are features of the role that have the potential of providing officers with types of satisfaction that are

TABLE 2.7 "What Features of CPOP Do You Dislike?"

Job Feature	Percentage Mentioned (N = 68)
Beat Book	33.8
Victim surveys	14.7
Trivial noncrime problems	11.8
Dislike by non-CPOs	10.3
Requirements of the job	8.8
Community pressure	7.4
Foot patrol	7.4
Paperwork	5.9
Other	13.2

> This area is very bad. It's all drugs and weapons and you're constantly battling with people.

> My attitude was somewhat negative. In patrol you're always meeting people at their worst, and they give you a hard time.

> The people that you dealt with on patrol were so negative. They didn't care what you were doing for them, but wanted to know why you aren't there when they needed you and why you weren't there 5 minutes earlier.

Another officer mentioned the apathy of the community: "Nobody wanted to get involved. They would say 'I don't care. That's your job; you do it.' Most of them were fearful too." Nearly a quarter of the officers (22.2%) described their attitude toward the community as neither positive nor negative at the time they joined the program; 54.0% said it was positive, or very positive (7.9%).

By the time of the initial research interview, only one officer felt very negative and two officers felt negative toward the community. Five officers (8.1%) were neutral, 58.1% felt positive, and 29.0% were very positive toward the community. The most common reason for change (17 of 26 who changed) was that the officer had become much more familiar with the neighborhood and had met many of the good people. Four officers indicated that they had changed their attitudes because the people liked them, and five officers gave other reasons.

When the CPOs were asked to characterize the attitudes of the community toward the police in general, nearly a quarter stated that at the time they joined CPOP, the people on their beat had a negative (16.4%) or very negative (6.6%) attitude toward the police. These CPOs stated that the community did not trust the police, because they did not believe that the police would solve problems, or they thought the police were brutal and abused their authority, or they were influenced by negative media coverage, or they did not understand police activities. As one officer explained:

> Their attitude was very negative because of the things that they see the police doing to people. They feel that cops have quotas and that cops are giving tickets and summonses for no reason. They think that cops think they are better than everyone else. People also think that the police abuse their authority. There are a lot of things that people just don't understand about the police.

Nevertheless, more than half of the CPOs indicated that, at the time they joined CPOP, the community attitude toward the police was positive (45.9%) or very positive (11.5%), while 19.7% stated that the attitude was neither positive nor negative.

In marked contrast, in assessing community attitudes toward the police at the time of the initial interview, only 4.9% of the CPOs reported that the people on their beat had a negative attitude toward the police, while 62.3% described the attitude as positive, or 24.6% as very positive; 8.2% indicated it was neutral.

Among the 25 officers who changed their opinions, 13 attributed the change to their being known by the people in the community, and another 11 credited the change to CPO follow-through on problems:

> Very positive. They know me, and I have helped them to understand the unknown. "What you don't know you fear." Once people understand the unknown, they have less fear. People now have a more positive attitude about the police because I explain to them why the police do certain things that to them may seem wrong.

Several officers believed that the goodwill fostered by CPOP has promoted a positive attitude toward the police in general. One officer described it as the "spillover effect." Another stated: "For many people I am the first cop they have ever had a conversation with. If the interactions are positive, it may carry over to other cops. I let people know there are other nice cops." Another officer summed up the situation as follows: "The fact is that through CPOP I've gotten a chance to go out in the public and find out that there are people who are positive about the police." He continued: "In turn, people who were once negative see this 'individual' officer trying to help them and it makes them more receptive to cops. We're not just kicking down doors or writing tickets anymore." When asked how the people on their beats felt about *them* personally, the CPOs' assessments were, with few exceptions, positive—49.1% very positive, 43.9% positive, 3.5% neutral, and 3.5% negative.

CPO Attitudes and Beliefs About the Program and the Qualities of a Good CPO

The question, "Are there any qualities or skills that you think are more important in CPOP work than in regular patrol work?" produced a wide variety of responses from the research subjects. Although the responses defied easy classification, a number of notions recurred throughout the comments. Specifically, while the CPOs believed that all patrol officers should be courteous, sincere, patient, articulate, and good listeners, they stated that these attributes are especially important in CPOP work. The following comments are typical:

> You have to have a cool head on your shoulders. You can't get pissed-off easily. It's the same in RMP though; you just can't have police who get mad easily and call everyone an asshole.

> You have to be able to adjust from being a scumbag to a nice guy. You have to be able to come from RMP to CPOP and learn that you can't talk nasty to everyone. You give more of yourself in CPOP. You give a little extra than you would in patrol.

the police and have the police presence in their neighborhood." Or as another officer said: "People in this area never saw cops before unless something was wrong. Now they're closer to the community than ever before. The quality-of-life problems are being addressed."

A few officers stated that one of the strengths of the program was that it gave the public a specific officer to call, so they were no longer dealing with an impersonal department: "I think they should have it in every precinct in the city. CPOP is a 'buffer zone' between the community and the police. It gives the community the chance to rely on at least one cop in the precinct—they know someone there." Or as another officer stated, "CPOP is productive. It actually works. It clears up problems; provides public education about police work; lets them know one police officer personally. This isn't exactly police work, but it's important." He continued:

> It definitely "pulls more than its weight." It gives people a feeling that someone is watching over them or can help them. They know if they call the office, someone will respond (unlike calling some unknown person). It also helps the community to get to know us, because we recruit block watchers and attend the community meetings.

Another officer emphasized the importance of developing a familiarity with the people in the beat, and how that led to an exchange of information: "You are able to be out there, and you know what is going on in your beat. You are capable of preventing situations because you learn who is 'dirty' and who isn't. There is a good deal of information exchange between cops and community."

Nevertheless, two officers who worked in beats where drug problems were very severe expressed reservations about the usefulness of CPOP in areas of that type:

> Well, the ideas are good, but I am not sure that it will work here. This place is all drugs, and a lot of the people don't care. The bad people definitely outnumber the good.

> It's just the idea that people think that CPOP can work in a place like this. There are so many drugs and the community is hard to define. It is hard to know who is good and who is bad. The ones that are willing to talk are very afraid. CPOP may work in 5 years, but it will take long-term change.

The percentages of officers identifying various features of CPOP as valuable are presented in Table 2.8.

Ways to Improve CPOP

When the CPOs were asked in an open-ended question to mention ways in which CPOP could be improved, 12 officers offered no

TABLE 2.8   Valuable Features of CPOP

Feature	Percentage Mentioned (N = 66)
Understand the community better	30.3
Able to follow through	27.3
Community likes it	24.2
People have a cop to call	18.2
Improving police image	16.7
Information source/exchange	13.6
Good experience for officer	7.6
Other	10.6

recommendations. However, 55 CPOs made one or more recommendations, which included more flexibility in patrol tactics (30.9%), smaller beats or more CPOs (29.1%), the use of scooters or other transportation (20.0%), and a short, more concise Beat Book (20.0%). The results are presented in Table 2.9.

The desire for more flexibility in patrol tactics generally reflected the belief of officers working in narcotics-laden beats that the department imposed too many constraints on the tactics that uniformed officers, including CPOs, are permitted to employ in attacking these problems. As is discussed later, the anti-drug strategies and tactics used by CPOP units were quite varied and differed across precincts.

In some of the geographically large precincts, especially in Queens and Brooklyn, beats sometimes encompass 50 square blocks. As a result, officers often believed that these beats were too large to cover effectively on foot, especially if the beat contained more than two or three areas with serious or chronic problems. This perception is reflected, as well, in those officers who wanted access to a scooter to provide them with the mobility to crisscross their beat during any given tour. Nevertheless, at the time of the research, the operational guidelines for the program prohibited the use of scooters, because it was feared that the officers would spend too much time patrolling the beat on the scooter, rather than walking foot patrol and dealing directly with the community.

TABLE 2.9   Ways to Improve CPOP

Suggestion	Percentage Mentioned (N = 55)
Flexibility in patrol tactics	30.9
Smaller beats or more CPOs	29.1
Use of scooters	20.0
Shorten the Beat Book	20.0
More training for CPOs and others	18.2
Eliminate victim notifications	12.7
More opportunity for promotion	9.1
More special programs; resources	7.3
Other	20.0

TABLE 2.11 Importance of Activities to CPOP Job (N = 52)

| | | Importance | | |
Activity	Not at all Important %	Somewhat Important %	Important %	Very Important %
Work as unit	—	—	23.1	76.9
Visibility	—	5.8	21.2	73.1
Priority problem	—	3.8	28.8	67.3
Information	—	3.9	41.2	54.9
Make arrests	—	19.2	32.7	48.1
Community needs	—	11.5	53.8	34.6
Community mtg.	3.8	11.5	48.1	36.5
Youth activities	1.9	23.1	50.0	25.0
Issue summonses	11.5	30.8	34.6	23.1
Security insp.	28.8	28.8	25.0	17.3
Block assn.	3.8	28.8	51.9	15.4
Victim notification	36.5	36.5	17.3	9.6
Patrol objectives	23.5	31.4	37.3	7.8
Beat Book	23.5	45.1	29.4	2.0

remaining 23.1% evaluating it as important. This finding is surprising in light of the fact that each CPO had direct responsibility for his or her own beat, and the finding that the same respondents estimated that only 8% of their time was spent "helping other CPOs." These findings suggest that "working as a unit" is considered important because of its relevance to unit morale, and that the officers may enjoy unit activities.

Another highly rated activity was maintaining visibility, with 73.1% of the CPOs classifying it as very important, 21.2% as important, and 5.8% somewhat important. Once again, the phrase used to describe the activity may be somewhat misleading. Officers in the NYPD are taught that maintaining a visible, public presence in order to deter street crime is the principal function of conventional foot patrol. However, CPO training emphasizes the differences between CPO patrol and conventional foot patrol. In CPOP, the officers are encouraged to develop problem-solving strategies that do not rely on the officer's personal presence to deter misbehavior. Thus, in CPOP, the visibility of the uniform is useful, not as a deterrent but as a means of maintaining one's accessibility to the public. The data do not clearly indicate whether the respondents were confusing the two types of patrol or stressing public accessibility when they attributed so much importance to visibility.

Working on priority problems was rated as very important by 67.3%, while 28.8% believed it was important or somewhat important (3.8%). At the other end of the spectrum, four activities were rated as "not important all" by a sizable segment of the respondents: conducting security inspections (28.8%) or victim surveys (36.5%), maintaining the Patrol Objectives Section of the Beat Book (23.5%), and keeping

TABLE 2.12 Attitude Change During Past Six Months (*N* = 52)

| | Direction | | |
Attitude re:	*More Negative* %	*No Change* %	*More Positive* %
CPOP	6.0	64.0	30.0
Community	5.8	69.2	25.0
Being a cop	7.7	73.1	19.2
Police Department	17.3	80.8	1.9

current other sections of the Beat Book (23.5%). As noted above, several of the CPOs found these activities objectionable.

Another area of interest in the T-2 interview centered around the CPO's perceptions of whether his or her attitudes toward CPOP, the community, the police department, and being a police officer had changed as a result of his or her experiences during the previous 6 months. The majority of the CPOs reported no change in any of these attitudes, and most of those who perceived changes reported them to be in a positive direction (see Table 2.12). It is striking, however, that the only variation from this pattern was that 17.3% of the CPOs reported that they had become more negative toward the police department, while 1.9% had become more positive. No data from either the qualitative or quantitative research explain this result.

In contrast, 6 months appeared to make a substantial difference in the CPOs' career aspirations for the next 5 years.[6] The data presented in this section pertain to the 47 CPOs who completed both the T-1 and T-2 interviews. While OCCB was the most desired unit at the time of the initial interview (with 23.8% wanting to move to that unit within 5 years), at the time of the T-2 interview, only 7.1% of the CPOs expressed that aspiration. The percentage of CPOs who reported that they wanted to be in CPOP in 5 years remained constant at 21.4%. The percentage indicating that they wanted to be in the Detective Bureau rose slightly, from 7.1% to 11.9%. None of these CPOs wanted to be in RMP or Anti-Crime in 5 years, while the percentage aspiring to RIP rose from zero to 7.1%, and the percentage of officers who wanted to be out of the NYPD rose from 2.4% to 7.1%. The percentage of officers who reported that they wanted to be in a specialized unit rose from 35.7% to 45.2%.

While at the time of the initial interview 60.3% of the officers aspired to the rank of sergeant within 5 years, at the T-2 interview only 37.5% said they wanted to be sergeants in 5 years. The percentage aspiring to reach the rank of lieutenant rose to 31.3%, and 16.7% hoped to become detectives; 10.4% wanted to remain police officers (and 4.2% responded "other").

In sum, by the end of the 6-month research period, the officers' aspirations regarding future rank in the department rose somewhat.

to the research subjects, their perceptions and attitudes toward the community became more positive from the time they entered the program through the time of the second research interview. In general, they claimed that the change was a function of their coming to understand more about the problems in the community and the desires of the residents to experience peace and order in their neighborhoods. The CPOs claimed that the program exposed them much more fully to the large number of good people who wished to correct the area's problems. Moreover, the respondents also believed that the attitudes of the community toward the police also improved over the life of the program.

Notes   1. Data describing selected demographic characteristics of department personnel as of July 1989 were provided to research staff by the personnel department's Data Unit. These data describe the composition of the department about 16 months after the data collection period for this research ended. It is assumed, however, that they provide a reasonably accurate description of the department during the research period since the hiring and attrition processes went on routinely during the intervening year or so.

2. The list contained eight precoded responses and an open-ended "other" category. The responses to the "other" category were coded during analysis.

3. Officers secure promotions up to the rank of captain through a civil-service testing system. However, there is an alternative through which officers may move to desired assignments without being promoted in rank. The end status in this alternative system is assignment to the Detective Bureau. Typically, a patrol officer reaches that status by moving through other assignments that involve increasing levels of investigative work and arrest activities. The first steps on the way to the bureau include precinct-level assignments to the Anti-Crime Unit and/or the Street Narcotics Enforcement Unit (SNEU). Effective performance in these units qualifies an officer for assignment to such investigative units as the Organized Crime Control Bureau and the Inspectional Services Bureau, from which most members of the Detective Bureau are selected. About 18 months after CPOP expansion began, assignment to the CPOP unit was formally equated with assignment to the Anti-Crime units for the purpose of movement along the career path.

4. These interviews were not conducted with coordinators or alternates or officers who had been CPOs in the precinct for less than 3 of the 6 research months; therefore, the sample size for most of the questions in the T-2 interview is 51.

5. The researcher explained to the officer that the average month should total 160 working hours and worked with the officer to help him or her adjust the estimates to total 160.

6. It should be noted that the sample responding to this question on the T-2 interview is substantially smaller ($N = 47$) than that for the initial interview ($N = 59$). Thus some of the differences in responses may be a function of the compositions of these two samples.

those in which the research was concentrated, as well as staff members from the Citywide CPOP Coordinator's Office, about the CPO role and its implementation. Access to these people helped provide perspective on the generalizability of the insights derived from the data collected in the research precincts. That perspective was important in light of the fact that the research precincts were not selected as typical of those in their respective borough commands, and in light of the fact that the expansion of the CPO program to other precincts and the articulation of guidelines for its operation continued throughout the entire data collection period.

Problem Solving

In general, the research indicates that the CPO role can be performed by regular patrol officers in the NYPD, and that they prefer the role over that of the regular RMP officer. Despite the fact they had no experience with, or training in, the problem-solving method prior to becoming CPOs, the officers were able to learn enough about it to identify problems, focus attention and resources on their solution, and secure widespread commendation from community leaders. Among the CPOs in the research precincts, there were a number of individual success stories and many more among officers operating in other precincts. Nine such success stories were written up in a document entitled *CPOP: Community Policing in Practice*, prepared for use in training new CPOP officers (see Appendix A). These stories and others like them make it clear that CPOs applying the problem-solving approach with persistence and ingenuity can appreciably alleviate festering problems on the neighborhood level, even very difficult problems such as widespread drug dealing, and thereby improve the quality of life experienced by the residents of the community.

The question addressed here, however, is not whether individual successes are possible, but how well the problem-solving process was implemented generally in the research precincts. The simple answer to that question is that it was implemented moderately well by most officers. The more complex challenge addressed in this chapter is the identification of those problem-solving tasks with which the CPOs appeared to have most difficulty, the exploration of why they proved difficult, and the consideration of how those tasks might be performed more effectively by the several hundred officers who are now serving as CPOs throughout the department.

Problem Identification

The CPOs were advised in the training program, and directed by their sergeants, to spend their first few weeks of patrol familiarizing themselves with their beat; identifying themselves to the residents, merchants, and organization leaders; and asking everyone they met to identify the most pressing problems in the community. They were told to probe about both the street crime and the quality-of-life problems with which the people were most concerned. In addition, the CPOs were advised to attend as many meetings of community organizations as they could during the first couple of months and to ask those in attendance to identify their concerns. The officers were also told to solicit similar input from regular patrol officers and Anti-Crime officers in the precinct. Finally, every morning each officer was given copies of the complaint reports for crimes committed in his or her beat during the preceding 24 hours. It was suggested that each officer maintain an updated spot map of selected crimes (e.g., robberies, burglaries, assaults) reported in the beat, and use the information contained in the complaint reports to learn something about the times, places, methods, victims, suspects, and situations associated with areas in which such crimes were concentrated. The designers of the program believed that CPOs could make effective use of information regarding the calls-for-service in their beats, but it was not technically feasible to make that information available on a regular basis.

The CPOs were expected to record this information in their Beat Books and, from it, to identify the three crime problems and the three quality-of-life problems that were most troublesome in the beat. It was on those six problems, or some of them, that the officers were expected to focus their problem-solving efforts. Their monthly work plans, developed with the approval of the CPOP sergeant, were to identify what the officer hoped to accomplish with respect to the chosen problems and to describe what he or she planned to do toward that end.

When the field researchers were first deployed, they were instructed to review the Beat Books of the officers in their precincts and, in dialogue with each officer, to identify between three and five priority problems on which the officer had chosen to work. The researchers were then to complete a PPR over the course of the ensuing few months for each of the problems identified. It was expected that this would produce a database of between 150 and 250 problems for analysis. This proved to be an overestimate. In fact, 102 problems were identified and described by the field researchers using this method. During the 6-month data collection period, most officers focused on two priority problems with a small number addressing either three or one. One thoroughly disaffected officer refused to identify even one problem, claiming that he was not working on any.

It seems likely that the expectations of the researchers in this regard were somewhat unrealistic. When, at the end of the data collection periods, the CPOs were asked to estimate how their time was distributed across a variety of program activities, they estimated that an average of 31% of their time went into general patrol and 28% was devoted to working on priority problems. In this context, general patrol means moving about the beat observing conditions, talking to residents and merchants, and providing assistance to those who seek it. With less than a third of their time spent working on priority problems, it is unlikely that many officers would get around to addressing more than two or three such problems in a 6-month period.

or merchants, or one or more community organizations, had identified the problem, so that he or she was merely reflecting the community's assessment. There was, however, at least some suggestion that the morale of the officers was adversely affected when they identified problems that were of only minor importance in their own eyes. It is not unlikely, moreover, that the taking on of relatively nonserious quality-of-life conditions as priority problems would become more troublesome in precincts where regular patrol resources struggled to meet the demands imposed on them.

This problem is likely to be dealt with more effectively by the department as it develops more experience with the CPO program and the diverse conditions it encounters in several hundred different neighborhoods throughout the city. At the same time, the prospect of establishing departmentwide criteria for according various problems priority status runs counter to the basic assumption that the police must identify and respond to the problems that are most disturbing to the people in their own neighborhoods.

This difficulty could be lessened considerably if the CPOs developed procedures for consulting regularly with groups of community residents and insisted that those groups actually debate the relative priority they want given to the various problems that they raise. The research suggests that this type of consultation between the CPO and a consistent group of community representatives does not happen often. Rather, the CPO typically counts the voices that he or she hears mentioning different problems, and then either accords priority to any problem mentioned more than a few times or tries to resolve judgments of relative priority her- or himself. Within the assumptions of the program, it would be more appropriate for the officer to insist that the community's representatives wrestle seriously with where, ideally, they would like him or her to focus attention.

Problem Analysis   The range of sources from which the CPOs collected information concerning their problems was wide. In addition to their own observations and the comments and explanations provided by people in the community, the officers were encouraged to speak to other police personnel, representatives of other public agencies providing services in the vicinity of the problem, and representatives of community organizations who were concerned about it, and to seek statistical or other archival information from the police and other agencies. They were told that the purpose of the problem-analysis task was to learn as much as could be learned about the problem with respect to its time and place of occurrence, the circumstances in which it was typically manifested, and the sequence of events or actions typically involved in its occurrence. They were also expected to learn the characteristics of those who were usually victimized or somehow adversely effected by it, and the characteristics of, and whenever possible the identities of, those suspected of causing the problem. In addition, they were to consider the origins, evolutionary patterns, and duration of the problem in the community; the past and current efforts of the police, other public agencies, community organizations, and citizens to combat the problem, their results, and the probable reasons for their failure; and the public and private resources that could be focused on the problem in a newly developed corrective effort.

In the research precincts, in many instances the CPOs used the range of available information well, but in general, the analysis of priority problems tended to be somewhat superficial. The officers were usually good at identifying areas of concentration, time and place of occurrence, and the reported characteristics of those responsible for the problem. However, for a few problems on which this kind of information would have been helpful and should have been readily available, it was not known or acted upon by the officer. The problem analyses by most of the officers were generally less impressive with respect to understanding the sequences of actions that produced the problems, the particular ways in which people were victimized or offended by the problem, historical variations in the frequency or circumstances of occurrence, and the nature and results of past efforts to solve the problem.

The superficiality of some of the problem analyses appeared to reflect the insufficiency and inadequacy of the officers' initial training in problem solving. Some of the officers saw problem analysis as an essentially academic exercise with little benefit or interest for them, more useless paperwork. These officers failed to appreciate that the whole purpose of the analysis was to identify points of potential intervention for future action and to learn from past experience what might help to correct the problem in the present. Having identified the problem and where it occurred, such officers were inclined to attack it immediately either by themselves or with other members of the unit.

Developing Problem-Solving Strategies

In developing strategies to correct or alleviate the problem, the CPOs were advised to consult widely with representatives of other agencies and with residents and merchants in the neighborhoods. They were told to think of themselves as planners and resource managers who were to prepare a plan to attack the problem, negotiate for the public and private resources called for by the plan, and then coordinate and monitor the implementation of the plan by those responsible for carrying it out. The training suggested that the CPO always consider the potential involvement of four types of resources—the CPO himself or herself, using all the authority and tools he or she possessed as a police officer; other police resources on both the precinct and the borough levels; other public agencies responsible for providing services to the community; and the residents, merchants, and voluntary organizations in the community.

Analysis of the strategies set forth to address the priority problems in the research precincts confirmed the connection between problem analysis and strategy development. In general, the broader and deeper the analysis, the more varied the strategies and the more they called for the involvement of resources other than the officer, including nonpolice resources.

The strategies described in the PPRs were coded to group the actions to be taken and the person or agency responsible for carrying out each action. Each action called for by the strategy was considered a separate element and, for each problem, up to three CPO actions, two activities by other precinct personnel, one action by other police personnel, and the presence or absence of activities by public agencies, private agencies, or community members were coded. Thus there were many more strategy elements than there were problem-solving strategies.

Forty-five percent of the strategies contained one or more elements that were to be carried out by an agent other than the CPO. In the vast majority of these cases, the other agent was to be another member of the CPOP unit, or, far less often, other precinct personnel.

Shifting focus from the strategies to the elements contained therein revealed that 76.7% of all the elements were to be carried out by the CPO and another 12.9% were to be carried out by other precinct personnel. Only 1.6% of the elements called for actions by other police units, usually the Narcotics Division; 2.3% of the elements were actions that were to be implemented by other public agencies; and 6.5% of all the strategy elements were to be performed by residents, merchants, or organizations in the beat itself. Private, nonprofit service organizations appeared to be ignored totally as a resource.

The most frequently used strategy element was high-visibility patrol, usually by the CPO; it appeared as an element in 77% of the strategies, while summonses were to be used with respect to 45% of the problems and arrests with respect to 22% of the problems. In 39% of the strategies, the CPO intended to refer the problem to other precinct or borough units for supplementary action, and 22% of the strategies contained one or more actions that were to be carried out by members of the community.

According to the CPOs, the average priority problem had been in existence for almost four years, and almost three quarters of the problems were said to have received some form of attention from precinct personnel prior to the advent of CPOP. The officers indicated also that they had been addressing the majority of these problems since they began work as CPOs, and for 83% of the problems, the strategy described in the PPR was the only strategy that the officer had tried on that problem. Finally, it should be noted that drug problems prompted the development of more multifaceted strategies, involving more elements to be implemented by more agents, than did any other type of problem.

Three other points deserve mention with respect to the CPOs' performance in developing problem-solving strategies. At least three of the types of problems identified—drugs, homeless people, and peddlers—are chronic, widespread problems and require citywide policies, structures, and resources beyond those of the police. Those policies are not always clear and unambiguous, and the resources are often not easily accessible. Under these circumstances, the CPOs are sometimes frustrated by not knowing what to do or where to turn outside the police department for assistance with the local manifestations of these problems. They realize that enforcement responsibilities with respect to the drug problem are theirs. But, working at the neighborhood level, they feel the need for preventive efforts directed at the children and treatment slots available for those seeking this assistance. And such services are scarce and difficult to obtain.

On some occasions, CPOs are hesitant to call for the commitment of other police resources to the resolution of problems in their beats. In some instances, this hesitancy reflects their belief that their commanding officers expect them to deal with the problems themselves and reduce, rather than add to, the demand for other resources. In other instances, CPOs may hesitate to seek other police resources because no routine means exist for doing so and they lack the personal connections that would be helpful in this regard. Finally, in some cases, the hesitancy reflects an officer's unwillingness to make a request because he has no idea what to do if the request is refused or ignored. Supervisors and commanding officers consistently encouraging CPOs to develop plans that call for the efficient use of other police resources would help considerably.

Finally, the analysis of strategies again suggested the utility of CPOs carrying on a regular dialogue with some stable body of residents, merchants, and organizations in the beat. Such a body might provoke the officer to think more broadly and creatively. It would also serve as a check against the inclusion of strategy elements that may have been tried without effect before, or that may be inadvertently offensive to a segment of the community. And a stable group of citizens may provide direct assistance to securing the commitment of nonpolice resources to the strategies developed.

Strategy Implementation   Using the notes of the field researchers, each of the strategy elements was coded as having been fully implemented, partially implemented, or not implemented at all. Almost two thirds of the elements that were to be carried out by the beat officer were described as fully implemented with another 12% partially implemented. The strategies to be carried out by other officers in the precinct were implemented even more often, as were those for which police personnel outside the precinct were responsible. A slightly lower percentage of the strategy elements that were to be performed by community members were implemented.

While these findings paint a rather rosy picture regarding strategy implementation, they should be interpreted with caution. They do not reflect judgments based on an independent, objective measure of implementation. Rather, the notes of the field researchers reflect a mix of their own observations and their conversations with the CPOs regarding the implementation process.

At the same time, there is no reason to believe that they distort the picture radically. As indicated previously, the CPOs were rather good in carrying out their own responsibilities, and over three quarters of the strategy elements were designed for implementation by the CPO. In addition, most of the remaining elements were to be performed by other precinct personnel, including other members of the CPOP unit. Research observations indicated that the members of the CPOP units were extremely cooperative in helping one another in their problem-solving efforts. On the other hand, most of the CPOs were not particularly careful in monitoring the implementation efforts of agents, including other police units, outside their own units. Had they been, it is likely that they would have found performance on these elements more incomplete than they realized. It is interesting to note in this regard that several officers said that they encountered more difficulty in obtaining action from other police units (excluding their own CPOP unit) than they did from nonpolice agencies.

Other positive observations should be noted here. The staff at the Community Boards not only applauded the presence of CPOP units, but also often proved helpful to the officers in securing cooperation from other public agencies. This was especially so with the assistance provided by the Sanitation Department in towing abandoned autos and in clearing out dangerous, abandoned lots. The Department of Housing Preservation and Development (HPD) proved quite responsive to the CPOs' efforts to attack drug locations. Many of these operations were located in abandoned buildings that had reverted to the city or empty apartments in city-owned buildings. Not long after expansion of the CPO program began, the HPD developed policies and procedures that encouraged their staff to cooperate with CPOP efforts to clean out and seal these drug locations. On the other hand, cooperative, joint efforts between CPOP and the Housing Authority Police occurred less often than might have been expected. Finally, facilitating the implementation of problem-solving strategies is yet another CPOP task that would be eased by regular dialogue between CPOs and stable groups of residents and merchants in the beats.

Review and Modification of Strategies   As part of the problem-solving process, the CPOs are expected not only to monitor strategy implementation but also to assess the effects of the strategy on the problem, review those assessments with their supervisors and members of the community, and modify the strategies accordingly. This task was rarely performed well in the research precincts and often not performed at all. As mentioned previously, the CPOs indicated that the strategy described was the only strategy they attempted with respect to 83% of the priority problems identified.

There were several reasons for the inadequate level of performance on this task. With respect to many problems, the goals and objectives set forth by the CPOs were vague and unspecific; for example, eliminate the problem, attack the problem, implement particular strategy elements. In the absence of fairly specific goals and objectives, it is difficult to think of specific indicators that would provide some measure of progress. A more specific sense of what one is attempting to accomplish is even more important when the problem is chronic and intractable, such as the drug trafficking and peddler problems in selected locations. Realistically, the officer may be trying simply to contain the problem by continuing to take some sort of action with respect to it. But rarely does the containment objective get translated into some indicators of accomplishment.

The absence of a stable group of community representatives with whom to consider the impact of one's strategies is relevant here as well. Such people are often useful barometers of community perceptions and sentiment, so that a regular sampling of their opinions may suggest whether changes are occurring in the scope or frequency of the problem, or in the nature and extent of the damage it is doing.

Finally, supervisors and commanding officers did not seem to demand much from the CPOs in this regard. This may reflect their own confusion as to how useful feedback can be secured. Or it may reflect an implicit view that some problems cannot be alleviated in any appreciable way, and, in those cases, simply ensuring that the officer continues to act on the problem is sufficient. It may also be another manifestation of their reluctance to obtain and pass on "negative" information. Whatever the reasons, the absence of periodic feedback is an important deficiency in a problem-solving process, and correcting that deficiency will require leadership from those on the command level.

Community Involvement in the Process

The importance and utility of greater community involvement has already been discussed with respect to each of the problem-solving tasks. While the CPOs had extensive contact with people in the community, sustained contact with the *same* people and the serious involvement of such people in all phases of the problem-solving process were rare. One of the reasons for that fact was that very few of the officers had any experience with or training in the skills of community organizing.

The need for such training was anticipated by the designers of the program prior to the start of the pilot project in July 1984. They invited the Citizens Committee for New York City (CCNYC) to assist in providing such training to the CPOs. For some time, this organization had served as an umbrella organization, information clearinghouse, and advocacy voice for thousands of citizens' groups throughout the city. CCNYC was asked to provide new CPOs with an orientation to the community organizing dimension of the role. They did so in a 2-hour segment of the initial orientation and training program.

After program expansion had begun, it became clear that the officers needed more assistance with this aspect of their role and that such assistance would be best provided in the form of a full-day workshop for each of the operating units. The workshops were conducted in the precinct, and they attempted to focus on some of the specific problems with which the officers in that unit were concerned. In addition, the CCNYC staff provided the officers with additional information regarding citizen organizations operating in that precinct and with suggestions for stimulating and sustaining citizen interest in participating in the problem-solving process.

CCNYC evaluated its workshop efforts, called the Police and Community Training Program (Chavis, 1987). The specific objectives of the workshop were:

1. To improve the participants' ability to develop creative solutions to crime problems by mobilizing community resources.
2. To help participants understand the potential that community organizing has for crime prevention on their beats.
3. To learn how to begin to organize.
4. To learn the resources available for participants to assist them in their community organizing efforts.
5. To develop realistic expectations of what CPOs and community residents can do for each other to improve the quality of life. (pp. 6-7)

The evaluation concluded that although the officers expressed satisfaction with most aspects of the workshop and claimed to feel better prepared to handle some aspects of the community organizing role, there was no evidence that this learning had much of an effect on their problem-solving performance. The evaluation staff concluded that the 6-hour workshop was probably not long enough and that the principles enunciated in the workshop should be reinforced by providing on-site assistance to the officers as they attempt to apply those principles to the problems with which they are actually dealing.

It seems likely that the CPOs need considerably more assistance with the community organizing dimension of the role. They come into the program without any training of this sort and with a basic shyness about reaching out to community organizations. Nevertheless, the researchers' observations indicate that an appreciable majority of the CPOs overcome that shyness and make contact with a large number of people in their beats within the first few months of operation. One CPOP sergeant summarized the evolution of attitudes on the part of the CPO and the people in the community as follows:

> I think they do well. I think they could do better. The first 6 months is tough. The second 6 months you start to pick up on things and you start to get a little bit entrenched. People know who you are, and then after that you're starting to move.
>   Within the community, they're learning to change their attitude from "What's your problem?" to "Hey, how're you doing?

How's everything?" And then the community has to respond the opposite way around. They say, "Hmm, he said hello to me. What's wrong with that cop?" You know, and then to finally get back to them saying hello. Six months. And now they have a good personal relationship. They have a nice rapport.

The evidence suggests, moreover, that these personal contacts with the officers are welcomed by the residents and merchants and that they contribute to the favorable assessments of the program, and of the police in general, expressed by community leaders.

Building on these contacts to develop effective working relationships with the people and organizations in the community is another matter. Some officers are not persuaded that such developments would be valuable, and many of those who are so persuaded are not sure of how to go about the process. In addition, some of the CPOs operate in beats that are quite disorganized socially, and in which many of the residents and merchants are afraid to participate in meetings, especially those involving police officials. Finally, many of the officers are not prepared for the ebb and flow of enthusiasm that is so much a part of citizen action efforts.

At the same time, there appears to be a need for organizational and support efforts on the citizen side of the ledger, as well. In some neighborhoods, citizen organizations may be suspicious of police initiatives to plan and act together. Moreover, in many communities, the citizen organizations have no more experience with or training in the problem-solving process than the police. And many community leaders are themselves uncertain about how to motivate and sustain participation among residents who are afraid of falling victim to the very problems they are so anxious to see resolved. Thus citizen groups need assistance to prepare them to participate constructively in the local problem-solving process to which they are invited by the CPO program.

Research Efforts to Measure Impact of Strategies on Problems

When this research project was designed, it was hoped that reliable empirical data could be brought to bear on the question of which strategies worked to ameliorate various types of problems on the beat level. Because the identification of conditions as priority problems emerges from the CPO's applying the problem-solving process in the beat, the research staff could not establish, a priori, a set of problems to be measured before and after the start of the program. In addition, the program was operational in each of the six research precincts for some period before the research began in that precinct. Thus there could be no single, objective means for determining whether the problem-solving actions of the CPOs effected actual changes in the conditions they targeted as problems. In the absence of such a single measure, the research staff attempted to measure the impact of the strategy on each priority problem using five separate impressionistic indicators in each case. They were (a) the CPO's own assessment of impact, (b) the CPOP sergeant's assessment of impact, (c) the field researcher's assessment of impact, (d) an assessment offered by residents and merchants living or operating in the area where the problem occurred, and (e) changes observed in relevant statistical indicators of the problem. While no one of these measures could provide the basis for a definitive judgment about impact, it was believed that a balancing of all five could produce a reasonable estimate of impact.

Regrettably, this approach to evaluating impact failed because it was virtually impossible to secure all of the indicators for each of the problems. The CPO's assessment and the sergeant's assessment were secured for each problem, and these supported one another in virtually every case. Independent assessments by the field researchers were possible for only some of the problems, either because the researcher was not able to observe the condition with sufficient care or frequency to determine whether or not change had occurred (e.g., nighttime parking problems, the tendency of prostitutes to frequent particular intersections in the late evening), or because safety considerations made it impossible for the field researcher to probe and observe the location of the problem (e.g., indoor drug locations).

Safety considerations also influenced the willingness of residents and merchants, who lived in close proximity to various problems, to discuss the problems with the field researchers. As a result, impressions from this source were rarely available for drug problems. And finally, official statistical data describing patterns and frequency of occurrence are simply not collected for a number of the problems with which the CPOs deal (e.g., peddler activity, most parking and traffic problems, homeless people congregating in selected locations, groups of young people menacing the residents of a particular block).

For these reasons, it is not possible to make any precise or demonstrable claims about the effects of the strategies on the priority problems. Moreover, the small size of the problem sample (approximately 100 problems) would not permit an analysis of the relative effectiveness of different strategies for addressing the same problem, even if objective and replicable impact measures were available.

It can be said that the CPOs and the sergeants believed that they were having some desirable effects on the problems they addressed and that those opinions were often shared by the field researcher. When the latter was not the case, the researcher did not challenge the police officers' assessments, but claimed that the information available to him or her was not sufficient to make a judgment.

In a number of cases the efforts of the CPO appeared to have had a desirable effect on a street drug problem. Specifically, consensus was that dealing at a particular location had been terminated completely or made substantially less frequent and less public. In some of these cases, implicit corroboration existed in the form of statistical evidence that the officially reported volume of robberies, burglaries, assaults, and larcenies in the vicinity of the drug location had dropped sharply.

Evidence, in the form of testimony from residents and merchants, also indicated that several of the parking and traffic problems and some of the problems with disorderly groups were alleviated through the efforts of the CPOs. Such successes were less evident when the problem involved a proliferation of peddlers or the congregating of homeless people. As indicated earlier, the officers had little hope that they could do more than move these people along for the relatively short time that the officer remained in the vicinity. Moreover, several of the CPOs were personally ambivalent about the plight of the homeless and the peddlers, and frustrated by their inability to act in what they perceived to be constructive ways in relation to these problems. Finally, the strong positive assessments of the program and the work of individual CPOs expressed by the community leaders (see Chapter 7) suggest that the officers had positive impacts that the research was not able to capture in other than impressionistic ways.

Other Aspects of the Role

The CPOs performed other tasks that were related to but separable from their problem-solving function. A few deserve comment here.

Information Gathering and Dissemination

The program designers expected that, because CPOs would be in the community establishing rapport with residents and merchants, they would become the recipients of information that would not normally be shared with the police. Sergeants and commanding officers in the research precincts, as well as many in other precincts, agreed unanimously that this expectation was realized fully. They insisted also that the personal contacts that the officers made and the personal trust that people vested in the them were responsible for this effect.

Of course, CPOs secured a good deal of information about problems, their locations, and the situations in which they occurred. The officers actively sought information of this kind. In addition, despite some personal risk, people told them about drug locations and drug dealers in the community and identified people suspected of involvement in other types of crimes. Information of this sort was shared by the CPOs with other police units, including Anti-Crime, SNEU, the Narcotics Division, and the Warrant Squad. In fact, commanding officers took pleasure in telling research staff that, after the program had been operating for several months, members of these special units would go directly to the CPOP unit when they were seeking leads on some important crime or looking for a particular suspect.

In the program design, these information-gathering tasks were seen as part of the information-link dimension of the CPO role. CPO performance on the other side of that dimension—disseminating information to the people in the community—appeared to be considerably more uneven. On the positive side, some community leaders specifically mentioned that some CPOs were quite honest in telling the people what efforts the police were making to correct a problem and in suggesting to them what could and could not be expected from those efforts (see Chapter 7). These leaders also expressed the belief that this behavior helped the community in two ways. The information provided by the CPOs was substantively useful to the people, and the openness and candor of the officer encouraged the people to believe that they could address their problems in a productive partnership with the police.

On the other hand, there were instances in the research precincts in which the CPOs clearly missed opportunities to inform the public. Some of the officers did not seem to realize that they possess, or can acquire, information about problems in the community and the situations that give rise to those problems that the people do not possess or understand. Moreover, police officers often have knowledge of how the police bureaucracy works, and how other public agencies work, that could be very useful to local residents and organizations trying to develop realistic plans for improving life in the neighborhood.

When CPO performance in providing information to the community is less impressive than it should be, the shortfall may be attributed to the officer's failure to recognize how much special and useful knowledge he or she possesses. In that case, a little additional training may produce notable improvements in performance. Alternatively, the CPO may be reluctant to make the extra effort required to obtain and organize the information for the people in the community. Additional supervisory encouragement would be appropriate in that case. Finally, however, CPOs may be afraid to provide information about police activities and responses to requests for assistance, because the information does not always show the police in a good light. It is reasonable to expect some degree of prudence in an officer's handling of this type of information, but it is necessary, as well, for supervisors and commanding officers to indicate that an officer's good-faith sharing of such information in an effort to develop effective problem-solving strategies will not work to the officer's professional disadvantage.

Handling Calls-for-Service

As explained earlier, CPOs were not available to be centrally dispatched to calls-for-service in their beats. They were equipped, however, with hand-held radios that permitted them to monitor the police radio traffic and to be reached by their supervisor or other precinct personnel when needed. In their training, they were encouraged to listen for calls in their beats when they were not tied up with other duties, and to respond to them whenever possible. One of the ways in which a call-for-service is coded in New York City indicates whether it is eligible to be handled by a single officer responding. (The overwhelming majority of calls can be dispatched only to two officer units because of their complexity or safety threat.) CPOs were encouraged to call off other units and to respond to such calls themselves. In addition, they were advised to respond as backup on other calls in their beats.

The program's rationale for taking the CPO "off the queue" was to prevent him or her from being "absorbed by the radio" and to provide him or her with the time needed to implement the unique dimensions of the role. Nonetheless, the program designers were sensitive to the possibility that the CPO might be defined invidiously by regular patrol officers because he or she did not have to "carry a load" of calls. The request that CPOs involve themselves with the calls-for-service work load was intended both to check those perceptions and to give the officer added insight into what was going on in his or her beat.

It was not possible for the research staff to collect data systematically on the extent to which this encouragement was heeded by the CPOs in the research precincts. However, the impressions provided through interviews with the CPOs indicate that sergeants and regular patrol officers in those precincts confirm the wisdom of the advice. CPOs who did this with some frequency felt that they were sharing the work load of the precinct, and regular patrol officers who were interviewed by the research staff occasionally credited a CPO whom they saw as willing to do this.

Nevertheless, the majority of CPOs in the research precincts did not appear to do this very often. To some extent, they may have feared that the practice would create an expectation with which they would have to live on a long-term basis. Some indicated that they were reluctant to identify themselves at all to the central dispatcher for fear that once they were identified, the dispatcher would treat them as any other available field unit. Finally, some of the officers appeared to be happy to be rid of the radio response duty and were not likely to pick it up unless directed to do so.

On the other hand, CPOs did handle a fair number of the calls that came into the precinct switchboard directly or were directed to the precinct commanding officer. These tended to be nonemergency calls, often pertaining to quality-of-life conditions, which do not require immediate deployment of a responding officer. Some of these calls were given to the CPOP sergeant, who would, in turn, give them to the appropriate beat officer for response. Many precinct commanders expressed the belief that CPOP was a significant help in handling these type of calls. That belief was evident in the oft-heard comment of the commanding officers, "My phone is no longer ringing all the time."

Services for Special Populations   The CPOs were encouraged, in their training, to identify groups in their beats who needed special assistance from the police. Such groups included elderly residents, teenagers, small schoolchildren, and homeless people. The program design suggested that these segments of the population might be more vulnerable to damage from crime and quality-of-life problems and that various types of crime prevention efforts might be especially productive with respect to them. Finally, providing special services to these groups was seen as a means of building goodwill in the community.

Special services for elderly residents, including crime prevention and safety lectures and escorted shopping trips, were implemented by many CPOP units. In some precincts, the CPOP units helped groups of teenagers get access to school or church facilities for social and athletic activities. In some, CPOs were actively involved in organizing and helping to manage athletic teams and sports leagues. In others, their efforts produced revitalized Police Athletic League chapters.

In some precincts, the unit helped to organize holiday festivities for small children. In one, the CPOP unit was primarily responsible for conducting a "Safe Halloween" party attended by over 2,000 children and their parents. In other precincts, CPOs became especially knowledgeable about the problems of tenants and the resources available, including housing courts, to help tenants secure their rights, resist the incursions of drug dealers, and reduce the risks of robberies and burglaries occurring in or immediately around their buildings.

Not all CPOP units became involved in providing services to special populations, but many did. Where they did, the reactions of the officers and the residents seemed to be unanimously enthusiastic. It is worth noting also that in the early years of the program, some command-level personnel in the department expressed concern that activities of this nature were not properly the responsibility of the police and that engaging in them would reduce appreciably the time and resources available for performing tasks of greater importance. Despite these reservations, the commanding officers in the precincts that did provide such services expressed the belief that their effects were all positive and that the personnel and supervisors in their precincts proved quite capable of preventing an excessive commitment of resources to these tasks.

Summary of Principal Findings

In general, the research indicates that the CPO role can be performed by regular patrol officers in the NYPD and that they prefer the role over that of the regular RMP officer. Within the context of this general finding, the research concentrated on identifying those tasks with which the CPOs seemed to have difficulty, and on considering ways in which those difficulties could be lessened in the future.

It was estimated that less than a third of the average CPO's time was devoted to work on the priority problems he or she identified. This is a lower percentage than the program designers expected and could probably be increased by supervisors seeking to reduce the amount of the officer's time spent on general patrol, and to increase his or her accountability regarding problem-solving activities.

In some cases, the CPO's analysis of a priority problem did not include information that could have been obtained, and consequently the analysis was somewhat superficial. The superficiality of some of the problem analyses appeared to reflect the insufficiency and inadequacy of the officers' initial training in problem solving. Some of the officers failed to appreciate that the purpose of the analysis was to identify points of potential intervention for future action and to learn from past experience what might help to correct the problem in the present. Having identified the problem and where it occurred, such officers were inclined to attack it immediately either by themselves or with other members of the unit. Nevertheless, the research revealed that in general, the broader and deeper the analysis, the more varied the strategies developed by the CPOs and the more they called for the involvement of resources other than the officer.

The analysis of strategies again suggested the utility of CPOs carrying on a regular dialogue with some stable body of residents, merchants, and organizations in the beat. Such a body could assist the officer in making judgments about the relative importance of the problems he or she identifies and could provoke the officer to think more broadly and creatively about strategies to correct them. It would also serve as a check against the inclusion of strategy elements that may have been tried without effect before, or that may inadvertently be offensive to a segment of the community. And a stable group of citizens may provide direct assistance to securing the commitment of nonpolice resources to the strategies developed.

The CPOs were quite successful in implementing the action elements for which they were personally responsible, but most of the CPOs were not particularly careful in monitoring the implementation efforts of agents, including other police officers, outside their own units. The CPOs rarely reviewed their experience with particular strategies or modified them accordingly. The absence of a group of community representatives with whom to consider the impact of one's strategies is relevant here as well. Such people are often useful barometers of community perceptions and sentiment, so that a regular sampling of their opinions may suggest whether changes are occurring in the scope or frequency of the problem, or in the nature and extent of the damage it is doing.

There is a need for organizational and support efforts on the citizen side of the ledger as well. In general, citizen groups are no better prepared for effective problem solving than police officers, who have not been specially trained for the function. Constructive participation will require adequate preparation for both parties.

In a number of precincts, the CPOP units provided special services for needy segments of the population, including elderly people, teenagers, small schoolchildren, and homeless people. The commanders of the precincts in which these services were provided believed that they had many positive effects and that they could be carried out without an excessive commitment of precinct resources.

Evaluating the Performance of CPOs

- Introduction
- CPOs as Problem Solvers
- Sergeants' Assessments of the CPOs
- Research Assistants' Assessments

Introduction   In the NYPD a sergeant is required to complete a performance evaluation form on each of his or her subordinates once a year. This is a standard evaluation form that focuses on qualities and activities expected of a patrol officer, regardless of his or her assignment. Although CPOP sergeants continued to prepare such evaluations in keeping with departmental regulations, Vera staff believed that, because they did not focus on the unique features of the CPO role, these evaluations were of limited utility for the purposes of this research.

After examining several performance assessment instruments used in other departments or in other research projects, the research staff concluded that none was sufficiently sensitive to the specific facets of the CPO role. Therefore, four approaches to evaluating the performance of the research subjects were used in this research, all based on instruments designed by the Vera staff specifically for application to the CPO program.

First, each CPOP sergeant completed an evaluation form on each member of the unit. The form consisted of 22 statements reflecting a broad range of personal qualities and skills requisite to the CPO role. Each CPO sergeant was asked to indicate the degree to which each statement accurately described the officer being assessed. Second, the research assistants were instructed to complete the same form for each of the officers in the units they studied. Third, the research staff developed an evaluation form to assess an officer's performance in carrying out the problem-solving process. Finally, data were collected (from Monthly Activity Reports completed by the CPOs) on a number of activities (arrests, summonses, community meetings attended, etc.) performed by each officer, and these were correlated with the assessment of the CPO as problem solver, the sergeant's assessment, and the research assistant's assessment.

Brief descriptions of each of the instruments and methods used are provided below, along with the results obtained from each of these approaches and the relationships among the assessments obtained using these varied techniques.

CPOs as Problem Solvers

As was described in Chapter 3, during the first month of the research period in each precinct, Vera research assistants approached each beat officer and explained that as part of the research the CPO would be asked to identify "priority problems" on which he or she was currently working. The researcher recorded each problem on a Problem Process Record (PPR) form. Then, during the course of the next 6 months, through discussions with the CPO and observations of the problem location, the researcher completed the PPR. The completed PPR served as a record of the process the officer used to identify and analyze the problem, the strategies he or she developed to deal with the problem, the degree of success with which the officer implemented these strategies, the impact of the strategies, and the extent of community involvement in the process.

The result of this data collection effort yielded 102 PPRs, each representing a single problem, identified by 53 CPOs.[1] An evaluation form was then devised to assess performance in each of four areas of problem solving: (a) problem identification and analysis, (b) strategy development, (c) strategy implementation, and (d) community involvement. Each PPR was assessed by the three senior members of the research team, and scores were computed for each officer's performance in each of the four areas for each of that officer's priority problems. In addition, *problem* totals were obtained by summing across the four areas, and *CPO* totals were computed by summing the officer's two highest problem scores.[2]

It is important to note that impacts on the problems were not considered as part of the officers' performance evaluations, in part because of the measurement problems described in Chapter 3. In addition, the research staff recognized that the impact on a particular problem could be affected by a wide variety of factors beyond the officer's control and unrelated to the quality of his or her performance or problem-solving skills. These factors included the varying degrees of difficulty involved in "solving" problems, which ranged in complexity from relatively minor but persistent parking problems to extensive narcotics trafficking operations.

TABLE 4.1 Mean Evaluation Scores by Precinct

	A	B	C	D	E	F	Overall
				Precinct			
Analysis	37.7	40.4	36.6	36.8	37.8	37.8	37.9
Strategy	23.3	33.5	27.1	22.6	28.4	26.1	27.1
Implement	25.9	33.5	26.9	22.0	30.3	26.3	27.8
Community	24.8	29.1	28.8	24.2	27.2	29.3	27.4
Prob. Total	111.8	136.5	119.4	105.6	123.6	119.6	120.1
CPO total	223.5	255.1	240.2	154.3	235.2	224.2	222.2

Problem Identification and Analysis

The 11 items used to assess problem identification and problem analysis (referred to here as the Analysis subscale), rewarded officers who specifically identified the behaviors or conditions that constituted the problem, the location, the time of occurrence, and the sequence of events leading up to the problem. In addition, CPOs were judged on how well they identified the characteristics of the people affected by the problem and those causing the problem. Finally, the officer's efforts to describe prior attempts to correct the problem, to identify resources for dealing with the problem, to assess the level of community concern, and to obtain information from nonpolice sources were evaluated.

In this evaluation, an officer could receive scores between 10 and 50 on each subscale. The overall mean for the Analysis subscale was 37.9. Across precincts, CPOs tended to perform better on the Analysis subscale than on any of the other three subscales (see Table 4.1). In addition, there was little variation among precincts. The mean scores ranged from 36.6 to 40.4, and differences among them were not statistically significant (meaning the differences might have occurred by chance). The means for the other three subscales were all approximately 27.

The reasons for this effect are unclear, although it may be that identification and analysis of problems is more within the bailiwick of the police officer, and therefore better addressed by the training obtained in the Police Academy and/or CPOP training, than are devising strategies and implementing them. It is also likely that the higher average scores on this subscale are partially attributable to the inclusion of a few items on which it was difficult *not* to score high—identification of the conditions that constitute the problem, geographical location, and time of occurrence.

Although the total scores for the Analysis function were rather high, this was not true for all of the questions measuring the various aspects of this function. (Table 4.2 shows the mean scores achieved by the research subjects on each of the items that constituted the Analysis subscale). For example, the officers were generally adequate in describing the behavioral details of the problems they identified and the sequences of actions and reactions involved in the manifes-

TABLE 4.2 Means and Standard Deviations on the Item Analysis for PPR Evaluations, Analysis Subscale

Attribute	N	Mean	SD
Behavior/conditions	97	48.6	3.6
Location	97	49.2	3.5
Time	97	46.7	5.9
People affected	97	39.3	7.2
Sequence	83	35.7	8.2
Perpetrators	85	37.3	7.4
Phys./soc. setting	96	36.7	8.4
Prior efforts	62	28.4	9.9
Local resources	97	23.9	10.9
Nonpolice resources	97	30.4	8.7
Community concern	96	36.7	8.5

tation of the problem. Nor did they seem to realize that such details could be useful in suggesting points of intervention.

The characteristics of the people causing the problem were sometimes known only in general terms, when a more thorough inquiry among the community residents might have permitted the identification of individuals or groups of perpetrators and a better understanding of the dynamics of the problem. This increased knowledge and understanding, in turn, might have provided insight into the ways in which community residents and local agencies could be mobilized to address the problem without relying on police officers and law enforcement tactics.

Finally, in performing the Analysis function, the CPOs were generally superficial in documenting previous efforts to address the problem, especially those undertaken by nonpolice organizations and individuals, and in considering what could be learned from such efforts about either the problem or the potential effects of various corrective strategies.

Strategy Development Each officer was assessed on his or her plan for correcting the problem; this assessment was based on how well the officer covered eight considerations involved in the development of a problem-solving strategy. Did the officer articulate a set of clear and feasible goals and objectives? Did the strategy recognize the important dimensions of the problem and previous attempts to address the problem? Also included in this dimension was the extent to which the officer used available resources such as other police officers, organizations, and neighborhood residents and merchants. Finally, the officer was evaluated on the basis of whether he or she had articulated a means of assessing the effects of the strategy.

As was indicated above in Table 4.1, scores on the Strategy Development (Strategy) subscale tended to be lower than those on Analysis; the overall mean was 27.1, suggesting that the average

TABLE 4.3   Means and Standard Deviations on the Item Analysis for
PPR Evaluations, Strategy Subscale

Attribute	N	Mean	SD
Goals/objectives	97	34.4	7.8
Important dimensions	97	31.7	8.6
Previous efforts	62	26.7	11.0
Police resources	97	28.2	14.0
Organizational resources	97	18.9	12.7
Community resources	97	20.4	10.8
Resource deployment	97	23.6	9.6
Effects assessment	97	30.9	9.9

officer obtained about half of the available points for this dimension of the problem-solving process. There was also more variation among precincts: The means for five of the precincts ranged from 22.6 to 28.4, while one precinct (B) had a mean Strategy score of 33.5. (The mean for Precinct B was significantly higher, at the $p < .05$ level, than those of three other precincts—A, D, and F.) The CPOs in Precinct B were generally very active and also tended to have higher mean scores than the other precincts on other subscales. None of the precincts stood out as having an especially low score on the Strategy subscale.

Generally, the strategies developed by the officers were designed to address those dimensions of the problem that their analyses had suggested were the most important. As is indicated in Table 4.3, the CPOs were somewhat successful in defining specific goals and objectives for their problem-solving strategies, and, as might be expected, they were notably better at identifying other police resources that might help correct the problem than they were at planning for the involvement of nonpolice resources.

*Strategy
Implementation*   Strategy implementation (Implement) was measured using just three items. These items reflected the extent to which the officer completed his or her own responsibilities under the strategy, whether the officer kept abreast of implementation efforts by other members of the police department, and whether he or she kept abreast of implementation efforts by nonpolice resources.

Mean scores on the Implement subscale were very similar to those on the Strategy subscale (see Table 4.1); the overall mean across precincts was 27.8, and the means for five of the precincts ranged between 22.0 and 30.3. The precinct with the highest mean Strategy score (B) also had the highest mean Implement score, 33.5. The precinct with the lowest mean Strategy score (D) also had the lowest mean Implement score. (The means for these two precincts, B and D, were significantly different from each other.) This suggests that those officers who were good at strategy development also tended to be good at strategy implementation, and these strengths appeared to be more concentrated in some precincts than others. It is not clear from the

TABLE 4.4 Means and Standard Deviations on the Item Analysis for PPR Evaluations, Implementation Subscale

Attribute	N	Mean	SD
CPO implementation	94	40.9	11.5
Police implementation	97	24.5	14.2
Nonpolice implementation	91	18.0	12.5

data, however, whether these differences are due to stronger training or supervision in some precincts than others, or whether they are attributable to differences in officer selection, or to other factors. Further discussion of these possibilities appears below in the section on Correlations Among Measures of Performance.

In general, the CPOs did carry out the actions for which they were personally responsible within the strategies they developed (see Table 4.4). However, they were considerably less successful in monitoring the implementation efforts of other police resources (except those of their own CPOP unit) and those of nonpolice resources. Thus the officers were often not precisely aware of the extent to which the strategies they had outlined were actually implemented, or how and why the efforts had failed. Moreover, the research field observations indicated that officers were not always clear as to what they would do with this type of information if they did have it on a systematic basis. In interviews, CPOs claimed that it was sometimes more difficult to get other units within the department to carry out their responsibilities within a particular strategy than it was to get other city agencies or community groups to carry out theirs. Pressing to get action from other units was sometimes seen as difficult and possibly risky to one's career in the department.

Community Involvement

The officers' performance on the community involvement (Community) dimension of the problem-solving role was measured using five items. Each CPO was rated on the extent to which he or she involved local residents, merchants, or organizations in identifying and analyzing the problem; used community members to provide information not otherwise available; showed evidence that he or she was aware of the level of community concern; involved community members as part of the corrective strategy; and made efforts to review the strategy and monitor its implementation with the community.

The pattern of scores on the Community dimension differed from that found for Strategy and Implement (see Table 4.1). Here, four of the precinct means were about equal and the other two were somewhat lower. None of these differences was large or statistically significant, however; the overall mean was 27.4, with the lowest mean being 24.2 and the highest 29.3. The degree of community organization in a precinct appeared unrelated to the extent to which officers involved community members in problem solving; mean Community

TABLE 4.5 Means and Standard Deviations on the Item Analysis for
PPR Evaluations, Community Involvement Subscale

Attribute	N	Mean	SD
Community ID/analysis	97	33.7	9.5
Community information	97	30.6	9.8
Community feelings	96	35.5	8.8
Community involvement	97	17.7	10.5
Community review	97	19.5	11.2

scores in some highly organized precincts were relatively high, but in
other highly organized precincts, they were relatively low.

The CPOs usually scored fairly well on the first item considered
in the Community scale—involving local people and organizations in
identifying and analyzing the problem (see Table 4.5). In addition,
they seemed reasonably aware of how strongly the community felt
about a particular problem. These items indicate that officers solicited and received information about the problem and the people's
feelings concerning the problem. They do not suggest that the officers
secured a large portion of the information that might have been
obtained from residents and merchants in the community, or that the
officers were thorough in tapping all segments of the population in
their beats. These concerns could not be measured quantitatively, but
they are discussed qualitatively in Chapter 3.

The CPOs were not very successful in involving community
residents in their problem-solving strategies, and when they did
succeed, the residents participated largely as members of block watch
or tenant patrol organizations. Moreover, only in a handful of instances did a CPO succeeded in involving local residents, merchants,
and organizations in a review of the implementation and effects of
problem-solving strategies. No structural models for this purpose
were established before or during the program, and few CPOs or
supervisors expressed awareness of how such efforts might be beneficial to the program.

Composite Scores   Scores on the four dimensions described above were combined to
form two indices—a Problem total and a CPO total. The Problem total
was computed by summing across the four subscales for each problem,
while the CPO total was computed by summing the CPO's two highest
total problem scores. The mean Problem totals and the mean CPO
totals are reported in Table 4.1 for each precinct. It is clear from the
data that the small but consistent differences evinced on the subscales add up to a more striking difference on the summary scores.
Performance in Precinct B stands out as superior to the others, while
the mean for Precinct D is considerably lower than the rest.[3] In fact,
the mean Problem total scores for precincts B and D were significantly
different from each other.

TABLE 4.6 Problem Evaluation Scores by Problem Type

Problem Type	N	Mean	SD
Drugs	28	131.5	28.6
Parking, traffic	16	107.6	25.2
Disorderly groups	14	121.1	24.5
Auto larceny	10	118.2	26.8
Prostitution/gambling	6	122.2	9.4
Burglary	5	123.1	40.9
Robbery	5	109.9	28.1
Homeless people	5	117.1	16.0
Peddlers	4	107.9	23.3
Misc. street condition	4	114.6	21.1
Total	97	120.1	26.6

Data were collected on the type of problem identified in each PPR, and an attempt was made to determine whether performance differed across different types of problems. This type of analysis was rendered unreliable by the large number of categories of problems (10) and by the high degree of overlap between precinct and problem type. As a result, while it is possible to see from the mean Problem total scores presented in Table 4.6 that the CPOs generally dealt more effectively with some types of problems than others, it is not possible to determine whether that is attributable to varying performance by *problem type* or varying performance by *precinct*. For example, 15 of the 28 drug problems occurred in one precinct and 6 of the 14 problems with disorderly groups were in another; it would be impossible, therefore, to separate the effect of problem type from that of precinct without a considerably larger sample.

Sergeants' Assessments of the CPOs

At the end of the research period in each precinct, the CPO sergeant was asked to evaluate the performance of each of his beat officers using a form devised specifically for the research. This instrument consisted of 22 items; the sergeant was asked to indicate on a four-point scale the extent to which each statement was descriptive of the officer. The items were designed to assess all the dimensions of the CPO role—problem solving, community outreach and organizing, information gathering, and so forth.[4]

Scores on the scale could range between 22 and 88, but the actual minimum was 56 and the maximum was 88. The overall mean was 76.1, and the standard deviation was 8.3. Thus, the sergeants tended to rate their officers quite highly, with little variation among the scores accorded to individual officers.

Although comparisons of CPOs' performance as problem solvers produced small but consistent differences among precincts, it is not meaningful to make such comparisons of the sergeants' assessments. Because each precinct had a different sergeant, a difference between two precincts might represent two different ways of using the scale rather than a real difference between the officers' performance in those precincts. More useful are the correlations among the various performance measures; these are presented and discussed below.

It is clear from the high mean and from inspection of the rating frequencies on individual items that sergeants are reluctant to give officers in their command poor ratings. The sergeants very rarely gave a negative rating to a CPO; rather, they used the two highest scores, 3 and 4, almost exclusively, and in no instance did a sergeant give one of his officers a score of 1 on an item. Thus, despite the research purpose of this rating form, the sergeants treated it as they do the standardized assessments that the department requires them to complete. As a result, in the sergeants' hands, the instrument did not discriminate between officers who were performing well and those who were not.

Research Assistants' Assessments

The field research assistants evaluated the CPOs in their precincts using the same form used by the sergeants.[5] However, the instrument was used somewhat differently by the research assistants; the overall mean was lower (66.5, $sd = 10.9$) and the range was greater—27 to 80—than when used by the sergeants. The same problem of comparison among precincts exists for the field researchers as for the sergeants; four research assistants worked in the six research precincts, and therefore differences between precincts may be attributable to the research assistants rather than to the officers' behavior.

Across precincts, the research assistants appeared more willing to evaluate individual officers negatively than did the sergeants. This may be partially a function of the fact that in no way did an officer's behavior reflect on the research assistant, while poor performance of an officer could reflect negatively on his or her supervisor. Thus it is possible that a research assistant could be more objective about poor performance. On the other hand, the sergeant should be more knowledgeable about an officer's performance, and perhaps better able to evaluate accurately his or her performance than would be a researcher stationed in the precinct for only 6 months. Again, the correlations among the various performance evaluation measures should shed light on this question.

CPO Activity Levels

One of the traditional ways that supervisors measure officer performance is through the levels of various activities they perform. These activities include arrests and summonses, and for CPOs they also include community-oriented behaviors such as community meetings attended, block watchers recruited, and block associations formed. Although CPOP is not generally an arrest-oriented unit, these data were collected because they are conventional measures of police performance and permit the examination of the relationship

TABLE 4.7 Unit Activity

Activity	Precinct					
	A	B	C	D	E	F
Felony arrests	8	21	20	1	6	1
Other arrests	<u>59</u>	<u>173</u>	<u>15</u>	<u>63</u>	<u>62</u>	<u>26</u>
Total arrests	67	194	35	64	68	27
Abandoned cars	6	23	123	114	44	62
Security surveys	1	2	1	31	8	42
Meetings attended	26	50	69	56	61	12
Intelligence	14	31	6	—	22	8
Summonses	785	1956	1610	769	564	932

between such traditional measures and the evaluation instruments created specifically for the current study.

For each CPO, field researchers collected data on the number of felony and other arrests made, summonses issued, abandoned vehicles towed, intelligence reports filed, security surveys conducted, and community meetings attended during the 6-month research period.[6] Data were collected for each officer and then summed across months to provide officer totals and across officers to provide unit totals.[7]

The activity totals compiled by the research subjects in the six precincts are presented in Table 4.7.[8] It is clear that the number of arrests made by the research units vary considerably, with Precinct B showing almost three times the number of arrests compiled by its nearest competitor. In general, CPOP units were not encouraged to make large numbers of arrests, but to be available to the community and to focus their attention on the problems, especially quality-of-life problems, which were of most concern to the people in the beats. Arrests were to be used as one among many tools that the officers might bring to the solution of these problems. Consistent with this theme, Precinct B was the most problem-ridden (at least with respect to drugs and conventional street crimes) of the precincts, and the most pervasive problem in the precinct was street narcotics trafficking. Thus the officers made many arrests and issued many summonses as part of their efforts to rid the streets of the narcotics dealers. On the other hand, abandoned cars were a serious problem in several beats in Precincts C and D, as reflected in the numbers of towed vehicles in those precincts.

Table 4.7 also indicates that conducting security surveys of private residences was a rather infrequent activity in the research precincts. In the program design, this was seen as an activity that might be useful as a preventive measure in neighborhoods with serious burglary problems, and more generally as an appreciated public service. Indeed, the CPOs were provided with some specialized training so they could conduct these surveys, but they were precluded from conducting the more technically demanding surveys of commercial premises. These were to be done by the crime prevention officers in the precincts. The limited number of surveys conducted appears to reflect a low demand for them among the public, a general reluctance among the officers to enter private residences unless asked to for an official purpose, and the officers' general inclination to avoid activities that required them to prepare additional paperwork.

The number of meetings attended was considered a rather important indicator of CPO activity by the department officials, who managed the expansion of the program, because of the program's emphasis on the officers becoming involved with the residents and their concerns. The data presented in Table 4.7 indicate that in four precincts the officers averaged approximately one meeting per officer per month. While this is considerably more than regular patrol officers, who almost never attend community meetings, it is probably a lower level of this activity than the program managers would consider desirable.

The research staff noted some ambivalence among the officers about attending public meetings. On the one hand, they enjoyed the fact that they were generally quite well received by the public when they did attend. On the other hand, many of the officers were uncomfortable speaking in public, and some were reluctant to change shifts or work overtime for the purpose of attending such meetings. Moreover, some worked in beats containing very few community organizations that met with any regularity, and some of these officers were not confident in their ability to stimulate such organizations. Finally, some officers believed that the principal reason they were being encouraged to attend community meetings was to ensure that they would be familiar with the problems that concerned the residents and merchants. This objective could be accomplished adequately, they believed, through the conversations they had with small groups of residents and merchants as they moved about the community on patrol.

The preparation and transmittal of intelligence reports occurred in the research precincts less frequently than expected. When it did occur, it generally involved a report on a suspected narcotics location that was passed on to the Narcotics Division for possible action. It is not surprising, therefore, that Precinct B would lead the others in the number of such reports prepared. It should be noted, however, that the research was conducted prior to any special efforts to facilitate good working relationships between the CPOP units and the various borough-level narcotics units. In such an atmosphere, many of the CPOs in research precincts did not believe that formal intelligence reports sent outside the precinct would accomplish anything. Thus they would make notes about various locations and conditions in their own records, bring information back to the CPOP sergeant, and pass it on orally to other officers and specialized units, such as Anti-Crime or the Street Narcotics Enforcement Units, on the precinct level.

The unit figures were translated into activity scores for each of the CPOs by calculating the proportion of each unit's activity for

TABLE 4.8 Correlations Among Evaluation Scores

	Evaluation Measure		
Variable	*CPO Total*	*Sergeant*	*Researcher*
Sergeant	.17	—	—
Researcher	.78*	.24	—
Arrests	· .02	−.10	−.08
Summonses	.12	.11	.19
Cars towed	.26	.07	.25
Meetings	.30*	.15	.38*

Note: *p < .05

which each CPO was responsible. However, when the unit's total for an activity was less than 10, that activity was dropped from the analysis for that unit.[9]

The research then sought to determine the extent to which these officer activity scores correlated with one another and with the previously described measures of performance evaluation. Because the CPO activity scores were not uniformly available for all precincts, only four activity variable were actually used in the correlation analyses—total arrests, summonses, abandoned cars towed, and meetings attended. There was very little relationship among the activity variables. The officer's contribution to the unit's arrest totals was not significantly correlated with his or her contribution to the summonses totals, nor with any of the other activity variables. Thus, no support exists here for the contention that police officers who are active in one area are active in all. In fact, the only significant correlation among the activity variables was that between the abandoned vehicles towed measure and the meetings attended ($r = .40, p = .005, N = 46$).

Correlations between the activity measures and the other three measures of performance—the CPO as problem solver (CPO total), the sergeant's evaluation, and the research assistant's evaluation—were calculated. The correlation coefficients for each performance measure with the others are presented in Table 4.8.

The most notable statistic in this table is the very high correlation between the CPO total and the researcher's evaluation ($r = .78$, $p < .0001, N = 48$). This indicates that these instruments measure similar aspects of the officer's performance as a problem solver, the central feature of the CPO role. It was that aspect of the role on which the researchers were asked to focus their data collection efforts. The data they collected describing the work of the CPOs were the data on which the senior research staff's performance assessments were based. Yet the assessment instrument used for that purpose was never used by the field researchers; nor was it seen by them before they collected the data. Rather, the instrument used to obtain the researcher's evaluation addressed more features of the CPO role and was identical to that used by the sergeants. Yet, the data in the table also indicate that no significant correlation exists between the sergeant's and the researcher's assessment, or the sergeant's assessment and the CPO total.

This lack of correlation might suggest a lack of validity in these three performance measures were it not for the previously mentioned fact that the sergeant's assessment did not discriminate between performance levels among the officers. Virtually every officer received a high score when assessed by the sergeant, indicating that the sergeant was not attempting to use the instrument seriously as a performance assessment device. Therefore, the fact that the sergeant's assessment scores do not correlate significantly with any other measure of performance or activity adds to, rather than detracts from, confidence in the CPO total and field researcher's assessment as valid measures of problem-solving performance.

In this regard, it is also noteworthy that the only activity measure that obtained a statistically significant correlation with these problem-solving measures was the measure of community meetings attended ($r = .30$; $p = .04$; $N = 48$, with CPO total; and $r = .38$; $p = .0063$; $N = 51$, with the researcher's evaluation). The meetings-attended variable may be a useful proxy for the extent to which the officer interacts with residents and merchants in the community, an activity that is also at the core of the CPO role.

Finally, this table of correlation coefficients also indicates that the levels of arrest and summons activity achieved by an officer are not necessarily good indicators of his or her effectiveness as a problem-solving CPO. This finding is also consistent with the program's contention that arrests and summons activity should not be seen as ends in themselves, but only as possibly useful tactics within problem-solving strategies.

Notes   1. For the purposes of the evaluation, 5 of the PPRs were dropped; thus the evaluations described below were conducted on 97 PPRs, representing 48 officers. One problem was dropped from this analysis because it was so idiosyncratic that it did not fit into the evaluation categories. Four other PPRs were eliminated because the problems had been identified by one officer (who subsequently left the unit prior to the end of the research period) and completed by his or her replacement. As a result, the data contained in each of those four PPRs represented the work of two officers and could not be used to evaluate the performance of either officer.

2. Reliability analyses (Cronbach's alpha) were computed on each of the four subscales and on the total scores; the results of these analyses indicated that the total score and the subscales were quite reliable. Descriptive statistics were computed on each of the four subscales, the problem total, and the CPO total, and then analyzed by precinct. For each of these analyses, except the CPO evaluation,

the sample size is 97; the analysis of officer evaluations (CPO totals) includes 48 CPOs.

3. The very low CPO total mean of 154.3 for Precinct D is substantially influenced by the fact that one CPO in that precinct did not identify *any* priority problems. When pressed by the Vera research assistant, he responded that he was not working on any problems; therefore, that CPO was assigned a CPO total score of zero. There were an additional three CPOs in this precinct who identified only one problem and received scores of zero for the second problem. Nevertheless, the mean Problem total score, which is unaffected by the number of problems identified by a particular officer, was lower for this precinct than for the remaining five.

4. Reliability analyses (Cronbach's alpha) showed the internal consistency of this measure to be very high (alpha = .95), indicating that the 22 items do form a scale.

5. Therefore it is not surprising that the reliability for this instrument was equally high (alpha = .96) when used by the research assistants.

6. The data were collected from a report prepared by each officer entitled "Precinct Community Patrol Officer's Monthly Activity Report." Attempts were also made to collect data on the number of block watchers recruited and the number of block associations formed. However, because the data were not collected uniformly, they were not useful for the purposes of this report.

7. If an officer was in the unit for at least 3 months but less than 6 months, his or her totals were prorated by simply assuming that the average level of activity (of arrests, for example) was constant across the 6 months and adjusting accordingly. For example, if an officer was in the unit for 5 months and issued 100 summonses during that time, it was assumed that he issued 20 each month and his adjusted 6-month total would be 120. Any officer who was assigned to a beat for fewer than 3 months was excluded from this phase of the data collection.

8. Because the activities of a few officers were excluded for reasons explained above, the actual totals compiled by the units were somewhat higher, in some cases, than those shown in the table.

9. Thus, as can be seen from Table 4.7, CPOs received scores for felony arrest activity in only two units, for security surveys in two units, and for intelligence reports in only three units. In addition, no abandoned-cars-towed scores were calculated for officers in Precinct A.

Supervision in the CPO Program

- Introduction
- Method
- Supervision in Regular Patrol, NPT, and CPOP
- General Perceptions of Sergeants and Commanding Officers Regarding Supervision in CPOP
- The Supervisor as Leader and Guide
- The Supervisor as Control Agent
- The Program's Efforts to Strengthen Supervisory Performance
- Summary of Findings

Introduction

In every precinct, the CPOP unit is a group of selected officers performing a specialized function under the direction of a supervising sergeant. Given the newness of the role and the differences between it and the conventional patrol role, the department relies heavily on the skills of the supervisor to ensure that the program is implemented effectively and with integrity.

The supervision function in police work involves a wide range of responsibilities. These include shaping the attitudes of subordinates in terms of the goals of the agency, teaching them how to apply those goals in their work, assessing the adequacy of subordinates' performance, using available incentives and training to correct deficiencies in performance, and monitoring subordinates' actions to control various types of misbehavior (Goldstein, 1977; Weisburd et al., 1988). The special challenges of supervision in the CPO program and how the function was performed in the six research precincts are described in this chapter.

Many students of policing have suggested that the growing emphasis on community and problem-solving policing will pose special challenges to line supervision systems (Brown, 1981; Goldstein & Susmilch, 1981; Barker & Carter, 1986; McElroy, 1987). They contend that the military model of organization adopted by most urban police departments presumes a large degree of predictability in the situations encountered by police officers, while many of the real-life situations cannot be anticipated, and the norms designed to define appropriate behavior by police officers often do not provide useful guidance in addressing those situations. Fashioning effective responses, especially if they are to bring genuine relief to the situations encountered, requires that community patrol officers operate with levels of flexibility, discretion, and imagination rarely permitted regular patrol officers.

Egon Bittner (1983) suggests that conventional police organizations implicitly define line officers as "soldier bureaucrats" for whom compliance with regulations and avoidance of trouble are of primary importance. This emphasis reflects organizational concern with the "legality" of their members' actions. Such concern is appropriate, but this approach to control ignores the importance of cultivating the spirit of "workmanship," which Bittner indicates "involves the maintenance of minimally acceptable levels of knowledge, skill and judicious performance" (p. 3). Such qualities are especially important to officers who are expected to be problem solvers (Goldstein, 1979).

With these considerations in mind, it is useful to think of the role of the police supervisor as consisting of two related, but somewhat distinct, dimensions—the supervisor as leader and guide, and the supervisor as control agent. As leader-guide the supervisor defines goals and encourages their internalization by subordinates, guides the officers substantively in addressing the problems they encounter, provides them with regular feedback on the extent to which their behavior contributes to the realization of unit goals, and defines and protects the interests of his or her subordinates within and outside of the larger organization. As a control agent, the supervisor makes certain that subordinates understand what constitutes appropriate and inappropriate behavior under various circumstances, attempts to prevent noncompliance by keeping subordinates out of situations in which rule-violative behavior is likely, monitors their behavior to assess compliance with regulations, and attempts to correct noncompliant behavior through various control techniques, including the imposition of authorized punishments.

The work of the scholars mentioned above suggests that, in fact if not always in rhetoric, police agencies place far greater emphasis on the control agent dimension of the supervisor's role, and this disproportionate emphasis will prove to be particularly problematic with respect to community-oriented, problem-solving initiatives such as the CPO program. This chapter considers how these two dimensions of supervision were manifested in the six research precincts and the special tensions experienced by the CPOP supervisor. The questions addressed include: how and how well the supervisors performed the leader-guide as opposed to the control agent function; what were the more notable achievements and failings of supervision in each of these areas; and what might be done to strengthen supervisory performance in the CPO program.

Method   The research staff used several techniques to address these questions. First, the field research assistants, who spent 6 months in each of the precincts, were encouraged to spend a good deal of time with the unit sergeants and to converse informally with them both in the precinct house and out in the street. These field observations and interviews enabled the research assistants to note the issues that were of principal concern to the sergeant and how he focused his attention on them. In addition, observations were made regarding the sergeant's interactions with the members of the unit, including informal comments he might make about their performance, strengths, and weaknesses. These observations were the subject of regular debriefing sessions with senior research staff. Those sessions identified follow-up questions and related issues on which the research assistants would concentrate when they returned to the precincts.

In addition, during the last month of the data collection period in each research precinct, two senior research staff members conducted an extensive interview with each CPOP sergeant and another lengthy interview with each precinct commanding officer. The interviews with the six sergeants lasted 2 to 3 hours, while the commanding officer interviews (there were actually seven because one of the COs was transferred during the research period) lasted between 1 and 2 hours. All of these interviews were taped, transcribed, and analyzed to produce the material presented in this chapter.

Finally, the data on the six research precincts were supplemented through informal observations of and conversations with CPOs, unit sergeants, and precinct commanders from precincts other than the research precincts. These observations and conversations took place before, during, and after the data collection process in the research precincts, and they provide a perspective for thinking about supervision in a community policing program.

The sergeants who served as supervisors in the research precincts, as well as their commanding officers, were assured that the data collected from and about them would be accorded the same confidential treatment as any other research data. Assuring such subjects that their names will not be used in research reports is simple, but not sufficient to prevent their being personally identified. Because there were only six research precincts, there were only six sergeants and seven commanding officers who served in them during the data collection period. Therefore, to decrease the likelihood that these subjects might be identified by department officials, the quotes used in the chapter are not attributed to a person or to a precinct. Moreover, supervisory practices that are judged deficient are not identified with a particular precinct, nor are comparisons drawn among the precincts with respect to the quality of supervision observed. This does not mean that such differences did not exist among the precincts. They did, but confidentiality concerns prohibit describing them in relation to specific precincts. Instead, the analysis presented here identifies those elements of supervisory practice that appeared to be effective and those that did not, and provides some insight into the effects of those practices and the circumstances that appear to support them.

In light of these confidentiality concerns and the limited size of the sample, no effort was made to identify factors in the background, perspectives, or attitudes of sergeants or commanding officers that might be statistically correlated with effective supervision. Nonetheless, the analysis presented here does permit the identification of both supervisory and command practices that appear to strengthen CPOP performance, as well as those that undermine it.

As previously indicated, community policing in general, and CPOP in particular, pose some distinctive challenges for the patrol supervisor. To identify and understand the nature of those challenges, one must first understand the crucial operational differences between CPOP and regular patrol in the NYPD and the implications of those differences for the demands imposed on the supervisors and the tools available to meet them. Those concerns are considered below, followed by the specific demands that the CPO program imposes on the supervisor attempting to be a leader and guide for his or her subordinates. Then the unique problems that the CPOP supervisor faces in his capacity as a control agent, and the ways in which these problems were met, or not met, in the research precincts are described. The chapter concludes with a description of the efforts made by program managers to understand the needs of CPOP supervisors and to provide services designed to strengthen supervisory performance throughout the city.

Supervision in Regular Patrol, NPT, and CPOP

Operations and Supervision in Regular Patrol

The role of the CPO sergeant differs from the traditional patrol sergeant in several ways, and to understand the importance of these differences it is essential to be acquainted with the patrol structure in a typical New York City precinct. Briefly, most patrol officers are assigned to one of the nine squads that operate on a very complicated scheduling system involving tour rotation across day, evening, and midnight tours. The officers working the "nine-squad chart" are primarily responsible for staffing the RMP cars responding to the 911 calls for service. Depending on the work load of the precinct, the size of the squads varies; however, in general, each squad has 8 to 12 officers. Each squad also has its own sergeant, who works the same hours as the officers and rotates tours with them.

In all precincts, for example, two squads and their sergeants are scheduled to work the day tour (8:00 a.m. to 4:00 p.m.). When all personnel are working and when other duties permit, the sergeants divide the precinct in half; one half takes the northern portion and the other takes the southern. In addition to monitoring the activities of the officers assigned to their squad, the sergeants also supervise officers assigned to traditional foot posts, scooters, or "conditions" cars. The deployment of personnel in the field may be as follows: 5 RMPs (in "sector cars"), 2 officers on scooters performing summons duty, 8 officers on traditional foot posts, and 2 conditions cars. Thus there may be 24 officers in the field to be supervised.

The responsibilities and tasks of the patrol sergeant and RMP officers and the procedures for handling a wide variety of situations are described in the Patrol Guide and the Administrative Guide. The sergeant rides on patrol with his officers to ensure that the officers are answering the 911 calls quickly and handling them expeditiously. If at all possible, the sergeant is expected to be present at the scene of serious crimes or arrest situations and to supervise incidents involving reported deaths (DOAs) or emotionally disturbed persons. These situations are complicated and time-consuming. If one sergeant is involved with such duties, then his or her squad is monitored by the other patrol sergeant. As a result, it is not uncommon for one sergeant to be supervising 20 or more officers, many of whom are not in his or her squad and therefore are unfamiliar to him.

In the absence of the sergeant, the officers' whereabouts can be monitored to some degree by the Central Communications Division, because their activities are tied to the 911 system and there is constant radio contact. Therefore, if a sector car on a 911 assignment does not radio in to the Communications Division within 30 minutes or cannot be raised on the radio, then it is assumed that something is wrong. However, these situations are very rare. Moreover, logistical factors limit the effectiveness of monitoring by Communications. At any given time, a single dispatcher may be responsible for 50 or 60 units in the field, and it is impossible for anyone to monitor dozens of units simultaneously. As one CPOP sergeant explained, the role of the regular patrol sergeant is often difficult, and he or she cannot rely on the vigilance of the dispatcher:

On the nine-squad chart, you work on a 6-week cycle. You're working with your same squad over time. Another squad you only work with 2 weeks out of the 6. And other squads you only work with 2 days here, 3 days there. . . . When you're out there supervising a platoon, you may be the only sergeant with 10 radio cars and 30 people. If I was on patrol I could get stuck with a homicide, or an EDP [emotionally disturbed person], or a DOA and I could get tied up there for 3, 4 hours. . . . In the sector car, the RMP's supposed to be in its sector, but they could be into something, or the radio sends them to the other end of the precinct. What happens between when the job is over and they get back to their sector? Again, the cops and the sergeant cover the whole precinct. I don't think the sergeant can control it as well.

While much of patrol work is routine, working with officers who are not known to the sergeant adds an element of uncertainty and unpredictability, thereby threatening his or her supervisory effectiveness. In addition, although RMPs are assigned to specific sectors, in the course of a tour they may be all over the precinct responding to calls. As the number of officers and units in the field expands, the sergeant's span of control increases, which in turn decreases the amount of time that the sergeant can devote to monitoring the activities of individual officers. Thus the level and quality of patrol supervision in any precinct at any given time is frequently less than ideal.

Dispatchers can only monitor the activities of the RMPs in a broad way: They know if calls-for-service are piling up and a precinct is in danger of going into "alert" or "backlog" status (calls backing up because precinct-based units are not available for central dispatching). Although the dispatchers are able to maintain radio contact with all units, they are not able to pinpoint the location of the officers, nor are they able to provide substantive assistance or oversight to the officers handling the call.

Finally, rules that specify where the officer should and should not be, and what he or she should and should not be doing, are an obvious aid in supervision:

> They provide predictability and clarity with respect to behavioral expectations, are presumably applicable to all patrol officers, provide predictable sanctions for violations, and may actually reduce the prevalence of opportunities for misbehavior. However, they also foster a mechanical form of supervision which, although meeting the needs of the supervisor, may lessen the substantive value of the supervision. (Weisburd et al., 1988, p. 35)

The Critical   Radio motor patrol is reactive, incident-oriented, and short-term.
Differences   Productivity is measured in terms of dispatch time and service time.
in CPOP   The Patrol Guide sets forth rules and regulations for police response to particular situations, but compliance is monitored by exception, and rarely is an effort made to determine whether the response actually helped to correct the problem that produced the call. The officers deal with the radio runs as quickly as possible (preferably in

20 minutes or less), resume patrol, and await the next call for service. In many situations, the solution is a "quick fix"; the officers cannot address the underlying problem, nor are they expected to. In addition, because of rotating tours and shifts in sector assignments, officers do not develop a proprietary interest in their sector. Moreover, even if an officer were concerned about a specific street condition, he or she might not be scheduled to work that tour or sector again for weeks. As a result, problem-solving patrol is generally not feasible under the nine-squad chart system.

Because the CPO role was designed to correct for some of these limitations, the tasks of the CPOP sergeant are more varied and non-traditional than those of the patrol sergeant. A very important difference between RMP and CPOP is that CPOs generally work flexible hours. On any given day, the CPOP office may be open from 12 to 14 hours, with the CPOs working staggered tours. The CPOP sergeants work 9-hour tours; thus for large blocks of time the officers are not under the direct supervision of their sergeant. In addition, some days the CPOP sergeant is absent due to sick leave, vacation, or court appearances. Whenever the sergeant is not on duty, the CPOs are under the supervision of the regular patrol sergeants if they are in the field, or the desk lieutenant if they are in the station house. However, at the time that the research data were being collected, no systematic efforts had been undertaken to acquaint non-CPOP supervisors with the CPO role, so they were not well prepared to supervise them effectively. As a result, in some precincts, the CPOs operated to some extent on the "honor principle." They had a great deal of autonomy, especially when their unit supervisor was absent.

The scope of the CPOP sergeant's role is broad, and the core is problem solving. The sergeant must be familiar with the problems in each beat, assist the CPOs in developing work plans and strategies for dealing with the problems, monitor the CPOs' activities, attend community meetings, assist in organizing community groups when necessary, handle correspondence, and file monthly reports.

The sergeants are advised to look on the CPOs' Beat Books as important supervisory tools. Theoretically, the sergeant could use the book to determine whether the officer was aware of problematic conditions that existed on the beat, and to review the officer's priorities, the input he or she was receiving from the community concerning them, and the strategies being implemented to correct them. The monthly work plan was to constitute the first section of the Beat Book, and it was to be a prospective digest of the problem-solving activities, including conferences with community residents, merchants, and leaders, approved by the sergeant for the officer to carry out during the coming month.

All patrol sergeants perform certain administrative tasks, such as reviewing accident and arrest reports filed by their subordinates to ensure that they are complete and accurate. The CPOP sergeants in the research precincts stated that much more paperwork and administrative work were involved in CPOP than in traditional patrol. They often mentioned the time involved in reading over the entries in the Beat Books, a task that they estimated required 3 or 4 hours a week. The sergeants are often expected to answer communications, a function that may be quite time-consuming and varies by precinct. "Communications" are generally letters or telephone calls received by the precinct about crime or quality-of-life problems. For example, the operations lieutenant may receive a letter stating that drug dealing takes place at a particular location. In some precincts the lieutenant will send a patrol sergeant out to investigate the situation and report on the problem. In others, the lieutenant will forward all communications of this type directly to the CPOP sergeant, who must then conduct the investigation and follow up on the problem. In certain instances, this requires the CPOP sergeant to write a letter or file a departmental report—a process that was seen as an ordeal by some sergeants.

In addition, the CPOP sergeant is expected to interview one citizen a week to obtain an independent view of problems and performance in each of the beats. At the end of each month, the sergeant also submits an activity report, which is a compilation of the unit's activity for that month. The six sergeants in the research precincts estimated that they spent 30% to 40% of their time on paperwork and administration. As a result, administrative time severely limited the amount of time that they spent on patrol. Nevertheless the sergeants reported that they spent another 30% to 40% of their time on patrol, driving around the beats, reviewing conditions, monitoring the field activities of their officers, and talking to residents and merchants. The remaining 20% of their time was spent, they said, conferring with the commanding officer, coordinating unit activities with other precinct or borough units, assisting individual CPOs, attending community meetings, and dealing with miscellaneous matters.

Supervision in CPOP and Supervision in NPT

As previously indicated, CPOP is only one form of community-oriented, problem-solving policing. In fact, it is not the only form of community policing with which the NYPD has experience. In the early 1970s, Commissioner Patrick Murphy introduced the concept of the Neighborhood Police Team (NPT) to the department. Indeed, a number of urban police agencies experimented with this form of community policing during that time. As a result, when CPOP was introduced, a number of more seasoned supervisors and commanding officers initially thought it was a replay of the NPT.

The designers of CPOP always recognized the philosophical similarities between the program and NPT. The CPOP training sessions pointed out that both programs shared many of the same principles, including the emphasis on continuity of assignment to an area, the value given to intensive interaction between the police and the residents and merchants in the area, and the importance of the police responding to the needs and desires of the local residents.

Despite the philosophical similarities, the two approaches differ sharply in operational and structural terms. The NPT was more akin to a task force with responsibility for providing all forms of patrol service to an area. As such, the most critical member of the task force was the sergeant. It was the sergeant who was responsible for identifying the problems, setting the priorities, and deploying the resources of the unit. In effect, the sergeant was to become the "neighborhood police chief." The role of the police officer was not changed dramatically, although he or she did experience greater exposure to the community and an assurance of working regularly in the same general area.

By contrast, the design of CPOP gives primary action responsibility to the CPO. It is the officer who has first responsibility for problem identification, problem analysis, strategy design, strategy implementation, and regular communication with community residents and leaders. In theory, the role of the sergeant remains critical, but more as a coach than as a starting player. He or she selects the members of the unit, assigns them to the beats, encourages them in their initial efforts to reach out to the community, provides substantive guidance in problem solving, helps them to relate effectively with people and groups both within and outside the department, and monitors their behavior against the rules and regulations of the department. The sergeants are instructed to resist the temptation to take over or to do for the CPO who is slow to master the role. In the context of this program, if there is anything akin to a "neighborhood police chief," it is supposed to be the CPO, not the sergeant.

Thus in the early days of the CPO program in New York, supervisors and commanding officers were trying to master not only the differences between this program and regular patrol, but also the differences between CPOP and NPT, its community-oriented predecessor. It was not always easy for either the supervisors or the COs to remember that the sergeant ought not be held responsible for "getting things done," in the sense of identifying and solving the problems in the neighborhoods, but should be accountable for directing and assisting others to do so. Nor was it always easy to remember that, toward that end, it was sometimes necessary to give officers more, rather than less discretion, and to encourage other police officials at various levels to listen attentively to the intelligence and recommendations provided by a police officer.

General Perceptions of Sergeants and Commanding Officers Regarding Supervision in CPOP

During the interviews with the sergeants, senior research staff asked them to describe what they saw as the essential differences between the supervisor's role in CPOP and in regular patrol, and to provide a summary assessment of their comparative difficulty. All of the sergeants were fairly precise in describing the differences between the two roles. They were a bit less certain about which of the two roles was more demanding; however, all preferred to continue with the CPOP unit than to return to regular patrol.

Overall, there was little consensus regarding the general difficulty of the role of the CPOP sergeant versus that of patrol sergeant. However, the sergeants in the research precincts agreed that CPOP supervisors, unlike regular patrol sergeants, have to show results; therefore, they are held to a higher standard of accountability. Neither the sergeant nor the officers can say, "Hey, my tour's over. It's not my problem." As one CPOP sergeant explained:

CPOP is a lot more involved. When you're on radio motor patrol, you're going to be responsible for that 8 hours and 57 minutes. You get them in their cars, and you're just listening to the radio in order to make sure they're answering the jobs, and they're doing it correctly. That's all you're really concerned about—that one particular tour you're on. Once you're out, you're gone.

In CPOP, there's a lot of long-term problem solving and long-term strategy to worry about. Things that I deal with today, I know I'm gonna have to get back to tomorrow or the next day or the next week. I have to deal with it. I have to make sure my people are producing.

Another CPOP sergeant described the situation as follows:

A regular supervisor really doesn't have to answer out to the community on a particular problem. He may get rid of that group hanging out on the corner on that particular day, but if they come back, he doesn't have to address it. In CPOP, if someone calls me up on a particular problem they're going to keep calling me until it gets taken care of. I'm gonna have to answer out to the particular person, the captain or whatever, what I've done to alleviate the problem. So there's definitely pressure to get things done, but to me that's a challenge.

The sergeants agreed that there are advantages to supervising a small unit and working with the same officers every day, especially that they quickly learn the strengths and weaknesses of their staff. Continuity in personnel also allows the sergeants to set up procedures for handling paperwork and processing routine matters:

In CPOP, you're working with the same 10 guys. It's easier here because you can get to know all these people, how they are. I mean, you handle people different too. You know how they are and you know how to get the most out of them. They know what you expect and they know what they have to do.

Accountability refers not only to getting the job done, but also to knowing where the officers are and what they are doing at various points during the tour. The large size of the beats, and the relative autonomy accorded CPOs, produced questions in the minds of some department officials as to whether it would be possible for the sergeants to monitor their units. Although the sergeants estimated that they spent perhaps 40% of their time in the field, none believed that field supervision was a problem. Each unit maintained a diary in which the officers recorded community meetings or other special events that they were scheduled to attend. Also the CPOs tended to develop routines, so there were patterns to their patrol. Nevertheless, the sergeants stressed the importance of being able to contact the officers on the radio, and some regretted that they were not able to spend more of their time in the field:

> With CPOP, my only job is to supervise these 10 men. If you drive around and you don't see them within a reasonable time, you ask for their location. And you ask them what they are doing there, and you get an answer. They do have more freedom than the normal cop. They can go into stores, they go to meetings. But if I know that on a Monday or Wednesday night this cop is going to be at this school from 7 to 9 with the Youth Council, or he's going to be at a meeting, I go there, and I've never had anybody that wasn't there yet. I'm not saying it doesn't happen, but I never found it. And, again, I really think they know their job.

The sergeants agreed that the primary measure of officer performance was whether the CPO was aware of conditions on the beat and problems were being addressed:

> I think that the biggest supervision that I do is talking to my cop and seeing what he's doing and seeing if he's doing what he says he's doing. "What's going on in your beat? You got a problem here? What are you doing about it? What's going on here?" A lot of the beats have school problems, so they are supposed to be at the school at a certain time. So I get feedback.

In the interviews, several of the sergeants indicated that, in the beginning, they were slightly intimidated by the uniqueness of CPOP and its supervisory demands, but they became more comfortable and more sure of themselves as time went on. The mechanical differences between CPOP and regular patrol could be mastered, and all of the sergeants liked the opportunity to work consistently with the same team of officers. The felt they were more accountable for correcting problems in CPOP, but, generally, they welcomed that feature of the job. The only persistent source of mild anxiety was their belief that they were more exposed than they would be in regular patrol if one or more of their subordinates became involved in a scandal of some sort. They all believed that such circumstances would lead to their removal from the CPOP post.

The Supervisor as Leader and Guide

This is the active, teaching, coaching dimension of the supervisor's role. As presented here, it consists of three components: (a) representing the unit within the department, (b) helping to represent the unit within the community, and (c) assisting the CPOs in the performance of their roles.

Each of these tasks is discussed in more detail below. Before turning to that discussion, however, it is important to provide some context for understanding the stage of program development at the time the research data were being collected. CPOP expansion within the department began in January 1985 and was not completed until the fall of 1988. During that time, the program staff at Vera and the central staff in the department were consumed largely by the demands of expansion and the early months of unit implementation. Most of the training and assistance provided to supervisors during that period focused on the efforts required to form a CPOP unit and get it off the ground. It was not until the fall of 1987 that the program managers at Vera and in the department were able to concentrate attention on the continuing performance of unit supervisors. Their observations at that time and the general comments of the research team helped the program managers develop a better understanding of the everyday demands of the supervisor's role and identify some of the areas in which the supervisors needed and desired additional assistance. Those efforts resulted in the production of the *Community Patrol Officer Program: Supervisory Guide* that was disseminated by the department in May 1988.

The major features of that document are discussed toward the end of this chapter. For now, it is important to note that the period during which the data for this research report were being collected (from December 1986 through February 1988) began and ended almost entirely before the program managers started to focus special attention on the needs of supervisors. While reading through the next two sections of this chapter, the reader should remember that the supervisory shortcomings identified here occurred rather early in the program's evolutionary process and helped to inform the content of subsequent supervisory assistance and training sessions. It is reasonable to expect, therefore, that some of the deficiencies mentioned here are less evident today than they were during the research period.

Representing the Unit Within the Department

As the supervisor of the unit, the CPOP sergeant was responsible to the commanding officer of the precinct. This meant not only that the sergeant had to account to the CO for the unit's actions, but also to explain the unit's mission, its underlying philosophy, and some of its more unusual operating principles.

Before a unit was created in a precinct, the CO was informed that his or her precinct had been chosen for the program and that he should choose a sergeant to head the unit. The CO, the sergeant, and the precinct's administrative lieutenant then attended an orientation meeting run by the Office of the Chief of Patrol. These sessions provided the COs with a general understanding of why the department was committing itself to community-oriented, problem-solving policing, how CPOP was expected to operate in the precinct, and the resources that would be committed to the program. Of course, the orientation session, which lasted from 3 to 4 hours, was no substitute for the detailed familiarity that the COs were expected to develop once the program began, and the principal person on whom the CO relied for that education was the supervising sergeant.

CPOP was a new operation not only for the CO, but for all the other supervisors and officers in the precinct as well. Therefore the administrative lieutenants and many of the regular patrol supervisors had to be provided with some explanation of the program to understand what supervisory actions they should and should not take with respect to CPOs when they encountered them in the precinct house and in the field. In addition, the sergeants heading the precinct's special units, such as the Anti-Crime, Street Narcotics Enforcement, and Total Patrol Concept (TOPAC) units, had to be introduced to CPOP because it was likely that such resources would be solicited to help in the problem-solving strategies developed by the CPOs.

None of the research precincts used a formal introduction and orientation session for this purpose. In most cases, the CO introduced and described the program, or had the CPOP sergeant describe it, during his meetings with supervisory personnel. Beyond that, the sergeant was expected to explain his unit's operation to other unit supervisors as he worked with them and to take some time to explain to the regular patrol supervisors how they should check on his people during his absence.

The sergeants in the research precincts felt that this informal process worked reasonably well. One of their principal concerns was that the CPOs not be pulled off their assignments and used to perform other precinct duties, such as manning radio cars when there was a shortage of regular patrol officers or covering a location to which a security officer had to be assigned for several hours.

In each of the research precincts, these non-CPOP assignments were something of a problem in the early months of the program's operation. Desk officers, who were responsible for finding personnel to fill the radio cars and meet all the other immediate demands, were initially inclined to see the CPOs as uncommitted resources that could be deployed to fill a hole when it appeared. While the CPOP sergeant was on duty, he could check this action by refusing to permit the reassignment of his people and reminding the desk officer that the CPOs were not to be pulled off their assignments except in the case of a serious emergency. The CPOs were more vulnerable, however, when their supervisor was not working. When reassignment happened under these circumstances, the CPOP sergeant would try to speak to the responsible supervisor the next day to discourage its repetition. These informal techniques were reasonably effective in the research precincts. In some instances in other precincts, however, the sergeants would speak to the CO and ask that he intervene either by speaking directly to those supervisors who were frequently troublesome in this manner, or issue a written order requiring supervisors to account to the CO for those instances in which they reassigned CPOP personnel.

The sergeants in the research precincts felt that this problem was brought under reasonable control after the program had been operating for three or four months. But the citywide CPOP Coordinator's Office believed that in many precincts this was a persistent problem that had to be monitored by holding COs accountable to the central office. Toward that end, each precinct was required to report on a monthly basis the percentage of tours worked by CPO personnel that were devoted to CPOP duties. The Coordinator's Office would look into the situation when the percentage reported fell below 85%.

This was an issue about which the CPOs themselves were sensitive. They felt frustrated in their new roles if they were reassigned frequently or reassigned to duties that they did not believe constituted critical functions. Reassignments were frustrating to the officers not only because they lessened the time available to them to perform their CPOP duties, but also because they perceived the reassignment reflected the low value accorded their work by others in the precinct. In this respect, it was seen as a challenge to the integrity of the unit, and the sergeant's success in fending off such interruptions was seen by some as a measure of his or her strength as a supervisor. The sergeants themselves considered it an important part of their responsibilities, but were quick to insist that their success in performing it was very much influenced by the attitudes and actions of the commanding officer. Thus, in general, CPOP sergeants favored the requirement that non-CPOP time be counted and reported "downtown."

Every precinct commander is required to submit monthly reports to headquarters that contain, among other things, the number of arrests made and summonses issued by personnel under his or her command. The monthly figures are compared with those for the same month in the preceding year, and the CO is expected to comment on any notable increases or decreases in the numbers. To most commanding officers, this accountability requirement is seen as a departmental encouragement to keep their arrest and summons numbers at least as high as they were in the past. All of the officers in the command are expected to contribute toward that end, and this was the source of another concern to the CPOP supervisors.

The order creating the program and the guidelines issued concerning it emphasized that the effectiveness of the CPO should not be judged on the basis of arrests made and summonses issued. Rather, these were viewed as techniques to be used as appropriate within the context of the problem-solving strategies that the officer was attempting to implement. Moreover, the nature of the CPO's duties were thought to limit the opportunities available to the officer for issuing summonses, especially those for moving violations.

Thus the sergeant had to find ways for the unit to make a reasonable contribution to maintaining the precinct's "numbers," without interfering with the demands of the CPO role. Neither the sergeants nor the commanding officers in the research precincts defined this as a difficult problem in their commands, although the levels of arrests and summons activity performed by these units varied considerably (see Chapter 4). The officers in the research precincts did not express resentment to the field researchers at having to produce more arrests and summonses than they felt were reasonable. They did indicate, however, that giving summonses for moving violations was extremely difficult for them because they worked on foot. In response, sergeants would sometimes permit two or three of the officers to go out in the unit's van together for a couple of hours expressly to give "movers."

However, at general meetings of CPOP sergeants from precincts other than the research precincts, several expressed concern about the arrest and summons expectations of their COs and the accountability system that made the COs so sensitive to the numbers. These sergeants indicated that, in some instances, the same "expectations" set for regular patrol officers were applied to the CPOs. Most of these sergeants said that they had discussed this problem with their COs on more than one occasion, but that the commander was unyielding. Under those circumstances, the sergeant felt he or she had no choice but to impose the expectations on the members of the unit, and to hope that the CPOP Coordinator's Office would "get the message across" to all commanding officers. The sergeants who complained most vigorously about this problem were not optimistic about its rapid resolution. They tended to sympathize with their COs, who, they felt, were victims of a "numbers game" sustained by the department's managers.

Another way in which the CPOP sergeant is expected to represent the unit within the precinct is to relay information up the chain of command about the problems being addressed by the unit, the extra-unit resources needed to address those problems, and the effects of the problem-solving strategies implemented by unit members. This responsibility involves both information sharing and a form of advocacy in which the sergeant attempts to secure the commitment of resources from other units to implement the problem-solving strategies developed by the CPOs.

The sergeants in the research precincts differed in the ways in which they approached this dimension of their role. All of them were eager to pass along information concerning those problems that the CO defined as precinct priorities. Sometimes this information concerned the locations in which these problems were concentrated or local situational patterns associated with their occurrence. Sometimes the information received from people in the community helped to identify the perpetrators of these problems and helped units other than CPOP to make important arrests. Finally, this information was often descriptive of the actions taken by the CPOP unit to address the CO's priorities.

On the other hand, all of the sergeants were reluctant to pass on what they thought of as "negative" information, and they varied in their willingness to do so. The types of negative information that were likely to come to the attention of the sergeant included information identifying neighborhood problems of which the CO might be un- aware, perceptions and opinions of neighborhood residents that were critical of the precinct's performance with respect to various prob- lems, information that could be interpreted as critical of the perfor- mance or cooperation of other units within the precinct, and informa- tion that reported the ineffectiveness of the CPOP unit's efforts to correct specific problems.

The sergeants in the research precincts also differed with respect to the extent to which they pressed for the commitment of other police resources to the problem-solving strategies set forth by the CPOs. The primary units on the precinct level to which the sergeants were expected to turn for assistance were the Anti-Crime (AC) unit; the Street Narcotics Enforcement Unit (SNEU), if one existed in the precinct; and the TOPAC unit. In addition, sergeants could ask that the regular patrol units pay some attention to specific local conditions when they were not responding to a call-for-service. The borough- based units on which the CPOP supervisors were most likely to call were the Narcotics Division and the Public Morals Division, both of which are within the Organized Crime Control Bureau (OCCB).

In the six research precincts, during the data collection periods, some instances of effective cooperation between the CPOP unit and the SNEU and TOPAC units did occur. CPOP seemed more often to provide information to the AC units than to receive aid from them in the research precincts, in part because the AC units were more focused on robbery and burglary than on other forms of street crime or quality-of-life problems. All of the CPOP units in the research precincts had at least some dealings with the Narcotics Division, because each unit had identified street narcotics as a problem in at least some of its beats. In some cases, the relationship between CPOP and Narcotics was close and effective, while in others it was strained.

Supervisors in both the research and nonresearch precincts claimed that their capacity to secure cooperation from other units depended to a great extent on their personal relationships with the supervisors in those units. If the CPOP sergeant was friendly with the other unit supervisor, he or she was usually successful in getting the cooperation he sought. If the personal relationship was not there, efforts to get action from the other unit were unpredictable and often unproductive.

On the precinct level, there did not appear to be a formal struc- ture that the CPOP sergeant could use to advocate for action by other precinct units. He or she could go directly to the other supervisor or to the CO with a request that he or she direct the desired actions from the other units. CPOP sergeants never went directly to the CO without first approaching the other supervisors. Indeed, they were very reluctant to go to the CO even after they were rebuffed by other unit supervisors. This reluctance reflected their unwillingness to do something that might create trouble for a colleague and their unwillingness to "create problems" for their CO. Thus, in the face of an impasse, the more passive CPOP sergeant would wait for something to change, while the more aggressive one would look for other ways to continue negotiations with the other supervisors. In any case, the sergeant's success in securing cooperation was often seen by the CPOs as a measure of the sergeant's effectiveness.

There was a formal structure available for precinct units to request action from the Narcotics and Public Morals Divisions, and it was used widely by the CPOP sergeants. Because street narcotics trafficking was so prevalent a problem, and because Narcotics possessed far greater resources and tactical flexibility than CPOP units, the units frequently submitted intelligence reports and requests for action to this division. The formal structure was designed to provide the division with an opportunity to establish priorities among the requests they received, because the demand for their services invariably exceeded their capacity to respond.

Nevertheless, the CPOP sergeants placed little faith in the responsiveness of that structure. They maintained that Narcotics was responsive to its own priorities so that, if they were targeting your precinct or specific beats within your precinct, your requests for action were apparently granted. Otherwise, you might never get a response, unless you "knew somebody." It was important, therefore, to cultivate relationships with Narcotics Division supervisors, and the more aggressive CPOP supervisors did just that. They were also much more willing to go to the CO with a complaint about the unresponsiveness of the Narcotics Division, both to show the CO that they were doing all they could to address the narcotics problems and to take advantage of whatever influence the CO might have.

Based on observations and interviews with the sergeants in the research precincts and on informal interviews with CPOP sergeants in many other precincts, it appears that some sergeants adopt a more proactive stance than others regarding the problem-solving activities of their units. This stance has two important consequences for how the sergeant represents the unit within the precinct and borough. The more active sergeants recognize the importance of this representational dimension of their role, and they work at it earnestly. They consciously cultivate relationships with other supervisors in the precinct, and even when they are not seeking specific actions from those supervisors, they are looking for opportunities to "do them a favor." Whenever they suspect that another supervisor misunderstands CPOP, or is down on it for some offense, real or imagined, they reach out to that supervisor to clear the air.

These proactive sergeants also appear to be more assertive in their relationships with the CO. They seek to meet with the CO on a regular basis and to review with the CO the activities and needs of the unit. They make a point of highlighting the activities of the unit that address the CO's priorities and the information secured by the unit that has proved useful to other police units. Within this context, they review various problem-solving strategies with the CO, and they point out where and when they are seeking the involvement of other units to get the CO's explicit or implicit blessing. That blessing, even if it is only implied, is very useful to the CPOP sergeant in negotiating with other supervisors inside and outside the precinct.

This active posture regarding problem solving permits the sergeant to represent the unit well within the department. It enhances CPOP's image as an active police unit, helps it to secure cooperation from other units, and strengthens the morale of the CPOs. Even in these instances, however, there is a strong reluctance to pass along negative information, and that reluctance probably limits the effectiveness of the unit's problem-solving capabilities.

Helping to Represent the Unit Within the Community

The planning that preceded the formation of a CPOP unit in any precinct involved some outreach to community organizations operating there, and the sergeant was a critical figure in establishing these initial contacts. In all cases, meetings were held with representatives of the Community Boards (public agencies that exert real influence on the allocation of city resources to the community) to announce the coming of the program, to elicit input regarding the design of CPOP beats, to identify key persons and organizations for individual CPOs to contact within their beats, and to begin the process of problem identification. In addition, the sergeants were responsible for arranging meetings as part of the CPOP training program between CPOs and various public and nonprofit agencies providing services in the community. Finally, the sergeants were expected to attend Community Board meetings regularly, and occasionally to accompany their CPOs to other community meetings.

The sergeants were expected to explain the operations of CPOP to the Community Boards and to assist individual CPOs in explaining it to other organizations. It was hoped that they would earnestly pursue the active involvement of residents, merchants, and organizations in the problem-solving process on the beat level and that they would actively encourage their subordinates to do the same. In addition, communications received from the community would be passed along by the CO to the CPOP sergeant for disposition by the unit. In some precincts, this practice was routine, while in others it was not. The sergeants were also expected to assist the CPOs in preparing information to share with local residents and organizations regarding the problems with which they were concerned and the strategies and tactics that could be employed to address them.

All of the sergeants in the research precincts accepted the fact that they and their subordinates were required to interact with members of the community and that representatives of the community had to be involved in identifying the problems on which the CPOs would work. The sergeants all encouraged their subordinates to spend time talking with residents and merchants in the beats and to develop a sense of the neighborhood conditions about which these people were most concerned. In short order, the sergeants also developed rather clear ideas about the relative importance of various individuals and organizations in the community, and they attempted to shape the unit's responses to suggestions and complaints accordingly. Finally, all of the sergeants understood quickly that they were expected to protect their commanding officers from the pressures and criticisms of community leaders and their organizations.

However, the sergeants in the research precincts varied in their feelings about this dimension of their role, in the amount of effort they devoted to it, and in the attitude regarding the community's involvement that they projected to their subordinates. Moreover, the level of community organization and the extent to which the COs were sensitive to it also varied considerably among the research precincts, from one precinct in which community organizations were numerous, often affluent, and politically influential, to another in which few community organizations were established and those that did exist were not actively involved with the police.

The observations and interviews with the sergeants in the research precincts, supplemented by informal discussions with CPOP sergeants in many other precincts, indicate that not all sergeants understood the full significance of the community in the design of the program. This inadequate understanding manifests itself in an essentially defensive attitude vis-à-vis community organizations and toward community residents perceived to be influential citizens. These sergeants may encourage their subordinates to talk with individual residents and merchants while patrolling the beat, but they tend to view organizations and group meetings as potentially threatening. As a result, even while they remind CPOs that they are required to attend meetings, they convey a rather passive posture toward this dimension of the program. They may stress the importance of respectful responses, especially to influential individuals, but they are not persuaded that active outreach to the community is either necessary or productive. They recognize the importance of community residents as sources of information, and even as participants in efforts such as block watch programs, but they have trouble thinking of them as active, productive contributors to the planning, implementation, and review of the problem-solving strategies themselves.

A sergeant possessing this set of attitudes in a relatively disorganized or moderately organized community can get by with a rather comfortable, minimalist approach to the community. The same set of attitudes in a highly organized community, however, is likely to produce a somewhat anxious and perhaps resentful sergeant who believes that he has to put too much effort into a relatively unimportant dimension of the program. Such attitudes are likely to be reflected by many of the sergeant's subordinates.

On the other hand, some sergeants understand that the CPOP design embodies a much more positive and less defensive view of the community. These sergeants are likely to emphasize the importance of the CPOs' maintaining a list of community organizations in their beats and a calendar of their meetings, and of attending as many of those meetings as possible. The sergeants will attend a number of these meetings with the CPO, encourage him or her to engage in active conversation with the residents, and even show the officer how to draw out problem-solving suggestions from the participants. They tend to be less defensive about sharing information with the public, including information that demonstrates the limits of what the police can accomplish working alone. They encourage their subordinates to become involved with nonpolice agencies that can provide needed assistance in specific problem-solving efforts, or even more general assistance to the residents of the beat. And they encourage their subordinates to develop problem-solving strategies that involve some form of active participation by residents and organizations within the community. Finally, these sergeants see these activities as being at the core, rather than the periphery, of the program and of their role as program supervisors.

This more positive and active view of the community appeared to be a minority view, although a substantial one, among CPOP sergeants at the time the data were being collected for this research study. However, the view was being articulated with increasing frequency at general meetings of CPOP sergeants. Moreover, there was some suggestion that sergeants matured to this view as the operation of their units became more stable and as they acquired more experience in attempting to implement problem-solving strategies, especially those addressing the more intractable local problems. Finally, this view is very clearly embodied in the supervisory guide produced in May 1988. It is likely, therefore, that this more active approach to community involvement is more prevalent among CPOP supervisors today than it was during the data collection period.

Assisting CPOs in the Performance of Their Roles   In addition to helping the CPO find his or her way around the community, the CPOP sergeant is expected to assist the officer in carrying out the problem-solving dimension of the role. This aspect of the sergeant's role involves helping the CPO to identify problems in the beat and to determine the information needed to analyze the problem and to assess its relative importance among the residents and merchants in the beat. Central to this helping function is guiding the CPO in interpreting that information and in making judgments about the priority that should be given to the problems; assisting the CPO to think through corrective strategies and tactics for each of the problems on which he or she will be working, and to make certain that the actions required by those strategies are consistent with departmental rules and regulations. The sergeant also encourages the CPO to carry out these analytic and planning functions with the assistance of residents and organizations in the beat; monitors the CPO's efforts to implement the strategy and assists him or her to prompt other police and citizen units with tasks to perform within the strategy. He or she reviews the implementation experience with the CPO and helps him or her to look for indicators of impact; helps the CPO to translate these efforts into a feasible and approvable work plan for the coming month, and to record actions taken in carrying out that work plan. This role also includes helping the CPO to understand the demands of other sections of the Beat Book and to schedule reasonable periods of time to work on them, and reviewing with each CPO the strengths and weaknesses of his or her performance and the actions that should be taken to improve performance. In short, the CPOP supervisor must be able and willing to provide a considerable amount of substantive assistance to his or her subordinates.

Effective performance of this aspect of the supervisor's role presumes that the sergeant has a fairly sophisticated understanding of the problem-solving process itself and the time and inclination to concentrate on its implementation by nine different individuals in nine different neighborhoods. Experience with the problem-solving process is an obvious benefit, as is knowledge of how alternative corrective strategies have fared with respect to various types of problems. Ideally, the supervisor should have at least some independent knowledge of the community against which to judge the CPO's effort.

At the time of the data collection, the sergeants in the research precincts and CPOP sergeants in general did not have a sophisticated understanding of the problem-solving process. They had not been exposed to it in prior training or in prior assignments within the department. Moreover, the exposure to the problem-solving process provided during the CPOP training program was no greater for the sergeants than it was for the CPOs. Nor was any systematic body of information made available to them concerning the relative effectiveness of various problem-solving strategies. Thus, for the most part, the sergeants were learning the process along with the CPOs.

Given this set of circumstances, it is not surprising that in the research precincts, the performance of the sergeants on this dimension of their role was quite varied. Some seemed to grasp the logic of the process and became comfortable with it rather quickly. These sergeants were reasonably good at working through the problem-solving process with their subordinates and, because they were involved with it in several beats at the same time, they developed a facility with it much more quickly than the average CPO.

Other sergeants did not grasp the essential differences between problem solving and incident response. As a result, their CPOs were more likely than those in other precincts to identify as problems what were really a handful of unrelated complaints. Problem analyses closely resembled a description of the circumstances in which the incident occurred. Corrective strategies were more likely to be brief descriptions of what the officer would do himself either to prevent similar complaints from arising, or in reaction to those that would arise. Lacking any substantial knowledge of or experience with problem solving, these sergeants did not often challenge their subordinates to do it better.

All of the sergeants spent a fair amount of time in the field checking on the whereabouts of the CPOs and, at least occasionally, attending community meetings with them. And, in compliance with departmental guidelines, all of the sergeants would talk with at least a few residents during the week about community problems and the efforts of the program. In addition, the sergeants were good to very good about requiring the CPOs to make entries in the Beat Book and to set forth a monthly work plan for their review. However, given the different levels of problem-solving sophistication among the sergeants, the quality of the Beat Book entries and the specificity of the work plans they accepted varied considerably.

The sergeants in the research precincts possessed expertise on different kinds of problems. Some were fairly knowledgeable about narcotics and departmental strategies and tactics used to address that problem. Some knew more about tactics used to combat street robberies and burglaries. Still others had some sense of what the department does in the area of community relations. These areas of special knowledge were usually developed through the sergeant's experience in previous assignments. Because the department had not been focusing on quality-of-life problems for some time, it is not surprising that none of the sergeants possessed any special expertise in these areas.

All of the sergeants recognized the limitations of their personal knowledge about how to deal with the wide range of problems brought to their attention. Therefore, most would have welcomed additional training and training materials regarding specific types of problems. Most also thought that additional training regarding the problem-solving process itself, and concerning useful techniques of community organization, would be beneficial for them and their subordinates. Finally, some of the sergeants in the research precincts and many in other precincts expressed the desire for some clarification of departmental policies applicable to specific problems. This was especially true with respect to what patrol units could and could not do in response to narcotics trafficking problems. Departmental policies in this area were often seen as ambiguous, confusing, and unnecessarily constraining. This state of confusion was thought to be especially problematic for CPOP units because of the frequency with which local narcotics problems were brought to their attention and the persistent need of CPOP personnel to be responsive to the demands of the people in their beats.

The sergeants in the research precincts differed with respect to the extent and nature of the feedback they provided concerning CPO performance. As previously indicated, a couple of sergeants worked rather closely with their subordinates on the substance of problem identification and strategy development. For the reasons explained above, however, this kind of involvement was not typical. Feedback regarding the use of patrol time, the maintenance of the Beat Book, and maintaining a reasonable level of summons activity was more common.

These general observations regarding the sergeants' provision of substantive assistance to the CPOs were shared by the research staff with the program staff in Vera and with the department and influenced their efforts to strengthen supervisory performance. Those efforts are described in more detail in the last section of this chapter.

The Supervisor as Control Agent

Although the CPOP sergeants were not entirely prepared for, or comfortable with, the demands of the leader and guide role, they were quite familiar with the concerns of the control agent. They understood clearly that failures of this sort—significant abuse of patrol or administrative time, frequent complaints by citizens of abuse, or a corruption scandal among their subordinates—could threaten the very existence of the program and their careers in the department. If they had any doubts about these risks, their commanding officers were quick to remind them that nothing can bring down a commander more quickly than a corruption scandal in the command. Thus the sergeants worked hard at, and were articulate in speaking about, the unique challenges posed by this dimension of their roles.

Officer Abuse of Patrol and Administrative Time

As noted above, in regular patrol, the sergeant, at least in theory, is out in the field with the officers and able to maintain constant radio contact with his or her squad. If a sector car is slow in responding to calls, the sergeant can talk to them directly over the radio, or arrange for a rendezvous. There are, however, opportunities for "cooping" (resting, hiding, or otherwise making oneself unavailable for assignment) during a quiet tour. Officers can park in an alley, turn out their lights, and half-listen to the radio. However, if the patrol sergeants are vigilant, cooping of this sort can be kept to a minimum.

The opportunities to coop appear to be more numerous in CPOP. CPOs are permitted to enter a store, drink a soda, and engage in conversation with merchants and customers for a reasonable period of time. This activity, which is generally prohibited for regular patrol officers, is defined as an acceptable way for CPOs to meet people in the community, establish rapport, develop contacts, and acquire information. It is impossible, of course, to draw a rigid line distinguishing between constructive and wasteful uses of such time, although the extremes, such as napping in the back room, are rather obvious. It is important, therefore, for the sergeant to remind his subordinates of the dangers of such "goofing off," to know his people, and to check out danger signs quickly.

In the course of our research, Vera staff saw some instances of abuse of patrol time. One of the more common forms was roaming around in the CPOP van without real purpose. For example, near the end of the month, three or four CPOs might go out in the van, ostensibly to issue summonses for parking or moving violations. Summonses would be issued, but, on occasion, a large part of the time would be spent cruising aimlessly around the precinct. To combat this type of abuse, two sergeants set up stringent rules regarding the use of the van. One, for example, always checked the odometer to determine whether the mileage accumulated was reasonable given the nature of the task. There were also instances in which officers were extending their meal breaks, or holding unnecessarily lengthy conversations with merchants or residents, but the researchers did not find a systematic or chronic pattern of evasion of work while the officers were in the field.[1]

In regular patrol, RMP officers are not supposed to be in the station house without a good reason. Acceptable reasons for returning to the station house include picking up equipment (e.g., rain gear), filing an accident or complaint report, processing an arrest, or taking a meal break. In all instances, the officers are required to sign in in the Interrupted Patrol Log, complete their task, and return to patrol quickly. This is considered legitimate administrative or break time.

In contrast, there are many legitimate reasons for a CPO to be in the station house on administrative time. The designers of the program realized that if the officers were to develop and update their Beat Books, keep in contact with community leaders, print fliers, and organize meetings, they needed access to typewriters, copying machines, telephone books, and their own office space. In addition, it was recognized that CPOs would be in the station house more often and for longer periods of time than officers assigned to traditional patrol. Although CPOP office space was often small, cluttered, and frequently shared with other units, CPOP nevertheless had its own turf.

Vera's field research indicated that these provisions for administrative time, though certainly necessary, could be abused in the absence of strong supervision by the sergeant. When that happens, the danger is that the CPOP office may become a clubhouse rather than a command post. The COs and CPOP sergeants were aware that abuse of administrative time could become a serious problem. One sergeant, who assessed the situation realistically and approached the problem pragmatically, explained:

> You don't want them to be goofing off totally all day, or even for a total hour. Everybody gets a cup of coffee and everybody has to make their little phone call. And conversation between cops on problems is a problem-solving method. You know, it's just like two days of bullshit about a problem and you come up with an answer.

He continued:

> One or two hang out a little bit extra or say "Jeez, I gotta walk
> back to my post, and I don't want to come back again, so maybe
> I'll make a few phone calls and I'll work on my Beat Book." Which
> is fine to a point. Okay, you're not going to gain anything by
> walking back out 20 minutes, and 20 minutes back, so you might
> as well stay the hour and go through your book a little bit and
> shoot some breeze. Now, I take advantage of that too. I use that
> as my down time to grab him and say "Well, what's going on, what
> have you got? What's happening out there?"
>
> I stop at an hour or two, that's more than sufficient. An hour
> is more than sufficient unless you have something specific, I
> mean you're working on a problem.

Each precinct dealt with this potential problem differently. The
CPOP sergeants agreed that the officers needed an hour at the
beginning of the tour to review the crime complaints, return telephone calls, set up appointments, update the Beat Book, or deal with
other matters. And, unless a CPO was working on a special project
requiring making up flyers or other materials, they believed that an
hour was adequate. In a few instances, COs indicated that the first
hour of the tour was the presumptive maximum time period for
handling administrative matters. After that time, all CPOs were
expected to be out in the field, unless a specific project required their
continued presence in the station house.

Abuse of administrative time is important not only because it
decreases the efficiency and effectiveness of the CPOP unit, but also
because it affects the prestige of the unit and the morale in the
precinct. As noted elsewhere, CPOP has to be sensitive to the image
of a do-nothing unit involved in nonpolice work. It is hard to combat
this image if the atmosphere in the CPOP office is perceived as
raucous and supervision is seen as lax. One respondent stated:

> Now [as a CPOP sergeant], I didn't think they goof off, but a
> regular cop has to wonder when you see three or four police
> officers sitting in an office and laughter coming out, and they
> lounge around for the first 2 hours of their tour and have their
> coffee. Something's not right. Or you walk in there for some
> reason, and their feet are up on their desks.

The research staff observed that the extent of abuse of administrative time varied among the research precincts, and reflected the closeness of the supervision provided. A commanding officer in a precinct
with a less active CPOP unit described the situation as follows:

> Yeah, goofing off is a problem. I think that they spend more time
> than they need to, you know, early on in the tour, talking and

this and that . . . and this is the sergeant's fault. And there's a perception, too, very often, which is a problem—and this is the sergeant's fault—that they have their own office, and you see them in there an awful lot doing their Beat Books and this and that. And I think that it probably, in more cases than not, requires a little bit more examination than what is on the surface.

In most work settings opportunities exist to relax, make personal telephone calls, or attend to other nonwork-related matters on company time, and CPOs should not be held to higher standards of productivity than other police officers or other workers. Abuse of administrative time, like abuse of patrol time, is not a problem in well-run units. If, however, the supervision is not strong, on both the unit and the precinct level, there are forces in operation that encourage officers to exploit the latitude provided by the program.

As was discussed above, CPOP hours are flexible, and often the CPOP sergeant may not be on duty during all or part of an officer's tour. And because CPOs do not always stand roll call with other officers, they may receive less attention from the patrol supervisors. Thus, on occasion, there may be no supervisors to chase the CPOs out of the station house. In addition, in the absence of the CPOP sergeant, CPOs may have no externally imposed sense of immediacy about getting out on patrol. In contrast to RMP officers, the CPOs do not have a car waiting and 911 calls to answer. The officer has to patrol alone, and little may be going on in the beat at eight or nine in the morning. Many of the stores in the commercial district are closed at that hour, and the people on the street are hurrying to work. Under these circumstances, it is sometimes easier to hang around the office drinking coffee or killing time on less than essential administrative matters.

Another concern of special relevance to the CPOP sergeant is controlling the tour hours selected by the officers. In regular patrol, these are determined by the tour rotation chart on which the officers work; however, for reasons explained above, the CPOs do not work on a standard chart. Thus they have considerable flexibility in establishing the times for their tours. This flexibility is provided to permit the officers and sergeants to establish these periods consistent with the specific demands of the beat to which the officer is assigned and the priority problems encountered there, rather than to meet the personal convenience of the officer.

Initially, CPOP sergeants in some precincts addressed this concern by requiring all their members to work the same hours and to change tour hours as a unit. This tactic left the determination of appropriate times in the hands of the sergeant and assured him or her that subordinates would be working the same hours as he or she did. However, it quickly became apparent that this tactic virtually eliminated the flexibility that the program was designed to provide and sometimes unnecessarily prevented CPOs from being on duty when they were most needed. Therefore, when the tactic was employed, it was usually abandoned after 3 months or so, with the encouragement of the CPOP Coordinator's Office.

The experience of the units in the research precincts and the comments offered by sergeants in many other precincts indicate that the control of regular days off (RDOs), tour time, and abuse of patrol and administrative times is best accomplished by the sergeant's close supervision of the monthly work plans of each CPO. By insisting that each officer identify priority problems and set forth specific plans for addressing them, the sergeant forces the CPO to provide substantive justification for the tour times. Moreover, through this form of substantive oversight, the sergeant is able to estimate the amount of administrative time needed by the officer in the next month and can recommend a schedule. Finally, review of the work plan also provides the officer and the sergeant with the opportunity to decide where and on what the officer will be working in the coming month and, thereby, hold to a minimum both "down time" and the time devoted to aimless patrol in the beat.

Checking the Threat of Corruption

Since the completion of the Knapp Commission hearings in 1972, which determined that corruption in the New York Police Department was widespread, the prevention and investigation of corruption has been a matter of utmost importance in the department. Therefore, when the CPO program was first proposed, some senior members of the department expressed concern about what they perceived to be the corruption hazards inherent in the program. Specifically, they feared that the friendly relations that CPOs were expected to develop with local residents and merchants would lead to the CPOs performing favors for them and expecting favors in return. They believed that this might make some forms of payoff seem like innocent expressions of gratitude. They were concerned also that the freedom of movement accorded the CPO would shield the officer from effective supervision in the streets and lessen the likelihood that corrupt activities would be detected.

With these concerns in mind, in our research we sought to estimate the extent of corruption complaints against the CPOs in the research precincts and to determine whether assignment to the program made such complaints more likely. In addition, the research staff discussed with the sergeants and the commanding officers their perceptions of the corruption risks in the program and their approach to preventing corrupt behavior among their subordinates.

Receiving and investigating complaints of police corruption is the responsibility of the Internal Affairs Division (IAD) of the department's Inspectional Services Bureau. IAD provided the research staff with a record of all such complaints against the CPOs in the research precincts through July 15, 1988. All complaints made during the officers' careers were identified, so it was possible to separate those complaints that the officers received during the assignment to CPOP units (referred to in the analysis as CPOP time) from those received before and after such assignments (referred to as non-CPOP time).

Thirty-one (44.9%) of the 69 officers had one or more corruption complaints during their entire career. Twenty-six (37.7%) of all of the officers had complaints filed against them before they joined CPOP or after they left it, and 10 officers (14.5%) received complaints while in CPOP. The 31 officers who had received complaints were involved in a total of 64 cases. Of course, substantial variation existed in the number of years the officers had been in the department and in their time in CPOP. To adjust for these differences, the average number of complaints per year was calculated for CPOP and non-CPOP time. The average number of complaints during CPOP time was 0.13 complaints per year, which means that an average officer would receive one complaint in the course of about seven and a half years in CPOP. Similarly, the average number of complaints received during non-CPOP time was very low—0.17—for an average of one complaint for every 6 years of service. Therefore, the hypothesis that assignment to CPOP increases the likelihood of corruption complaints is not supported by these data.

The research sought to compare the disposition reached in complaints made against CPOP and non-CPOP officers. However, given that there were only 50 non-CPOP and 14 CPOP cases, the numbers were too small to produce definitive conclusions. Only 11 (22%) of the non-CPOP cases resulted in substantiation of the charges, while only 1 of the CPOP cases was substantiated.

The department uses 13 categories to classify corruption complaints. Again, because the number of complaints against research subjects was so small, a useful analysis of their distribution by type was not possible. Suffice it to say that in 7 of the 14 CPOP-time complaints it was alleged that the officer had taken property, usually money, from the complainant. In some of these cases, the complainant had been arrested by the officer. In all of these cases, the disposition reached was either unfounded or unsubstantiated.

Corruption may be viewed as a continuum ranging from minor incidents such as taking free food and cigarettes, to midrange activities such as buying cameras, small appliances, and other items at prices discounted for the officer only, to serious criminal activity involving systematically shaking down gamblers and drug dealers, setting up a pad, and running extortion rackets. The Knapp Commission, using terms familiar to police, distinguished between *grass-eaters* and *meat-eaters*. Grass-eaters are basically opportunists who take advantage of situations as they present themselves. They are amenable to accepting gratuities in the form of free food, haircuts, discounts, and any other benefits that may happen their way, but their approach is passive. In contrast, the commission defined meat-eaters as officers who "spend a good deal of their working hours aggressively seeking out situations they can exploit for financial gain, including gambling, narcotics, and other serious offenses which can yield payments of thousands of dollars" (p. 65).

Police officers, regardless of assignment, are constantly offered free food. Department policy on the taking of free food is very clear—it is forbidden.[2] The logic is simple and compelling: today it is a free coffee, tomorrow a free dinner, the next week a case of liquor, and soon the officer is indebted to the restaurateur.

Clearly, CPOP provides many opportunities for grass eating of the sort described above, although it is not clear that these opportunities are more available to CPOs than they are to regular patrol officers. In fact, shopkeepers are often delighted to have a police officer in their store, because they know that while the officer is there they and their customers are safe. Some merchants actively encourage the patronage of police personnel by providing incentives in the form of discounts on merchandise or food. Vera field researchers witnessed several situations in which free food was offered to CPOs. For example, an officer entered a coffee shop and ordered a soda. He placed 75 cents on the counter and the owner said, "Your money is no good here." The officer explained that he could not take any gratuities. The owner said, "Please, please, I love having you here. It is the least I can do." The officer explained department regulations and engaged in more conversation. The officer left the 75 cents on the counter and said, "Consider it a tip."

In another instance, the officer bought a slice of pizza, gave the owner a dollar and received four quarters in change. Another officer went into a delicatessen and bought a pastrami sandwich for $3.75. When he opened the bag, he found two pastrami sandwiches, a container of coleslaw, and a cup of coffee. In none of these instances did the officer solicit the free food. Often these are difficult situations for the officer and the merchant, especially when the merchants are immigrants who do not understand why the officer would refuse their hospitality.

Several of the CPOP sergeants conceded that CPOs may be accepting free food, and a few expressed ambivalence toward the department's stringent attitude regarding such gratuities. As one respondent explained:

> To me, this corruption thing is overplayed, and when I hear about it, it makes me sick. As far as getting a cup of coffee or something like that, I'm sure they're eating pretty good on the beats and maybe they are getting a little special consideration, but I rarely delve into that. It's not a major, major problem. The job is tough enough as it is.

He continued:

> They're always out there. And you know, basically they may be going in there talking with a guy and he says, "You want a cup of coffee?" I don't really know if that's corruption. They're doing a lot of favors for people all the time. They're doing their job, which for an average cop might be considered a favor. They might be going out of their way for a particular individual over a

particular problem, whereas if the cop on patrol did it, the department would look at it and say "He's spending an inordinate amount of time on this."

The consensus of the supervisors was that while the opportunities for corruption might be more prevalent in CPOP than on regular patrol, the CPOs were no more likely to succumb to the temptations than were other officers. Moreover, the sergeants expressed the belief that if an officer wanted to be corrupt, he or she would find or make opportunities regardless of the assignment. As one respondent explained:

> I think that if anybody wants to be corrupt, they can be corrupt. I say that's anybody, not only CPOP. And I would say the temptation is more so in CPOP because "It's my post, my area, my people. I see them every day." There's a possibility that could exist, could happen. It doesn't happen. Why? Because CPOP is a good deal, better than most. It gives the cops something. It fits in with the "Gimmes. Gimme weekends off. Gimme days off. Gimme my flexibility." I'm afraid to lose that. And I'm not going to give that up for a sandwich or a pair of shoes, or a ten dollar discount. It's not worth it. And the ramifications of narcotics, now I'm talking about jail, and these people don't want to go to jail.

One respondent noted that violations may not pertain to corrupt activities in the form of payoffs, but to abuse of patrol time: "If there's incidents, more than likely it's going to be minor violation-type things. Maybe he'll get too friendly with a store owner and sit in the back of the store for a couple of hours—that kind of thing rather than hardcore corruption." The respondents agreed that it was extremely unlikely that a CPO would become involved in setting up pads and extortion rackets, because the risk of detection was too high. One CPOP sergeant described the situation as follows:

> It depends on what kind of corruption we're talking about. There would be more opportunity for a CPOP guy to be a grass-eater, where he could pick up a bottle at Christmas or maybe get a free meal or a free cup of coffee. The meat-eater concept was the guy who's not getting gratuities, he was selling his shield.

He continued:

> It's difficult for a CPOP officer to be a meat-eater, because he's not an anonymous entity anymore. He is the guy on the street every day. There's no anonymity anymore. He's not given the opportunity to go into a situation and make a quick kill, because they'll maybe get his number, maybe get his name. "Oh, I know him. He comes in here all the time. I know his name. I know everything about him."

The seven commanding officers and six CPO sergeants interviewed as part of this research agreed that the first line of defense against corruption is to select trustworthy officers. As one commanding officer stated, "There's more opportunity. That's why I think that picking people is critical. And you have to keep an eye on them, too. Not that I suspect that anybody's doing anything. But I would be a fool if I didn't keep an eye on them." Or as another commanding officer stated:

> First of all, they're selected officers. I'm familiar with all of their jackets. I've gone through all of their personnel files. I'm familiar with them personally as people now, and I know just about how much I can trust them. I'm aware of some of them that I still say, "You, I'm keeping a little more of an eye on, because you may have some kind of interest that could lead me into a deep suspicion of something."

One commanding officer, who is very strong proponent of the program, said:

> I always try to let them know that what they're doing is special. And CPOP is special and they have to feel that. I guess you're walking a very fine line, because they have a lot of latitude, and if you've got a bad guy out there he could destroy it. But if they know that they're special and that there's a lot of trust placed in them . . . you have to have a good sergeant, and you have to pick good guys for the program, and you have to let them go out there and do the job.
>
> You know, this is a revolutionary idea, giving a guy 25 or 40 square blocks. He could be anywhere. He could be doing anything. You really have to treat them with trust.

Although none of the supervisors reported taking any special measures to ensure the integrity of their officers, they did state that the CPOs were continually warned about corruption hazards and the severe penalties for infractions. As one supervisor stated:

> You have to let them know, he's not allowed to do anything. He's not allowed to take any money. He's not allowed to take meals. He's not allowed to get involved in anything that a regular cop isn't. And that if you do, and you're caught, you're gonna lose your job. And you have to put it very blunt and specific, and you have to keep them aware of it.

In addition to selecting the right officers and warning them regularly against the dangers of corruption, several of the sergeants and COs expressed the belief that the public exposure to which a CPO is subjected is a deterrent to serious corrupt activity. As one commanding officer explained:

As a matter of fact, I think it might be harder for a CPO because of the fact that everybody knows him. He's not the faceless man in blue that's riding around in a radio car. He knows people. I do believe that it's one thing to shake down somebody you don't know, but it's something else if it's somebody you see every day. Plus the fact he's there every minute. He can't do what he wants to do and leave. It's not regular patrol.

Another supervisor suggested that an officer cannot win the respect of the community if the people suspect that the CPO is involved in the local rackets:

People in the neighborhood know what's going on. If they see you going into a spot that they know takes numbers . . . if you go in there every week or every day, there's gonna be talk. "Hey, he's in there." It's not that he's going in there one day. You're in there all the time, and people know what's going on, and people write letters now. . . . Plus, I feel if these guys build up the people's confidence, if they know that you're going in there and you're making any kinds of deals with this guy or anything, it's going to really knock your credibility to Hell, because they say, "If you're dealing with him. . . ." You know.

All of the respondents believed that any suspected or real corrupt activity on the part of the CPOs would be brought to the attention of the sergeant or the CO very quickly by the community:

But I think the real check might be that I think I would hear it from the community. I really believe that. I think I have that kind of relationship with the community where they would tell me if they thought somebody was up to no good. They would let me know. And I'm not talking about an anonymous letter to the precinct. I think somebody would let me know. So perhaps that's the biggest check.

The following statement from the commanding officer in one of the research precincts serves as an overview and summary of the opinions expressed during these interviews regarding the corruption hazards inherent in CPOP:

You can get so concerned about corruption, you can have a Simon Pure operation but be ineffective. You can't do anything. I've always been a very aggressive precinct commander. I've always pushed for collars for street drugs, drinking, on everything. Corruption's not something I go home and worry about. You just have to accept it as part of the turf. If it happens, it happens. You can get so tied up with concerns about corruption that you can't do anything. You just stop functioning.

As far as corruption, if a guy is corrupt, he's going to go out there and he's going to do what he wants to do. He's going to shake down drug dealers; he's going to do whatever he wants to do.

When you talk about corruption, this program couldn't exist if we became obsessed with corruption. You have to be concerned about corruption, but we've come to the point where if we're not going to be operational and effective, we shouldn't have the program. If a guy wants to be corrupt, there's no way you could stop him. And if he has 50 square blocks of a beat, he could do you in, there's no doubt about it. There are certain risks you should accept. If a guy is an out-and-out corrupt guy, he's gonna go public one way or the other. But I believe in the CPOP program, it would surface a lot quicker than it would in other programs, because the cop is so well known in the area.

Checking Abuse of Authority   The purpose of CPOP is to develop long- and short-term strategies for dealing with crime and quality-of-life problems. The CPOP sergeants, precinct commanders, and the community want results. The field research indicates that the CPOs often expressed frustration from encountering the same "mutts," "skells," and "perps" on the street day-in and day-out. These people may be teenagers hanging out in front of a video arcade, derelicts or homeless people camping out in parks, or the ubiquitous street-level drug dealers. The officers may disperse a group, knowing that within minutes it will re-form there, or at another corner, or park, or storefront. Thus the officer who must return again and again in an effort to remove or substantially alleviate the problem may be tempted to take action that exceeds his or her lawful authority.

This was another concern of department officials in the early days of the CPO program. The concern was intensified by their recognizing that local residents and merchants are often less sensitive than the police to the constraints on action contained in law and regulation. It was believed likely, therefore, that the CPOs would sometimes be exposed to citizen pressures that could lead to abuses of authority and a consequent raft of civilian complaints.

With these concerns in mind, the research staff examined the experience of the CPOs in the research precincts to determine whether the evidence substantiated the fears that this form of policing would produce a disproportionate number of civilian complaints. In addition, the CPOP sergeants and the commanding officers in the research precincts were asked to describe how they perceived the threat of civilian complaints in the context of the program, and the special steps they took, if any, to counter that threat.

The Civilian Complaint Review Board (CCRB) is a body established by the City Charter to receive, investigate, and dispose of complaints against police personnel brought by civilians that allege that an officer has behaved improperly in his or her dealings with a civilian. Four types of alleged misconduct fall within the jurisdiction of the CCRB: (a) improper (either unnecessary or excessive) use of force, (b) abuse of authority, (c) discourteous talk or actions, and (d) ethnic slurs. Other types of alleged misconduct, including allegations of corrupt behavior, are handled by other bodies, including the district attorneys' offices when the allegations are of a criminal nature. The CCRB conducts an inquiry to determine whether the allegations can be substantiated and, if substantiated, recommends a sanction to be imposed on the officer, up to and including the formal lodging of charges. The CCRB maintains a record of all allegations made against police personnel and of their disposition. Commanding officers are held accountable for controlling the number of complaints made against members of their command, and an officer's record of civilian complaints is reviewed by department managers when that officer is being considered for various assignments defined as desirable by the work force. Thus police officers, supervisors, and commanding officers are concerned about the number of civilian complaints associated with them.

The research staff obtained from the CCRB the record of civilian complaints against each of the 69 CPOs in the research precincts. All complaints made during each officer's career through July 15, 1988 (the cutoff date for data collection) were counted. The overwhelming majority of the cases in the sample contained only one allegation, although some contained two or more. The most serious allegation contained in each complaint was coded for type, based on the following ordering of seriousness: force, abuse, discourtesy, and ethnic slur. Similarly, each case was coded for disposition according to the disposition reached on the most serious allegation. The disposition codes were investigation closed (no definitive disposition reached because of unavailable or uncooperative complainant); conciliation (complainant agrees to have the case closed by a CCRB official discussing the matter with the accused officer); unsubstantiated (evidence insufficient to find either for the complainant or for the officer); unfounded (evidence indicates that the alleged event never occurred); exonerated (evidence indicates that the officer acted properly); or substantiated (evidence supports the complainant's allegation). Finally, each of the complaints was coded as to whether or not it occurred during the officer's tenure as a CPO. This was the basis for distinguishing between CPOP and non-CPOP complaints.

Of the 69 officers in the sample, 29 (42%) had no non-CPOP complaints during their careers. Of the 40 officers (58%) who had at least one such complaint, the number of complaints received ranged from 1 to 22. The three officers who had 10 or more non-CPOP complaints during their careers also had at least 15 years of service on the job. The average number of non-CPOP complaints per year of service for these 40 officers ranged between 0.1 and 1.8 per year, while the overall average of non-CPOP complaints per year of non-CPOP service was 0.48 for the entire sample.

Of the 69 officers in the sample, 54 (78.3%) did not receive any civilian complaints during their tenure as CPOs. Of the 15 officers who received at least one complaint, the range was from one to three complaints. The average number of CPOP complaints per year of CPOP service for these 15 officers ranged between 0.3 and 1.5, while the overall average of CPOP complaints per year of CPOP service was 0.18 for the entire sample.

The probability of receiving civilian complaints varies with the nature of the duties assigned. For example, complaint rates are highest among people assigned to traffic enforcement duties. The number of officers in the research sample was too small to permit useful comparisons between complaint rates for the CPOP assignment and those for other special assignments in patrol (e.g., traffic, Anti-Crime, SNEU, RMP). Nevertheless, it is clear that the data presented here do not support the hypothesis that assignment to CPOP is more likely to produce civilian complaints when compared with all other patrol officer assignments taken together.

In 75% of the CPOP complaints and 61% of the non-CPOP complaints, the most serious allegation concerned unnecessary or excessive force. The number of CPOP complaints (24) is too small to determine whether a meaningful difference exists between these percentages. (If only three of those complaints were categorized differently, the entire percentage difference would be eliminated.) However, conceivably, the likelihood of CPO involvement in dealing with street narcotics problems, and the arrest and stop-and-question tactics attendant to it, may mean that the complaints that are received by CPOs are somewhat more likely to allege misuse of force. This may account, as well, for the fact that 50% of the CPOP complaints were withdrawn or closed because of an unavailable or uncooperative witness, a percentage considerably higher than the 22.5% of non-CPOP complaints that were disposed in that manner. No difference was evident between the two types of complaints in terms of the percentages that were substantiated—5.3% of the non-CPOP complaints and 4.2% of the CPOP complaints—but 12.5% of the CPOP complaints, as compared with 2.6% of the non-CPOP complaints, were exonerated.

The sergeants and commanding officers in the research precincts believed that pressures unique to CPOP could result in a large number of civilian complaints. Because the officer is known in the community and returns to the same neighborhoods every day, he or she is likely to feel additional pressure to correct persistent problems. In the face of that pressure, the officer may be tempted to intervene more forcefully than is appropriate, or may receive more complaints simply because he or she is making more arrests, issuing more summonses, or moving people from suspect locations more frequently that the regular patrol officer. As one sergeant explained:

> It can be very true. You can find yourself caught up in a situation where there's a lot of pressure from the community on a particular problem, and you can become very aggressive. I've had that

with our narcotics problem. . . . It was like a personal affront every time we went back up there that they were still up there. But that's when you begin to take a step back and you've got to try to control yourself. And I think that's where having officers that are well-rounded, that you put a little more trust in them.

Another sergeant advised his staff to approach situations cautiously and to be sensitive to the context of the interaction, but to recognize that assertive action may be necessary nonetheless:

I know if I was a cop on the street and had the same beat and stuff like that, that I'd have to eventually make a stand, because I wouldn't be able to accomplish nothing if they thought that I wasn't going to do anything to anybody doing wrong. You gotta make a stand sometimes. I try to explain to the CPOs to go in there easy, because people don't know they're doing wrong. So you don't go in there swinging nightsticks on Day One. Go in there a little gingerly, talk to them, explain the situation, and give it a little time. You have to start working your way up to chasing them, giving them summonses and then, bottom line, if that doesn't work, you have to make arrests.

Yet another sergeant suggested that despite the threat of a civilian complaint that a police officer faces when taking action against someone on the street, the consequences of avoiding that risk by doing nothing are even more destructive to police/community relations:

It's a big question; there's a few things working. What basically is being brought out here is that you're putting a cop in a situation where instead of being a robot, he should be a thinking individual. So, what's wrong with that? Would you rather have a cop out there who was standing there being window dressing, having junkies falling all around him because he doesn't know what the hell is going on, and he doesn't care what's going on?

He continued:

Being out there with a gun and a shield and a uniform and doing nothing to me is ludicrous—it sets back any kind of police/community relations. I told my guys point blank: You get to a block, you do whatever you can do. And I expect over and above everything to get these people organized and get information. And we'll do what's needed to show our good faith.

Despite the fact that the sergeants and commanding officers in the research precincts recognized the dangers of CPOs abusing their authority in relation to civilians on their beats, they indicated that this problem had not arisen in any significant way in their commands, and they doubted that it would because of the care taken in choosing officers for this assignment. As one commanding officer stated succinctly, "You've got to be selective. I'm not gonna get some swaggering guy with notches on his nightstick." Or, as a CPOP sergeant explained:

> We're back to selecting people for CPOP. Some guys in RMP every second word is "asshole" or something, you know. You can't have guys going out there who talk like that to people and aggravate them. You've got to have a guy that has a high boiling point. You can't have somebody that's going to go out there and start like gangbusters. . . . If it's an arrest, it's an arrest. But, again, you can do it in a way that you're not going to go out there and drag people through the street. You're gonna make an arrest, get in the van, and then you're gone. You can't have anybody going out there thinking that they're Matt Dillon, that they're running Dodge City.

Thus officers are selected for CPOP because they are courteous, patient, and flexible:

> CPOP is very good in that respect, with steady officers. They don't overreact to situations. Because of their ability to deal with people; that's how they get into CPOP to begin with. We don't have any problems in that regard. . . . With RMP officers there's more likely to be a problem because they haven't been screened for their ability to deal with the public as much as CPOP has. Some RMP officers tend to use an authoritarian approach. They're much more rigid than CPOP officers who are able to deal more readily with the public.

Several supervisors mentioned not only the selection process, but also the importance of CPOP training, and their awareness of the various resources that can be brought to bear in certain situations. As one commanding officer stated:

> I think that they're better trained in those chronic problems. I think the average cop usually says, "If there's a problem, I'm gonna solve it. I'm gonna do it." Whereas a CPOP cop is aware of the whole—not just criminal justice—but the whole governmental network of places to refer people, places to call themselves and get that other agency involved. And I think they use that more often than average.

Other supervisors noted that CPOP, unlike Anti-Crime, is not an arrest-oriented unit; therefore the tone and style of the units promote conciliation rather than confrontation. Thus, although the officers are under pressure, they are less likely to abuse their authority than are RMP officers. Another commanding officer said:

There's avenues to redress the problems that they have on their beats. When they go to a block association meeting and they hear about this narcotics place or whatever, it just encourages them ... yeah, it might encourage some individuals to become overzealous, but it hasn't happened yet. We don't have an arrest-oriented group in CPOP. I know some of the other CPOPs make enormous numbers of arrests. We don't have that.

During the course of this research, sergeants and commanding officers in research and nonresearch precincts expressed a different type of concern regarding civilian complaints and the CPO program. Several of these police officials expressed the belief that persons associated with the drug trade register groundless civilian complaints against CPOs whose persistent efforts disrupt the dealer's business. The dealers, they claim, know that an officer's chances of getting desirable assignments in the future, such as assignment to the Organized Crime Control Bureau, could be damaged by a record of frequent civilian complaints. In addition, it was suggested that dealers also know that commanding officers are held accountable for the number of civilian complaints registered against members of their commands and are anxious, therefore, to hold that number to a minimum. The respondents suggested that this knowledge leads dealers to make, and to encourage others to make, frequent complaints against active CPOs.

The sergeants and COs who spoke on this matter were concerned that active CPOs, especially those with serious drug problems in their beats, were vulnerable to such tactical use of civilian complaints. They noted that the officers were aware of this danger, and the COs and sergeants feared that this awareness might discourage the CPOs from attacking narcotics problems aggressively. They were fearful, as well, that some commanding officers might feel themselves threatened by such tactics, and, in self-defense, might move the more active CPOs to less active beats.

The research staff was not able to undertake the extensive analysis of civilian complaints against all CPOs and a comparison sample of non-CPOs citywide that would be required to subject these concerns to careful research. Research staff did speak to a few officers in the research precincts and to some officers and sergeants in nonresearch precincts, who claimed that they, or other members of their CPOP units, had been the targets of such tactical complaints. In at least two instances, research staff were informed by supervisors in nonresearch precincts that CPOs in their commands, who were actively attacking narcotics locations and receiving civilian complaints related to that activity, were pulled out of those beats by the precinct commanders.

The belief that CPOs are especially vulnerable to the tactical use of civilian complaints, whether it is empirically demonstrable or not, is a genuine threat to the effective functioning of the program. It is widely believed that civilian complaints are potentially damaging to a police officer's career, regardless of their final dispositions. This is because police officers believe that supervisors and commanders are swayed by the mere number of such complaints an officer receives when he or she is being considered for desirable assignments. This belief could be a strong disincentive to an officer's active involvement in identifying local narcotics problems and in implementing strategies to attack them. It seems important, therefore, that senior managers in the department monitor the breadth and intensity of this belief among CPOs, and make a special effort to determine whether officers careers are being adversely affected by groundless complaints submitted by people attempting to neutralize the officer's work in the community. If this is happening, the processes of investigation and accountability regarding those complaints should be modified in some way to prevent the situation from continuing in the future. If the managers conclude that the belief is erroneous, a special effort should be made to demonstrate that fact to CPOs and patrol officers from whom future CPOs will be recruited.

The Program's Efforts to Strengthen Supervisory Performance

Throughout the research period, the program staff at Vera and in the department continued to introduce the program to additional precincts and to monitor implementation in the precincts in which it was operating. These efforts provided the staff with a regular flow of information regarding program operations and with useful insights into the strengths and weaknesses of the implementation process. This information was supplemented by the research staff's sharing of its general observations regarding dimensions of the program design with which the units seemed to be having difficulty. This regular review of operations produced various efforts by the program staff to strengthen aspects of CPOP operations, including program supervision. Several of these efforts are worth noting here.

In the fall of 1987, the police commissioner asked that a program be developed to orient and train all command-level personnel (captains and higher) in the Patrol Bureau in the principles and operations of CPOP, its relationship to other forms of community and problem-solving policing in the United States, and the reasons why the department thought it wise to move in that direction. Vera staff, assisted by the staff of the Police Academy, after consulting with two dozen precinct commanders who already had the CPOP program, prepared an orientation guide and designed a 3-to-4-hour training program for that purpose. The materials were disseminated, and the program was presented to approximately 180 command personnel throughout the winter of 1987 and the spring of 1988.

The training program focused on the principles of community policing and problem-solving policing and the reasons for their current influence on urban policing policies in America. In addition, it described the structure and operations of the CPO program, the various dimensions of the role that the CPO is expected to perform, and the particular importance of the precinct commander to effective program performance. Toward that end, the guide recommended that the CO meet regularly with the unit sergeant and with each of the CPOs to review the performance of individual officers. To assist in that review, the guide set forth a list of over 60 questions, organized around the different dimensions of the CPO role, for use by a CPOP supervisor and/or a precinct commander. The training program also stressed the importance of the CO seeing CPOP as an intelligence resource that could be used to inform his resource deployment decisions and of his working to ensure the effective integration of CPOP with regular patrol and other specialized units in the precinct. After the training program was presented to the existing command staff in the Patrol Bureau, it was made a regular part of the Department Executive Training curriculum.

During the fall of 1987, Vera's program staff began a series of small-group meetings with the sergeants in the existing CPOP units. Typically, these meetings involved no more than four or five sergeants and were held away from the precincts at Vera's offices. The meetings were intended both to identify operational and supervisory problems perceived by the sergeants and to develop, with their assistance, guidelines for dealing with those problems. In addition, time was devoted to reviewing the administrative demands imposed on the sergeant. As a result of these meetings, a supervisory guide was produced and disseminated in the fall of 1988. The guide contained, among other things, the list of more than 60 questions to assist the sergeant in reviewing the performance of his or her unit members.

As indicated in an earlier chapter, by the spring of 1987 the program staff at Vera, armed with some general observations by the research staff, realized that the performance of the average CPO in carrying out the problem-solving process was not as strong as had been hoped. The deficiencies were explained, at least in part, by the inadequacies of the problem-solving training provided to the CPOs. In addition, it was recognized that, in most cases, the sergeants had no more training or experience with problem solving than the CPOs did. That meant that the supervisors were not well prepared to provide real, substantive assistance to their subordinates regarding the core element of their role.

To bolster the training and assistance provided to both CPOs and their supervisors, Vera staff proposed the development of training materials and a training program in problem-solving methods. With funding assistance from the Guggenheim and Norman Foundations, the Chase Manhattan Bank, and the Philip Morris Companies, a *Problem-Solving Guide* was prepared (see Appendix B). A full-time trainer, who is a retired member of the police department, was hired in the spring of 1988. Training curricula and procedures were developed first for CPOP sergeants and later for CPOs, and the training program was presented to all CPOP sergeants during the fall of 1988.

The presentation of a 4-day training program to be presented to the CPOs in each precinct was begun toward the end of 1988. The plan called for the presentation of this program in one precinct per week by the Vera trainer, and the gradual incorporation of Police Academy personnel in the hopes of completing the program in all 75 precincts within a 2-year period.

Most of these efforts were carried forward after the data for this research project were collected. Therefore, no effort was made by the research staff to measure the content of what the sergeants and CPOs actually learned or the impact of the training on their performance in implementing the problem-solving process. However, it was clear that the sergeants wanted more training in problem solving and that their performance as supervising leader and guide could only be strengthened by increased mastery of that sort.

Summary of Findings

Supervision in the CPO program imposes a somewhat different set of demands on the unit supervisor than does supervision in regular patrol. The leader-guide dimension is especially important in CPOP supervision, because it demands that the sergeant develop more substantive knowledge of the neighborhoods, of the problem-solving process, of the operations and priorities of other special units in the department, and of the strengths and weaknesses of his subordinates in the unit.

One of the principal responsibilities of the CPOP sergeant as leader-guide is to represent the unit within the department. This responsibility has several dimensions, including the obligation to relay information up the chain of command about the problems being addressed by the unit, the extra-unit resources needed to address those problems, and the effects of the problem-solving strategies implemented by unit members. All of the sergeants were reluctant to pass on what they thought of as "negative" information; this reluctance stems from a fear that such information will result in damage to someone's career in the department. This situation is a threat to the long-term effectiveness of CPOP in that problem solvers must be able to recognize implementation failures and incorrect assumptions to make the changes required to alleviate problems.

Some sergeants adopt a more proactive stance than others regarding the problem-solving activities of their units. Such sergeants recognize the importance of the representational dimension of their role, and they work at it earnestly. They try to meet with the CO on a regular basis to review the activities and needs of the unit. They highlight the activities of the unit that address the CO's priorities and the information secured by the unit that has proved useful to other police units. Within this context, they review various problem-solving strategies with the CO, and they indicate where and when they are seeking the involvement of other units. This active posture regarding problem solving permits the sergeant to represent the unit well within the department. It enhances the unit's image as an active police unit, helps to secure cooperation from other units, and strengthens the morale of the CPOs.

Another responsibility of the CPOP sergeant as leader-guide is to help represent the program to the community. This is a task with which police sergeants generally have less familiarity, and with which they are somewhat uncomfortable, at least initially. The observations and interviews of the research staff indicated that not all sergeants understood the full significance of the community in the design of the program. This inadequate understanding manifests itself in an essentially defensive attitude toward community organizations and toward community residents perceived to be influential citizens. Nevertheless, there are sergeants who understand that the CPOP design embodies a much more positive and less defensive view of the community.

The last task of the CPOP sergeant as leader-guide is to assist the CPOs in carrying out their problem-solving responsibilities. At the time of the data collection, the sergeants in the research precincts and CPOP sergeants in general did not have a sophisticated understanding of the problem-solving process. It is not surprising, therefore, that the performance of the sergeants in the research precincts on this dimension of their role was quite varied. A couple seemed to grasp the logic of the process and became comfortable with it rather quickly. The other sergeants did not really grasp the essential differences between problem solving and incident response. Lacking any substantial knowledge of or experience with problem solving, these sergeants did not often challenge their subordinates to improve their problem-solving skills.

The CPOP sergeants were better prepared to assume their responsibilities as control agents. In this regard, the need to control the abuse of patrol and administrative time presented some unique challenges because of the relative freedom of movement enjoyed by CPOs. However, the research did not reveal a systematic or chronic pattern of evasion of work while the officers were out on their beats.

Abuse of administrative time is important not only because it decreases the efficiency and effectiveness of the CPOP unit, but also because it affects the prestige of the unit and the morale in the precinct. Abuses of this sort typically involve spending more time on paperwork than is necessary and hanging around the station house for no apparent reason. Abuse of administrative time, like abuse of patrol time, is not a problem in well-run units. If, however, the supervision is not strong, on both the unit and the precinct level, there are forces in operation that encourage officers to exploit the latitude provided by the program.

Control of these types of abuse is best accomplished by the sergeant's supervising closely the monthly work plans of each CPO. By insisting that each officer identify priority problems and set forth specific plans for addressing them, the sergeant requires the CPO to provide substantive justification for the tour times and RDOs. More-over, review of the work plan also provides the officer and the sergeant with the opportunity to decide where and on what the officer will be working in the coming month and, thereby, hold to a minimum both "down time" and the time devoted to aimless patrol in the beat.

When the CPO program was first proposed, some senior members of the department expressed concern about what they perceived to be the corruption hazards inherent in the program. The research staff collected data regarding corruption complaints made against all of the CPOs in the research precincts. The analysis of these data did not support the hypothesis that assignment to CPOP increases the like-lihood of corruption complaints.

The seven commanding officers and six CPO sergeants inter-viewed as part of this research agreed that the first line of defense against corruption is to select trustworthy officers. In addition to selecting the right officers and warning them regularly against the dangers of corruption, several of the sergeants and COs expressed the belief that the public exposure to which a CPO is subjected is a deterrent to serious corrupt activity.

Departmental officials were also concerned about the extent of public exposure that the officers would experience and the possibility that their work would increase the number of civilian complaints alleging that the officers had been abusive in some way. To explore that possibility, the research staff collected data regarding all civilian complaints ever made against the CPOs in the research precincts. These data do not support the hypothesis that assignment to CPOP is more likely to produce civilian complaints when compared with all other patrol officer assignments taken together. Despite the fact that the sergeants and commanding officers in the research precincts recognized the dangers of CPOs abusing their authority in relation to civilians on their beats, they indicated that this problem had not arisen in any significant way in their commands, and they doubted that it would because of the care taken in choosing officers for this assignment.

Notes   1. The CPOP unit in one of the research precincts was the focus of an investigation by one of the department's central investigative units. Several members of the CPOP unit were found to be violating regulations by abusing patrol time, and they were removed from CPOP and transferred to other precincts. In addition, the CPOP sergeant was replaced as unit supervisor. These open positions were filled with new people and the unit continued in operation. This is the only instance of a unit being disciplined that has occurred since CPOP expansion began in January 1985.

2. Although the department's prohibition is clear and emphatic, such behavior is not universally prohibited by police agencies. The Knapp Commission recognized the ambivalence about officers accept-

ing free food: "the Commission feels [that these gratuities] cannot in the strictest sense be considered a matter of police corruption, but it has been included here because it is a related—and ethically border-line—practice, which is prohibited by Department regulations, and which often leads to corruption" (New York City Commission, 1972, p. 66).

CPOP in the Context
of the Patrol Structure

- Introduction
- Perceptions of CPOP Held by Non-CPOP Officers
- The Pivotal Importance of the Precinct Commander
- The Police Commissioner's Support of CPOP
- CPOP's Future as Seen at the End of the Research

Introduction　　The CPO program was introduced into the NYPD as a special demonstration program within the Patrol Services Bureau. The designers of the program hoped to demonstrate that the CPO role, embodying the principles of community-oriented, problem-solving policing could be implemented by patrol officers and could produce benefits to both the police and the community. It was further hoped that, based upon the results of the demonstration project, the department would expand the program and eventually integrate the functions of CPOP fully into the patrol operation at the precinct level.

While demonstration programs are a common occurrence in large police departments, not everyone is convinced of their utility as a method for introducing organizational change. On the positive side, they provide a reasonably nonthreatening opportunity to test a proposed change and to modify a program model until it works in that particular department. Usually, they can do this without requiring any major modification in existing services, policies, or procedures. An effectively implemented demonstration project also provides the evidence and the time needed to persuade policymakers, often including the chief executive officer of the municipality and members of the legislature, that it can be adopted with benefits and without significant losses.

Paradoxically, these valuable features of a demonstration project can be the very reasons for its being an ineffective method of change. Because the demonstration project does not attack the existing procedures, structure, or culture head on, it does not create the sense of foment that often appears necessary for significant changes to take root. In a large organization, the organizational culture may provide the members, especially middle management, with the cynical view that the demonstration project is simply the pet project of the new administration or some "bright boy" within it, and, like hundreds before it, it will collapse of its own weight if it is largely ignored. The fact that a demonstration project is mounted in a manner that shields the regular operation from its influence creates a barrier that must eventually be overcome, while providing its opposition with time and ammunition either to undermine it or to strengthen the resistance to its eventual adoption (see Moore & Trojanowicz, 1988a; Sparrow et al., 1990).

The designers of CPOP were aware of these dangers in the abstract and, over the years they had seen, on more than one occasion, those potential deficits neutralize efforts to introduce worthwhile changes into the NYPD. Nevertheless, they believed that an alternative method was not realistically available for CPOP. First, it was necessary to articulate the specifics of a role that existed only on paper and, even in that form, represented a dramatic change from the role of the regular patrol officer. Of course, embodying as it does the principles of community-oriented and problem-solving policing, CPOP also represented a significantly different way of defining the police function and of organizing and delivering some police services to the community. To sell the idea, it was believed necessary to spell out the specifics and demonstrate that they could be implemented by patrol officers.

Furthermore, the program designers recognized that the tasks that CPOP would require could not be performed unless the officer was assured of some continuity in his or her assignments and was given the time to do things other than respond to calls-for-service. But the tour rotation procedure in the NYPD (weekly change among three shifts for most regular patrol officers), the enormous volume of calls-for-service, and the use of central dispatching that ignored the sector assignments of RMPs and simply assigned the next available car, meant that a conventionally deployed patrol officer *could not* have the continuity and time needed to test the CPO role. Finally, it was believed that the scale of CPOP, a unit of 10 officers and a sergeant, was large enough to be noticed on the precinct level, where a commander would typically have about 150 police officers under his or her command.

Thus the choice of the demonstration project method as a means for seeding the principles of community-oriented and problem-solving policing in the NYPD was taken for several reasons. Yet the course of CPOP's expansion within the department did not follow the route one expects of demonstration projects. Normally it takes a year or so for a demonstration project to begin, shake out the quirks, and stabilize its operations. During that period, information is collected about the operation and its effects, and additional time is spent by the managers of the demonstration and policymakers within the department considering whether or not to continue and/or expand the demonstration procedures. If an affirmative decision is made with respect to expansion, a plan for accomplishing it is developed, and the implementation is begun. In the NYPD, it is not unreasonable to expect these processes to take the better part of 2 years. If the procedures are to be adopted throughout the patrol service, expansion to all 75 precincts is likely to take at least a few years more.

In the case of CPOP, the decision to expand from the single pilot precinct was made, a plan for the expansion was developed, and implementation of that plan was begun before the pilot was 6 months old. And CPOP units were operating in all 75 precincts only 4 years after the pilot project began, despite the fact that expansion was suspended for the better part of a year during a fiscal crisis in the city. At the time the report on this research was being completed, on the precinct level CPOP involved the daily efforts of approximately 750 police officers and 75 sergeants.

It was clear also that the role was being performed, with varying levels of efficiency and effectiveness, in hundreds of communities throughout the city, and that many leaders in the communities and officials in the department had been persuaded of its beneficial effects. Athough CPOP was initiated as a classic demonstration project, its expansion throughout the department was effected more along the lines of mandated organizational change. Therefore it is important to ask how that was accomplished.

Nevertheless CPOP remained a special unit within precinct commands. The members of the unit continued to perform tasks that the precinct's regular patrol officers do not perform, and to avoid other tasks that consume most of the regular patrol officers' time and energy. Therefore it is important to consider the nature of the relationship between CPOs and non-CPOP officers in the precincts, and the role of the commanding officer in integrating the efforts of the various types of resources in the command.

Finally, given the course of implementation and expansion that CPOP has followed and the fact that it remains a special unit on the precinct level, one must consider how its future place within the department is envisioned. These are the concerns addressed in this chapter, beginning with a description of the relationship between CPOs and non-CPOP officers in the precincts.

**Perceptions of
CPOP
Held by
Non-CPOP
Officers**

The program designers at Vera and in the department were sensitive from the outset to the possibility that CPOs could be isolated in the precincts because of the differences between their responsibilities and those of the regular patrol officers. It was recognized that such isolation could flow either from the regular patrol officers perceiving CPOP as involving nonpolice work that is irrelevant to the overall patrol function, or from their perceiving it as an elitist unit. Steps taken to prevent this from happening included placing the CPOP unit clearly under the command of the precinct commanding officer; selecting officers and supervisors to staff the unit from within the command, whenever possible; and insisting that the members of the unit be subject to the regular supervisory structure of the precinct, especially when the CPOP sergeant is not working. They also include insisting that the CPOs be assigned their share of out-of-precinct details, which are often seen as undesirable by the regular patrol force; encouraging CPOs to handle calls-for-service within their beats whenever possible; encouraging CPOs to make reasonable contributions to the productivity expectations ("numbers") of the precinct; and encouraging CPOs to provide information and assistance to other patrol units in the precinct, whenever possible, and to request that assistance be provided to them in implementing problem-solving strategies.

To determine how non-CPOs perceived the project, the research staff interviewed 10 RMP officers in each of the research precincts. No attempt was made to select officers randomly; rather, the sample consisted of RMP officers who happened to be available on the days these interviews were conducted and who agreed to respond. (Officers in specialized units such as Anti-Crime were not interviewed.) The interviews were conducted at the end of the research period in each precinct. The interviews were *not* tape-recorded; the interviewers read the questions and recorded the answers on the interview schedule. All of the questions were open-ended, and, wherever possible, content analysis was used to calculate percentages for types of responses to particular questions. Otherwise, the responses were analyzed qualitatively.

Although the interviewees were not selected randomly and the data are qualitative, the results are interesting and consistent with the findings reported in other sections. Specifically, officers appear to be aware of the strengths and weaknesses of the CPOP unit in their precinct.

For the officers in the sample, time on the job ranged from 2 to 22 years, with a mean of 5.1 years (comparable to the mean of 5.7 years for the CPOs in the research sample). Time in the precinct ranged from 6 months to 16 years, with a mean of 3.4 years as compared to 3.3 years for the CPO sample. No other demographic data were collected on the sample members.

*The Perceived
Purpose of CPOP*

The majority of the respondents indicated that CPOP was designed to improve the image of the police department and to promote police-community relations:

Community relations. To enhance the confidence that the public has in the police. To show the public that the police are willing to help and to provide an area of safety to the public. The CPOs work with the business people and the youth in the area.

The goal is to improve public relations with the community and to make the police more visible. CPOs go to community meetings, work with the youth, and participate in community events.

Several officers mentioned that CPOP addresses quality-of-life issues:

To help improve areas of the community. Take care of disorderly groups and other conditions in the neighborhood. They work on the problems that are minor and that regular patrol does not have time for.

Nobody really knew what CPOP was about at first. Right now, I'm seeing that their purpose is to help promote the police department—help the community to feel better about us. They do that by taking care of the little things that piss folks off, like abandoned cars. That's a big thing in this precinct and RMP guys don't really have time to handle it.

The Perceived Differences Between CPOP and RMP

When the officers were asked to describe the ways in which CPOP and RMP duties differ, the majority mentioned that CPOs are not responsible for 911 calls-for-service and that they patrol on foot:

RMP primarily handles jobs and makes radio runs. When you're on patrol, you don't get to stay at a job for very long. On the other hand, CPOs can stop and talk. The big difference is that we're in a car and they're on foot. If people want to talk to us, they have to wave the car down. They are more willing to talk to a cop on foot.

Several officers explained that CPOs are much more familiar with the neighborhood and accessible to the public because they patrol on foot: "CPOP is more familiar with the community. They're on a one-to-one basis with them and care more about the individual. In the car you don't get to know people. You go from job to job and just get the work done."

Another officer noted the problem-solving and crime-prevention capacity of the unit:

It's a lot different. They're not on the radio. When you're in RMP you handle all kinds of jobs—maybe ones that just happened.

CPOP can handle long-term problems or past problems. For example, bums in the park. They may be able to work on problems or conditions they can prevent.

The Perceived Difficulty of CPOP Assignment

Some of the most interesting and insightful responses pertained to the officers' perceptions regarding the relative ease or difficulty of the CPOP assignment when compared to RMP. Responses varied widely. Fifty-two percent of the officers expressed the belief that CPOP was an easy assignment; 28% believed that it was as difficult as RMP; 15% thought it was more difficult; and 5% could not answer this question.

Several officers believed that CPOP was easier because the officers are not "slaves to the radio" and as a result they can structure their time and select their assignments: "It's easy because they're out of the mainstream. They don't have to answer the radio. We have to respond to every job—CPOP doesn't. They pick and choose their work. They have more time off and don't have to go around the clock." Or as another officer explained: "I think it is an easy assignment because they don't have to respond to radio runs, take reports, and put up with the aggravation of responding from one job to another for eight and a half hours."

One of the themes in the comments of officers who believed that CPOP was *not* an easy assignment is the notion that working with the public is demanding:

CPOP is more difficult because you become more personal with the people you deal with. It's more of a challenge. On patrol the job is over in 15 minutes and you may never see that person again. In CPOP you deal with things on a daily basis. You get to know and work closely with the community.

A few officers, while stating that motor patrol was more difficult, believed that CPOP was "not a piece of cake": "Patrol is the most difficult. CPOs don't have to deal with the criminal element as often, but they do a lot of investigating and have to be on their feet all day. They work hard in a lot of ways."

Other officers indicated that the degree of difficulty involved in the CPO role depended on the whether the officer saw the assignment as a challenge or as an opportunity to slide:

It depends on what the police officer wants to make of it. It could be easy or hard. It depends on how involved they get. They can get very involved, or put in their time and leave.

You can make it as easy or difficult as you want. If it's done the way it's probably supposed to be done, it's probably not easy at all. But, it's the type of assignment you can also "skate" in.

Perceived
Characteristics
of the CPOs
Themselves

The respondents were asked, How would you describe the cops who become CPOs? Are they different from other patrol officers? The consensus was that CPOs are no different from other officers; they are not "supercops." They are just "regular guys" who volunteered for and were selected for the program. This finding is not surprising given that most of the respondents believed that the CPOP assignment was easier or no more difficult than motor patrol. However a few respondents described CPOs as perhaps being more "community-oriented" or "outgoing," or having more of "a gift for gab" than RMP officers:

> They have to be more inclined to deal with people in a patient manner. They have to be able to deal with people and like to talk. If someone is shy, they can't do the job. They're probably more sensitized to the community and their integrity is high. They have the ability and talents to deal with the community on a personal level.

Again, in keeping with the notion of CPOs as ordinary cops, several respondents stated in essence "some are good; some are not so good":

> I would like to think that they are more motivated than other officers. However, I believe that some of them join mainly for the hours.

> It depends on the individual officer. Some are more motivated and knowledgeable about the neighborhood. Some are not productive and just want to hide.

> Generally they are officers who don't want to work as hard and are looking for an easy way out of patrol.

Many officers stated that one of the attractions of CPOP is the working schedule, and that made it a "comfortable" assignment. Nevertheless, one officer recognized this factor, yet believed the officers changed with time in CPOP: "They join CPOP for personal reasons like flexible hours but once they're in there they are transformed by the work they do." In contrast, another officer stated: "I don't think they're different at the beginning. But I think after being in CPOP they slack off a bit and lose a bit of their street-sense."

Perceived
Activity Levels
of the CPOs

One of the ways in which patrol officers evaluate each other is in terms of "activity" levels. For RMP officers, activity levels are measured by the type and volume of calls-for-service handled, the willingness and frequency with which RMP officers serve as backups, and the number of "good" as opposed to "bullshit" collars (arrests) an officer makes. Factored into this equation is an assessment of the officer's attitude toward the job and his coworkers: Is he just going through the motions, or does he really want to get the job done?

When the interviewees were asked whether CPOs were as "active" as RMP officers, 53% stated that CPOs were less active; 30% thought the activity levels were about the same; and 5% said that CPOs had a higher activity level. Twelve percent could not answer this question.

As might be expected, officers who tend to judge performance primarily on the number of calls-for-service answered believed that CPOs were less active: "Less active. They're not required to answer the radio. They can choose to stay in the office all day and do paperwork instead. We can never make that choice." Several officers believed that the activity levels were equal, but the form that the activity takes is different: "They do different activities, so you can't really compare their activity level with that of other patrol officers." Or, as another officer explained: "CPOP wasn't designed to generate high activity. It's not the purpose of the program to issue summonses or make collars. It's usually difficult to make an arrest on foot. Most arrests are made when you drive the complainant around and they point out the perp."

Perceptions of CPOP's Relationship With the Community

When the interviewees were asked whether CPOP's relationship with the community was different from RMP, the overwhelming majority (83%) stated that CPOs had a better relationship, while 12% said it was the same, and 5% could not answer the question. The thread that runs through these comments is that, because RMP officers are tied to the 911 system and busy responding to calls-for-service, it is difficult for these officers to establish rapport with the community. Further, when they are not responding to calls, they are expected to perform random preventive patrol in their sectors. Thus the officers believe that they do not have the opportunity to become acquainted with the public. In addition, a few noted that in RMP the officers generally encounter a narrow segment of the population—criminals and their victims, and people who are angry, emotionally disturbed, or injured.

In contrast, the respondents believed that CPOs have the leisure, obligation, and opportunity to work with the stable elements in the community, the "good" people, and people who are not in trouble:

Sure. They're closer to the community because it's their job to talk to people on their beats. They're always meeting people on a positive note, when everything is fine. We respond to problems and a lot of negative situations.

CPOs have a closer relationship with the community because they get to talk to people at meetings and speak with members of block associations. On patrol you go to a job and see people at their worst.

Others mentioned the visibility and accessibility of the CPOs, which brings them into daily contact with merchants and residents:

> The relationship is different. The community sees them all of the time. The relationship is less superficial. There is more familiarity and a one-to-one relationship between the CPOs and the community. The CPOs are not so far removed from people like RMP officers are.

> It is much better. RMPs don't have time to deal with the community. People feel better when they know an officer personally. Sometimes when we go to a job, people specifically ask for a CPO that they know.

Nevertheless two officers commented that an officer should handle her- or himself in a professional manner regardless of assignment:

> No, the relationship with the community is not different, because it is not based on the detail you are in, but the attitude of the individual officer.

> Any good officer gets to know people in his area. The exception in CPOP is that the commanding officer wants you to get to know the people, while on regular patrol you are required to constantly be moving; otherwise, it looks like you are not doing your job.

Perceptions Regarding CPOs' Treatment of People

Because CPOs work in the same area every day, the designers of the program believed that the CPOs would be more aware of and sensitive to the conditions in an area than RMP officers and, therefore, respond more sympathetically to the problems and complaints of the community. Curiously, although most of our respondents believed that CPOs have a better relationship with the community than do the RMP officers, their opinions were divided when they were asked: "Do you think that being a CPO would make any difference in the way you deal with people in the street?" Specifically, 47% of them said Yes; 50% said No; and 3% could not answer this question:

> Yes. It would force me to be a little more attentive to them. You can't just dismiss them if they're in your beat.

> Yes. In CPOP you're more interested in the individual. You care more about the person because that's your job. Your focus isn't just to get the job done. In CPOP you're looking for a preventive approach.

Perhaps, because the question pertained to "you," as opposed to a more impersonal term such as "an officer," several respondents seemed to take umbrage and interpreted the question as, at least implicitly, challenging their personal fairness, sensitivity, or competence in handling situations. As one officer stated succinctly: "No. It should be about the same. We are all supposed to be courteous to the public."

Perceived Capacity of CPOs to Obtain Information About Criminal Behavior

Some 72% of our respondents stated that CPOs were more able than RMP officers to obtain information on the street about criminal behavior; 22% did not agree with that opinion; and 6% could not answer this question.

Officers who answered in the affirmative attributed the CPOs' ability to gather information to walking a foot post, daily contact with people, and a positive relationship with the community:

> Yes. Because they get to know people in the community better than other officers. CPOs see certain people every day. Some of these people will not talk to RMPs.

> Easier for the CPOs because they have more contacts and are on foot. But really anyone can have a good rapport with the community.

> Yes, because they have responsibility for a specific beat, meet with the people on a regular basis, and have the confidence of the public.

Again, some officers seemed to be offended by this type of question: "No, this is not true. Most information is generated by regular patrol officers who are out in the street." Overall the theme in these and other responses is that CPOS are "regular cops"; however, the circumstances of their assignment provide them with opportunities to develop positive relationships with the community, sources of information, and time to make inquiries and work on specific problems.

Perceptions Regarding CPOs' Ability to Distinguish Between "Perpetrators" and "Ordinary" Citizens

Some 60% of the non-CPOs stated that CPOs were no better than an RMP officer at distinguishing between "perpetrators"and "ordinary" citizens. However, 30% said Yes and 10% could not answer the question.

The respondents who answered in the negative emphasized the importance of "street smarts"—a skill that they believe can only be acquired through police experience in dealing with a wide variety of people. As some of our respondents indicated, an officer either has the requisite experience or he does not: "CPOs are no better than any cop who knows what he's doing. Experience is the only thing that can teach a police officer the difference."

Other officers indicated that because CPOs are confined to a foot post and tend to encounter primarily law-abiding people, their experience tends to be narrow: "No, because CPOs are limited in their experience. They deal with the same people all the time. Patrol deals with the criminal element more."

Curiously, although some RMP officers believed the view from a foot post is narrow, others thought it was broad. Some saw the glass as half-empty, while others saw it as half-full. Consider the following pair of comments:

No, probably less because they're on a foot post. They don't see as much as when you're in a car racing around from job to job.

Yes, because they walk the same post all the time and know who lives there and who does not.

Perceived Autonomy/Freedom of the CPO Role

The overwhelming majority (88%) of the respondents believed that CPOs have more freedom than RMP officers, while 8% thought they had the same, and 4% thought they had less. Many of the respondents saw the greater freedom as a product of the CPOs' not being tied to the 911 system, and therefore able to determine for themselves how they patrolled their beats:

They have more freedom because they aren't monitored by the radio and have only one sergeant who spends most of his time doing administrative work. Also CPOs can roam around their beats. They have more freedom to decide what they will do from day to day.

More freedom because they don't always have the sergeant looking for them and the shoofly [a field inspector] doesn't bother them as much. Being on foot helps them to become less visible for supervision.

They have a little more freedom. We have to respond to assignments. They just have to respond to their beat. They don't have to be as accountable at any time of the day like we do.

A lot more freedom. The supervision isn't so intense. CPOP is an elite group, so they're trusted more.

Perceptions Regarding the Integration of CPOP Into the Patrol Force

It appears from these interviews that the regular patrol force was not informed in any systematic fashion about the purposes and activities of CPOP. Rather, the RMP officers learned about the program through informal discussions with the CPOs and their sergeants and by interacting with them in the station house and on patrol. In considering the following comments, it must be remembered that RMP officers work rotating tours, and as a result, they encounter CPOs at irregular intervals. Although the working hours of the CPOs are flexible to some extent, they tend to work the day or early evening hours, when the stores are open and people are on the street. As a result, CPOs are most frequently in contact with officers who worked fixed day-posts (e.g., schools), are assigned to summons details (traffic enforcement), or other precinct-based details (e.g., Anti-Crime).

The research staff were primarily concerned with determining whether CPOs are viewed as part of the patrol force, or as a unit that one officer described as "off in their own little world." Although 47% of the non-CPOs said that CPOP was well integrated into the patrol force, 43% indicated that it was not. Ten percent could not answer this question.

Whether an interviewee believed that CPOP was well-integrated in the patrol force seemed to depend on several of factors including: whether CPOs stood roll call with other officers in the precinct; whether CPOs were perceived as spending inordinate amounts of time in their office (doing nothing); whether the CPOP office was perceived as being an exclusive club; whether the CPOs interacted in a friendly manner with non-CPOs; whether the CPOs were perceived as contributing toward the "productivity goals" of the precinct by issuing summonses or making arrests; and whether they shared information about precinct conditions or suspected criminals:

> Yes. They are expected to generate a certain amount of activity too.

> Yes. Everyone gets along well. Other officers understand their problems and vice-versa. CPOP is not seen as exclusive.

> No, because they are really considered a separate unit and take a lot of flak. There is some resentment and jealousy directed toward them.

> No. I see them more as a separate unit in the precinct like Anti-Crime. CPOP's daily activities don't really involve us unless they pick up a radio job.

> I don't think they're well integrated. I think if it was done properly, they would be a tremendous source of information. Other units aren't really aware of what information they have about the community.

> Yes, because they provide good information and sometimes work with patrol.

> No, because there is a lack of communication between CPOP and RMP.

> We really don't come into contact with the CPOP guys that much. They're a special unit and so you never know what they're doing.

The Perceived
Usefulness of
CPOP

Some 90% of the non-CPOs stated that CPOP provides useful services to the police department and the community; only 10% believed it does not. The following comments express these assessments, as well as some of the reservations held by RMP officers:

> It's public relations—people like to see police on the street and to talk to them. In reality it doesn't really probably do that much to help the community. We don't get much feedback about the program. All their activities and intelligence reports go right to the borough, so we don't benefit from it.

> They help solve the community's problems and are a good resource for patrol. They pass on helpful information.

> CPOP takes some of the stress off the RMPs by cutting down the number of jobs that have to be answered. The program also helps to improve police/community relations.

> It is beneficial to have a unit that deals with the community. It makes my job easier and reduces my work load. CPOs can address certain problems which patrol can't.

> Yes. It helps the community by making people feel that the police care. The positive feelings that people have toward CPOs is extended to other cops.

> It's good for the community, but it's a waste of manpower for the police department as far as regular patrol. CPOP can't be touched when RMP is short and a car has to be taken out of service.

> I don't really believe in it. I think Community Affairs and foot posts could do their job. The CPOs could probably do more if they were in a squad car.

Perceived
Advantages and
Disadvantages
of Assignment
to CPOP

By far, the most commonly perceived advantage of the CPOP assignment pertained to the hours that CPOs worked—77% of the non-CPOs mentioned matters related to hours worked—flexible hours, weekends off, not having to work midnight tours, or not having to go around the chart. Fifteen percent of the respondents mentioned not having to respond to 911 calls-for-service, and 8% said that CPOP provided an opportunity to help people. Other factors that were mentioned by only one or two officers included the ability to follow up on problems, feel a sense of pride and accomplishment, experience freedom and flexibility on patrol, and to advance one's career.

Some 42% of the interviewees could not think of any disadvantages to the CPOP assignment. Twenty percent said that they dislike foot patrol, while 13% specified that they would not want to walk a foot post in inclement weather. Ten percent stated that they thought

CPOP would be boring, and 15% indicated that they did not want to deal with the public on a close, personal basis. Some 47% indicated that they had considered joining CPOP, and 53% said that they had not. Finally, 65% of the RMP officers believed that service in CPOP would be advantageous to a career in the department, while 18% believed it would not be, and 17% did not have an opinion.

In sum, the RMP officers in the research precincts, interviewed at the end of the data collection periods, seemed reasonably accepting of CPOP. They saw the principal difference between the CPO and the RMP roles as the CPO's lack of responsibility for call-for-service and his or her greater freedom in determining how to patrol the beat. For that reason, a majority of the RMP officers thought of CPOP as an easier assignment, although a notable portion of the respondents thought it was harder than RMP duties because of CPOP's demands for working with the public.

The majority of the RMP officers thought of CPOs as generally like themselves, but perhaps a bit more outgoing or community-oriented. The overwhelming majority (83%) thought that CPOs had a better relationship with the community because it was their job to develop such a relationship, because they had more time to meet and cultivate the people in the community, and because they had less contact with the criminal element in the neighborhoods. And 72% of the respondents believed that CPOs were better able to obtain information about criminal behavior in the community because they had more contact and better relationships with the people.

The respondents were evenly split on the question of whether CPOP was effectively integrated into the rest of the patrol force. Nonetheless, 90% saw CPOP as providing a useful service to both the department and the community.

It is noteworthy that very few of the regular patrol officers identified the problem-solving mission of the CPO as a distinctive element of the role or identified particular problem-solving tasks when considering the relative ease or difficulty involved in implementing the role. This suggests that the general understanding of the role among non-CPOs was somewhat imprecise and inadequate. This imprecision may be expected, because the regular patrol officers had never been given any formal orientation to the CPO role. Under these circumstances, knowledge of what the role entails is transmitted informally and grows as more officers perform it and return to regular patrol duties. At the time the research data were being collected, that was still a rather rare phenomenon.

The Pivotal Importance of the Precinct Commander

The role of the sergeant in the CPO program is described and analyzed in Chapter 5 of this book. That material indicates that one of the sergeant's responsibilities as leader and guide is to represent the unit within the department, especially in relation to other supervisors in the precinct and to the precinct commanding officer (CO).

Several ways in which the ability of the sergeant and the CPOs to carry out their roles depends on the understanding and support of the CO are discussed in that chapter. Those points are obviously of relevance to the concerns of this chapter—the CPO program in the context of the patrol structure—but they need not be repeated. It is useful here to focus some attention on the ways in which the precinct commander can foster or block the integration of CPOP into the rest of the patrol operation.

First, a CO who sees CPOP as yet another special exercise mandated by headquarters and depriving him or her of 10 cops and a sergeant who could have been used productively in other ways is likely to convey that attitude to others, with disastrous consequences to the CPOP unit. On the other hand, a CO who believes in the potential utility of CPOP is likely to act more positively toward the program from the beginning. The CO is likely to select the unit sergeant with care and insist that the supervisor recruit the members in similar fashion. Obviously the trustworthiness of the officer is important, but so is the suitability of the officer for intensive work with the community, and for learning and mastering the elements of the problem-solving process. The officer's record and reputation as an energetic worker are also important. If the officers chosen are identified by others in the precinct as "coasters," the unit's need to be accepted will be that much harder to satisfy. Alternatively, the recruitment of active, energetic officers suggests the seriousness of the CO's intentions and triggers the interest of other officers if for no other reason than to discover what it is about CPOP that attracts the real workers.

Second, the CO must recognize that the non-CPOP officers and supervisors in the precinct are likely to need some orientation to the purposes and procedures of the program, especially its problem-solving dimension. Many COs have left this to be handled informally, and many CPOP sergeants have done a good job in this regard. It seems wise, however, for the CO to make some structured arrangements for orienting the rest of the command. At the very least, these arrangements would help the sergeant and the CPOs to explain themselves. More important, this kind of involvement by the CO signals the importance he or she gives to the program and provides the CO with an opportunity to define for all members of the command what he or she expects from them in relation to CPOP's efforts. Finally, to the extent that the CO participates in the orientation, he or she has an opportunity to identify the misconceptions that might exist among members of the command and to provide official clarifications.

Third, some COs accord the CPOP unit a great deal of autonomy and, in the proper amount, this autonomy is consistent with both the principles of the program and modern principles of effective management. There is a danger, however, that the CO will step back too far; that he or she will simply turn the program over to a sergeant and insert himself or herself only at the signs of trouble. This relative noninvolvement of the CO can have a variety of undesirable consequences. It may be interpreted as a sign of low interest, thereby reinforcing the initial negativism common among the non-CPOP supervisors and patrol officers. It may adversely affect the morale of the CPOs by suggesting that they have embarked upon an unimportant enterprise that is not likely to help their careers. And it may suggest to the officers and the CPOP sergeant that slackening off will not be a problem as long as they avoid any serious trouble, submit the right reports, and maintain some level of positive contact with the community. All of these consequences are likely to produce an unproductive unit, scorned by peers in the precinct and staffed by an increasingly cynical group of officers in the process of becoming completely disaffected from the CPO role. In this set of circumstances, the better officers will abandon the CPOP ship as soon as possible.

Fourth, the CO can assume a very different stance if, after becoming familiar with the objectives, assumptions, and procedures of the program, the CO envisions it as his or her resource to respond to the needs of the precinct more effectively. In this scenario, the CO would think first about the precinct's priority concerns and how CPOP can help to address them. The CPOs can be seen first as an intelligence source capable of providing the CO with information about priorities that the CO is not likely to get from any other source. Second, the CPOs can be the precinct's ambassadors to the community, helping to maintain good relations and a flow of information helpful to both parties. Third, the CPOs can become the CO's planners by taking the time, which he or she cannot commit personally, to develop sensible strategies through which the range of the CO's resources might be deployed to attack the problems that the CO defines as priorities. And finally, the CPOs can become the CO's resource managers, keeping him or her informed about how the plans are being carried out and providing suggestions as to how they might be implemented more fully and effectively.

In this posture, the CO would meet regularly with the CPOP sergeant and periodically with each member of the unit to discuss the problems in the beat and the levels of community concern regarding them. The CO would convey a personal sense of the relative priority that should be accorded to these problems and, in that way, make the CPO aware of the specific conditions in the beat about which the CO is most concerned. These sessions would enable the CO to review and discuss the problem-solving strategies, indeed, to infuse them with his or her own vision, experience, and wisdom. Such a review from the CO would encourage the beat officer to take the problem-solving demands of the CPO role seriously and to prepare reports carefully, and would also serve as a check on the CPO's judgments about the relative importance of the problems he or she has identified. The review would also provide a regular opportunity to discuss whether, how, and when non-CPOP resources could be committed to address the problems in the beat. As a result, the officer would derive a sense of the importance of CPOP work he or she is undertaking and have a reasonable estimate of the assistance that could be expected from other police resources. The CO would get a better sense of the officer's performance and potential, an increased awareness of conditions and community sentiment in the beat, and some specific ideas about the ways in which other resources in the command might be deployed, and advocate for the commitment of borough resources to achieve the objectives. Also, this awareness would enable the CO to focus the contributions that RMP officers and special units in the command could make toward addressing the precinct's priority problems.

A CO who understands and uses CPOP in this manner is likely to integrate the CPO unit into the rest of the command effectively. All precinct personnel would be required to recognize and address, in some way, the precinct's priority problems. The CPOs would provide the commander with the target conditions on the neighborhood level and suggestions about how the various precinct units might contribute to correcting them. They would also enlist the nonpolice resources in the effort. The commander would use this information in setting priorities for the various units and would arrange their work loads to make it possible for them to make problem-solving contributions. The commander would keep all units informed about the progress being made with respect to the priority problems so that everyone in the precinct, whatever their principal responsibilities, could derive some satisfaction from participating in the problem-solving process. Finally, an integrated effort of this sort, led by the precinct's commanding officer, would provide a very substantial incentive for the CPOs to master the problem-solving process and sustain the involvement of local residents, merchants, and organizations in that process.

The Police Commissioner's Support of CPOP

The proposal for a CPOP demonstration project was developed by Vera staff and submitted to senior officials in the department in the fall of 1983. Their reactions were generally positive; however, movement on all new proposals was slowed by a change in the administration of the department. Commissioner Benjamin Ward assumed office in January 1984 and, within a few months, approved the proposal. The demonstration project began in July 1984 and enjoyed the attention of the commissioner from the start. By the early fall, the commissioner had decided to move to expand CPOP beyond the pilot project and called for the preparation of a plan to do so. The plan called for expansion to groups of five or six precincts every 3 or 4 months beginning in January 1985. By the end of September 1988, CPOP became operational in the last group of the city's 75 precincts. Why and how was a program, begun as a single precinct demonstration, expanded so rapidly?

The simple answer to this question is that the commissioner liked the program, ordered its expansion, and controlled the pace at which the expansion was carried out. This answer raises the further questions of why he supported CPOP as he did and what steps he took to assure the acceptance of the program within the department.

Commissioner Ward's written and oral comments over the years clearly indicate that he is an ardent advocate of the principles of community-oriented and problem-solving policing. He believes firmly that police agencies must be aware of and responsive to the needs and desires of the people, including their desires to improve the quality of life they experience in the community, and that those needs can differ substantially from one neighborhood to another in a city as diverse as New York. He believes that the police must receive and respond to calls-for-service, but that this function is capable of absorbing virtually all of the patrol resources, leaving none to address neighborhood problems in a systematic fashion. He believes that police officers, if given the time and incentive to do so, will identify with the neighborhoods in which they work, make the concerns of the people their own concerns, and use their considerable ingenuity and energy to help the people deal with their problems. He believes, as well, that most of the problems on the neighborhood level can only be alleviated by an energized public assisted by the police in a variety of ways.

Commissioner Ward saw CPOP as reflecting all of those beliefs and as a means for making them operational on the precinct level. For the commissioner, CPOP was never merely another special program, but a means for advocating his principles of policing throughout the department and the city. The early experiences of the pilot project suggested that police officers were capable of implementing and growing in the CPO role. They also indicated that the reactions of community leaders on the neighborhood and precinct levels were overwhelmingly positive. Indeed, by the fall of 1984, local political leaders were beginning to take notice of the program and to call for its replication in their districts. It was in this context that the commissioner decided to expand the program and to do so at a relatively rapid pace.

In an organization as large and complex as the New York City Police Department, introducing procedures that differ in dramatic ways from the traditional requires more than a single decision by the commissioner. As the following explains, Commissioner Ward continually expressed his interest in and support for CPOP.

The CPOs and sergeants in each group of expansion precincts were introduced to CPOP through an orientation and training program of several days' duration. The commissioner would appear personally before each group of new units, usually on the first day of the training program, and would speak to the officers enthusiastically about the benefits that CPOP could produce for the department and the city, and about the kinds of satisfactions the officers could derive from this type of policing. Earlier in his career, the commissioner had been a member of the force for over 20 years, and his ability to speak from that experience gave his words an added measure of credibility.

It was noted also that the CPOP training was the only training program in the department at which the commissioner regularly made a personal appearance.

After the first year of CPOP expansion, the commissioner created a unit within the Patrol Bureau called the Citywide CPOP Coordinator's Office and staffed it with a full inspector, a captain, and six sergeants. The purpose of the office was to coordinate the further expansion of the program, monitor its operations in precincts throughout the city, and provide technical assistance to operating units. The fact that the commissioner gave the responsibility to a full inspector signaled to the department's command staff the importance of the program to the commissioner. Consistent with this view, the first person to assume these responsibilities was an officer with over 30 years in the Patrol Services Bureau, who had commanded several high-activity precincts, including two in which he had a CPOP unit, and who appeared to be well respected by his peers.

In various ways, the commissioner made it clear within the department that the CPO program was instrumental in securing political support and favorable budgetary decisions for the department. Thus personnel at all levels could see that, after the hard years of contraction during the late 1970s and early 1980s, CPOP was contributing to the growth of the department.

After the expansion had been under way for about two and a half years, the commissioner became concerned that its effectiveness could be blunted by a lack of adequate understanding and support at the command level of the Patrol Services Bureau. He pointed out that no special efforts had been made to orient this level of the department to the program, and he directed that an executive development training program be created for that purpose and that all personnel in the bureau at the captain level and above be required to participate in that training. As a result of that directive, almost 200 commanders were trained in approximately 6 months; an orientation guide for command personnel was produced and disseminated throughout the department; and the training program became a permanent feature in the department's Executive Development curriculum.

The commissioner recognized the need to provide CPOP sergeants and CPOs with improved and expanded training and assistance in mastering the problem-solving process. He encouraged Vera staff to develop such a program, supported their efforts to secure outside funding for that purpose, and committed the resources of the Police Academy to assist in the delivery of the training at a point when such involvement was appropriate and feasible.

Finally, over the course of the 4 years, the commissioner maintained the pressure for the continued expansion of the program and insisted that the integrity of the individual units be maintained at all costs. It was the commissioner who insisted that CPOP not be made part of any arrest-and-summons numbers "games" within the department, and that precinct desk officers be strongly discouraged from reassigning CPOs to RMPs or other regular patrol duties except in dire emergencies. While the Coordinator's Office was responsible for monitoring compliance with these directives, their task was made easier by the fact that commanders in the precincts and the borough offices knew that the commissioner had issued the directives personally.

CPOP's Future as Seen at the End of the Research

The report of our research was completed and disseminated very soon after Commissioner Ward left and before Commissioner Brown assumed office. As we indicated in Chapter 1, Commissioner Brown launched an ambitious plan to build on CPOP and restructure the whole department around the principles of community policing. It is worth noting that much of that plan's trajectory, and even some of its specific implementation objectives, are quite consistent with the future course for CPOP and community policing in the NYPD as it was described, in 1990, in the text below.

CPOP now seems well rooted as a special part of the patrol operation within the NYPD. Many precinct commanders seem to consider it a useful addition to their range of resources, although there may not be any who use it, and integrate it, quite as fully as suggested in the section on The Pivotal Importance of the Precinct Commander in this chapter. Some COs feel that the constraints on their power to reduce the size of the unit, or to reassign CPOs temporarily to other duties, are unnecessarily burdensome, especially in commands with complements of only about 100 police officers. These commanders suggest that their resources are so limited that they are regularly tottering on the brink of a calls-for-service backlog, and a unit of 10 officers not available to help avert such a backlog is a luxury they cannot afford. With this caveat, however, there seems to be considerable support for CPOP among the precinct commanders.

Support for the continuation of the program seems widespread among community and political leaders as well. Indeed, during the 1989 mayoral campaign, the successful candidate indicated he would seek to double the number of community patrol officers if elected. It seems reasonable to expect, therefore, that CPOP will continue for the foreseeable future. Thus the principles of community-oriented, problem-solving policing will continue to be given expression in the New York City Police Department, and it is possible that CPOP will not be the only medium for that expression.

As indicated earlier in this chapter, the designers of the program at Vera and in the department believed that these principles could best be given their initial implementation in the NYPD through a special program. The department receives approximately eight million calls-for-service annually and dispatches responding units on approximately half of them. It is unlikely that this volume will decrease appreciably in the future, so it is reasonable to expect that the vast majority of patrol officers in the department will continue to have radio response as their principal duty. Moreover, at the time

that CPOP was designed, the majority of patrol officers in all precincts rotated tours every week, worked with different groups of
officers and supervisors on different days, and experienced little
continuity of assignment to the same section of the precinct. Under
these circumstances, in 1984, it seemed impossible for regular patrol
officers to develop the familiarity with people, problems, and terrain,
and have the time necessary to perform problem-solving roles. It was
hoped, therefore, that by creating the necessary working conditions
for a small group of officers and training them as community patrol
officers, community-oriented, problem-solving policing could be introduced into the precinct.

But over the last few years, some of the obstacles to a broader
adoption of problem-solving policing efforts in the NYPD have begun
to change. In the early 1980s, Vera helped the department experiment
with a "fixed tour" system in which the patrol personnel in a precinct
volunteered to continue working the same tour for at least a year.
This made it possible for the same squads and supervisors to work
together on a continuous basis. In the same precinct, the department
introduced a different management system, using lieutenants to
serve as platoon commanders on each tour, with the authority to set
priorities, allocate resources, and hold the personnel working on that
tour accountable for various performance goals. The new system
proved to be very popular with the patrol officers, produced some
reduction in measured stress levels among them, and was deemed to
offer a number of management advantages over the conventional
system of precinct management (Cosgrove & McElroy, 1986).

In 1988, the department began to expand this system to other
precincts so that the combination of fixed tours and platoon commanders would soon be operating citywide. The continuity of command, of
supervision, of coworkers, and of tour that this system provides
appears to offer a more hospitable structure for involving the entire
patrol force in some form of community-oriented, problem-solving
policing. Within this structure, it should be possible to assign RMP
officers to the same patrol sectors from one day to the next and to
arrange for them to spend more time within the boundaries of those
sectors. This should make it possible for them to develop more knowledge about and spend more time working on the problematic conditions in those sectors during their tour. The CPOs should be able to
continue coordinating information regarding the problems and developing strategies for addressing them on each of the tours. Under the
new system, however, assigning tasks within a problem-solving strategy to RMP officers and using the platoon command structure to hold
them accountable for performing those tasks should be feasible. Thus
the challenge of relating in a meaningful fashion to the residents,
merchants, and organizations in a neighborhood, and of working with
them to alleviate their more pressing problems, could become a
responsibility of the entire precinct patrol force.

Precisely how the roles of the RMP officers and their supervisors, as well as those of officers in other special units, such as Anti-Crime and SNEU, should be changed to reflect the more community-oriented and problem-solving mission was not clear at the time of this writing. Nor were the support services that might be needed by the officers, or the structural arrangements that would be required to ensure precinctwide coordination of the problem-solving effort. However, the department, assisted by Vera Institute staff, had begun a pilot project in a single precinct designed to explore these issues more carefully and to test new procedures, roles, and relationships for diffusing the practice of problem-solving policing in New York City throughout the entire patrol force. The products of that pilot project should become available during the next couple of years. (That project is under way in the 72 Precinct, in Brooklyn, and is known in the department as the "Model Precinct Project.")

The Perceptions of Community Leaders

- Introduction
- Methods
- Levels of Community Awareness
- Perceptions of CPOP's Purpose
- CPOP Response to Crime and Drug Problems
- Summary

Introduction

The essence of CPOP is not only problem-solving policing, but also community involvement in the problem-solving process. Although some elements of CPOP as it evolved in New York City are unique to this city, CPOP incorporates several features that the designers believe are common to all community policing programs. These include:

- Insistence that the unit develop and maintain a knowledge base regarding the problems, cultural characteristics, and resources of the neighborhood
- Emphasis on the importance of the unit's reaching out to the neighborhood residents and business people to assure them of the presence and concern of the police
- Use of formal and informal mechanisms to involve community people in identifying, analyzing, and establishing priorities among local problems and in developing and implementing action plans for ameliorating them
- Emphasis on increased information flow from the community to the police and on the use of that information by various

elements of the police agency to make important arrests and to develop intelligence on illegal enterprises in the community

- Sharing with representatives of the community accurate information on local crime problems and the results of ongoing efforts to address them (*NYPD Orientation Guide*, 1987, p. 2)

The manner in which the CPOP units in the research precincts attempted to implement these features and the extent to which they succeeded was described in earlier chapters of this book. Those descriptions were based on the observations of the research staff and police officers and supervisors directly involved in program operations. In contrast, the perspective in this chapter is that of the community in the six research precincts.

By interviewing community leaders in each of the research precincts, Vera sought to answer a number of questions, including the following:

- What did representatives of the community perceive to be the purposes and methods of CPOP?
- What was the level of these representatives' awareness of the CPO program?
- What was the nature of conventional street crime and quality-of-life problems with which the community representatives were concerned?
- What did the community leaders perceive to be the police response to these crime and quality-of-life problems both before and after the advent of CPOP?
- To what extent was the community's perception of problems characterized by ambiguity and ambivalence, and how did the community leaders see CPOP dealing with these features of the community?
- How did the community leaders describe the effects of CPOP on police/community relations in the research precincts?

Methods   Early in the planning phase of this research project, a decision was made to address these questions by conducting intensive interviews with individual community leaders in each of the research precincts. This strategy had been used very successfully in a separate research project that Vera had conducted for the NYPD (Cosgrove & McElroy, 1986). In that project, the community leaders were found to be both knowledgeable and articulate regarding community problems and the police response to these conditions. In fact, the community leader interviews were far more illuminating than the large-scale telephone surveys of citizens that were conducted in the same project. Based on that experience, it was believed that the leaders would be more likely than randomly selected residents to provide useful insights into the strengths and weaknesses of the CPO program. Moreover, this strategy could be carried out with the resources available to the project.[1]

The plan called for extensive interviews with 10 community leaders in each of the six research precincts, yielding a total of 60 interviews. The respondents were identified by the CPOs, the CPOP sergeant, or from lists provided by the Precinct Community Affairs Officer. Each potential respondent was contacted by a research assistant, who explained the purposes of the research and assured the potential respondent that his or her responses would be kept confidential. The respondent was also offered the option of conducting the interview in person or over the phone.

Although Vera had planned to conduct 60 interviews, it was possible to complete only 48. In a several instances, the potential respondents indicated that they were too busy for an interview or that they were not adequately familiar with the program. Others, particularly in minority neighborhoods with severe drug problems, did not want to discuss matters with an interviewer associated with the police department. In many of these instances, the potential respondent feared that the fact of his or her cooperation in the interview would become known to drug dealers in the neighborhood and would provoke retaliation. Moreover, in these neighborhoods there were often language barriers and/or an absence of even block-level or tenant-level associations.

Some 45 of the 48 interviews were conducted in person, and 11 interviewees allowed the discussion to be tape-recorded. The respondents included merchants and business people, members of the Community Planning Boards, members of the Precinct Community Councils, officials in local tenant or block associations, civilian patrol organizations, and local clergy. Some 80% of the respondents were white, and two out of three were men. They ranged in age from 40 to 70, and the vast majority were homeowners; most had lived in their community for 20 or more years. Many belonged to two or more community organizations, and almost all were heavily involved in local civic affairs. Poor people, members of racial and ethnic minorities, young people with families, and people who had recently moved into their neighborhoods were clearly underrepresented in this sample of respondents, as they are among community leaders at the precinct level.

Although the sample of respondents seems to be reasonably representative of those people who were identified as community leaders in the six research precincts, they are clearly not representative, in demographic terms, of the populations served by the various precincts. Moreover, it is not possible to determine whether their perceptions and assessments of local problems, and of the activities of the police in general and the CPO program in particular, reflect a consensus among the residents of the community. Nevertheless their perceptions and opinions are of some importance both because these individuals exert some degree of leadership in their neighborhoods and because they are people to whom the police in the local precinct were attentive. Thus the interviews provide some insight into the reactions of the local community to CPOP.

Levels of Community Awareness

An analysis of the comments made by the interviewees suggests that there are four levels of awareness in any given community. The first and highest level of awareness is among business people, merchants, civic activists who are interested in police matters, politicians, and office holders in block and tenants associations. These citizens frequently contact the CPOP office to seek assistance or advice, and some communicate with the officers on a routine basis. These people are very familiar with the program and know the name of the sergeant and one or more of the CPOs. Several of the respondents were officials in local merchant and business organizations, and they agreed unanimously that the members of the business community were well aware of CPOP, welcomed the institution of this form of policing, and felt that CPOP contributed to the economic vitality of the community:

> The merchants are aware of CPOP, and we put out a newspaper. I am sure that merchants are all aware of the program. There are people that don't know about CPOP. You always get that, but I think it's apathy on their part. They just don't care. It's not that the word isn't out there. They just don't pick up on it.

The second level of awareness is among people who may be termed the "informed" public; that is, citizens who read local newspapers and attend community meetings. These people may not remember the name of the program or specific details, but they know that the program exists and that the police are doing "something." As one businessman stated: "People who attend meetings and read newsletters are probably aware of it. Other people probably think CPOs are regular foot cops, but they are still aware of what they do and that's the important thing." Or, as another respondent indicated, "I heard about it at meetings. I'm very public. I also read about it in the local newspaper and was introduced to a CPO. No, the community is not really aware of it. Unless they have a problem, they just know there's a cop on the block."

The third level of awareness is among residents who see the CPO patrolling the neighborhood. They may not know that there is a program, but they are aware of an increased police presence:

> I have a feeling that a lot of people think CPOs are just foot patrol officers who are wandering around. That's fine. I think that the important thing is that the community sees a visible police

presence on the street watching. You don't get the same sense of the community being watched and cared for by two guys riding by in a patrol car. They are detached. They are sitting there in their own little air-conditioned comfort and they might as well be watching it on TV.

The fourth level is nonawareness. A few community leaders stated that CPOP should have done more to develop community awareness: "People know about CPOP if they go to the precinct community meetings. If they don't, then they think CPOs are just regular foot cops. I think the police department should have posted more fliers about CPOP and should have launched a better public relations campaign. "

Based on this survey, it is impossible to determine the extent to which awareness of CPOP has filtered down to the average precinct resident. Undoubtedly, a percentage of the population in each precinct have no idea that the program exists, and it is impossible to estimate the magnitude of this group. Nevertheless, the findings suggest that community leaders and informed citizens are well aware of the program and speak very highly of it.

Perceptions of CPOP's Purpose

The respondents were very familiar with the purposes of the CPOP program: They frequently mentioned that CPOP was designed to promote police/community relations, that it increases the information exchange between the police and the community, that the officers become acquainted on a more personal level with the residents and merchants, that it involves heightened police presence through foot patrol, and that the officers work with individual and neighborhood groups to solve problems. One of the most comprehensive descriptions of the multiple purposes of CPOP was provided by the district manager of a community planning board. This interviewee's response is particularly interesting because she highlighted the ways in which the activities of CPOs differ from those of RMP:

> I have no doubt that CPOP is a direct response to the community boards' demands for more visible police to address crime, because the CPOs on the street do things that other officers weren't allowed to do. The other officers, your job was to go out there and catch people and arrest them if they are doing this or that wrong. Your job was *not* to get to know the grocery stores, and who's in the grocery store, and the block associations. That wasn't the role of the police department. As far as I can see it, the role of the police department as I perceived it was numbers. Tickets. Crime. It was reaction. Not prevention.

She continued:

I think the community sees CPOP as a combination of that visibility, that link between the community and the police, someone they can call on for help, and someone that they have confidence to call on for help. They understand that CPOP works with regular officers, the community relations officers. Some may see it as a continuation of that. Visibility. Getting to know the areas where there are specific crimes that CPOP can address, which the regular police patrol cannot. Surveillance. They identify hot spots for the community board and the police. They are the eyes and ears of the police. They are an excellent public relations device for the police. They are crime preventers able to filter information back to the police and the Youth Officer and assist him or her.

Conventional Crime Problems and the Police Response

The respondents were asked to describe the major crime problems in their neighborhood 2 years prior to the interview, and to describe current problems. They were also asked to describe and assess the response of the police in general, and that of the CPOP unit in particular, to these problems. The researchers were attempting to determine whether the leaders perceived any positive changes in the problems, or in the police response, with the arrival of the CPOP unit.

The respondents' views on the crime and drug problems and the general response of the police to them are presented in this and the next section of this chapter. That material is followed by a presentation of the respondents' views concerning CPOP's response to these problems.

With few exceptions, the perceptions of past and current crime and drug problems remained largely unchanged. Moreover, the respondents' assessment of the general police response to these problems was largely negative, though often sympathetic. On the other hand, the community leaders' assessments of the CPOP responses to these problems was considerably more positive.

In this regard, it is important to remember that in the early part of this decade, the police department was just recovering from the city's budget crises and rebuilding its capacity to respond to local crime and quality-of-life problems. For several years prior to that time, the police struggled to control the problem of street robberies, to sustain a reasonable level of felony arrests, and to keep up with the ever-increasing volume of calls-for-service received over the 911 system. Indeed, the department's decision to create and expand the CPO program reflected its desire to use some portion of the new resources to become more deeply involved in addressing problems at the neighborhood level. Thus the very positive response of the community leaders to CPOP was seen as confirming the wisdom of the department's decision to take this initiative.

Very few respondents who lived in predominantly white, middle-class residential areas identified robbery or burglary as problems. Specifically, they believed that these events were isolated incidents that, while unfortunate for the victim, were not a major source of anxiety for the average resident. As one interviewee explained, "The community outcry isn't that great. These are crimes that affect you most when they happen to you." Similarly, a former community board district manager stated: "I am not concerned about crime problems. I don't have statistics at my fingertips, but I would say that, generally speaking, crime problems remain pretty constant as far as burglaries are concerned. I get more involved with quality-of-life issues." Several respondents believed that the police were *not* able to prevent certain types of property crime such as the theft of car radios or batteries, because these are crimes of stealth that happen very quickly: "The police try to keep track of the crime problems and assign their patrol efforts to the hottest vicinities. But things like battery and radio stealing is 'in and out' kind of stuff, so that before any kind of patrol car comes along the perpetrator is gone."

The loss of a car battery or radio has a high nuisance value in and of itself. It is, however, even more aggravating when the perpetrator smashes the windshield or otherwise vandalizes the car in a frustrated attempt to steal property. Although most of the car owners in these neighborhoods were insured against theft or vandalism, they were reluctant to report the crime to their insurance company because they believed that their rates would be increased.

Nevertheless another interviewee described a recent rash of burglaries and car break-ins in his affluent neighborhood and stated that he was very dissatisfied with the police response:

> I would say the police, in general, did very little to address these problems. In fact, most police officers will come right out and tell you there is nothing they can do. I can recall one time when we discussed the occurrence of burglaries at our block association meeting. Some residents voiced the opinion that we should ask for additional police presence for a while. The typical response from most people was cajoling, because when these people had called the police at the time they had been burglarized, some were told that the likelihood of their property being recovered or the thief being caught was slim; that it wasn't worth reporting. In addition, police told people that they could always report this in person, at the station house. It is very disturbing to be told this and tends to create a negative attitude toward the police.

Moreover, burglaries and larcenies in middle-class residential areas may in fact be isolated events that are crimes of opportunity—a bicycle is stolen from a porch, a lawn mower and power tools disappear from an unlocked garage, clothes and suitcases are taken from a car left on the street at night. The president of a merchants' association in a predominantly white, middle-class area summed up the situation as follows:

"Is there a crime problem now?" Yes. We have eggs splattered on our store windows, but we don't have stick-ups. Commercial crime involves shoplifting and pickpocketing in the larger stores. There is also residential crime, which involves burglaries. But no, we don't have a crime problem of any grave consequence. And, people here don't like to prosecute, which doesn't help the police.

Drug Problems and the Police Response

While many respondents seemed to accept some theft and vandalism as the price of living in New York City, they were less tolerant when they believed that the cause of theft and violence was drug-related. It must be noted that in New York City, drugs are the quintessential bridge between crime and quality-of-life problems. Unlawful possession and sale of drugs, "controlled substances," is a crime problem per se; however, it is also associated with relatively high rates of conventional street crime, including robberies, assaults, and thefts. At the same time, it is a quality-of-life problem, because open drug trafficking on the street mocks conventional norms and is believed to contribute significantly to the general deterioration and lawlessness of the neighborhood. As one respondent from an affluent neighborhood stated:

Street conditions have gotten worse, especially with the increase in the crack traffic in the past 4 years. We've had some relief in the crack situation in the last year. A lot more attention has been focused on low-level drug dealing and enforcement. The community has put a lot of pressure on the NYPD to deal with the situation.

Similarly, others, primarily homeowners in transitional neighborhoods, asserted that conditions in their neighborhood had deteriorated as a result of "spillover" from nearby crack-plagued areas. They believed that the burglary and larceny rates were rising, and as a result, their property values were declining. The president of a homeowners association in Brooklyn stated: "While certain areas of this borough are being revitalized, I think that this community is on the decline. The main problem is crime. People are investing more and more in security devices. People are more afraid, and there is a general mistrust of the minority population." He continued, "The police are making arrests and trying hard, but it's a losing battle, and we have to come to the conclusion that certain parts of this community are beyond salvation."

Some of the respondents represented minority neighborhoods where street-level drug trafficking, primarily in crack, had become blatant and pervasive. The following pair of comments were made by interviewees who lived in what were once viable, working-class neighborhoods that have been destabilized by the crack trade:

Conditions have gotten much worse in the last couple of years. Crack has been the main contributor to increasing the amount of crime and delinquency in our area. We have more people roaming around like zombies now and many more homeless. We have lots of unsavory characters hanging out because of drugs.

Another interviewee stated: "Drugs are the root of all the problems. Burglaries are a serious problem for people because they feel as though their privacy is being infringed upon."

According to our respondents, one of the ancillary effects of the drug industry has been an increase in the level of fear, particularly in minority communities. One leader who represented an area with severe drug problems stated:

We've had quite a few homicides as a result of the drug problem. People are afraid of being shot while just being innocent bystanders. There is general fear. People don't want to have to sit in their house and close their doors. They want to be able to live and enjoy their lives. They want their children to be able to play outside. They want to come home at night and not be fearful.

Several of our interviewees commended the police for trying seriously to combat drug trafficking; nevertheless, they were dissatisfied with the results. As one respondent stated:

The police are trying to do something about the drug problem. It may take a long time, but they are addressing it. People get impatient, because they want an immediate response to their problem. They know that the police are trying and that makes them happy, but they want more and they want it now.

Although our respondents acknowledged the complexity of the drug problem, some believed that the police tactic of concentrating on a particular building or block simply displaced the problem—shifted it to another building or block. Thus the basic problem remained:

We do have problems with drugs, as probably every community in the city has. While the police do a good job in trying to deal with the situation, it is something that is far gone. I mean they will take care of a block and clean it up, but these people go to the next block. The police just move it to a new location and that has been ongoing. There are times when it is worse than others. And there have been times when things get very quiet. I guess you can attribute it to arrests being made of specific people who are involved, but someone else just takes their place.

Similarly, another respondent focused specifically on what he perceived as the futility of the police effort in trying to curtail the drug trade by relying on "sweeps"—a form of law enforcement in which uniformed and plainclothes officers descend on a building, make arrests, and confiscate weapons, drugs, and drug paraphernalia:

> I think there's even a deeper cynical attitude toward it, that sweeps don't do any good, because if they get swept up, two hours later they are back in business, because either they manage to get through the court system and get released on bail, or there's a backup crew that moves into the same site, and just resumes operating as usual. The problem is more intractable than can be handled by just a simple sweep up and down the street and I think most people in the community recognize that.

As described above, in discussing the drug situation, the respondents often commended the police for making arrests and conducting sweeps, even though they realized that these enforcement tactics provide only temporary relief from the problem. The overwhelming majority of the respondents were sympathetic toward the police and believed that their failure to make serious inroads into the drug problem was in part attributable to a lack of resources. Several respondents placed the blame for the drug condition on the "turnstile justice" of the criminal court system. This sentiment was not limited to one precinct or borough. The following comments are illustrative:

Manhattan

> They've done sweeps and cleaned up our street, but the crackheads leave and come back. The justice system isn't conducive to the police doing anything. The dealers are out in a few days. The police aren't miracle workers.

Brooklyn

> The police, in my opinion, have been excellent, but they can't put a cop on every corner in Brooklyn. Many of the drug problems are out of hand. They make arrests, but what really happens to the criminal? They get let out.

Bronx

> I know in many cases the situation with drugs gets to the point where people feel that nothing is being done, or not enough is being done. One of the problems is that the residents don't realize that there is red tape or the bureaucracy at court. And what annoys them is the fact that someone is arrested and in many cases the person is out in a couple of days, so it seems like the police aren't doing anything. They want to blame someone, so they blame the police instead of the judges and the courts.

CPOP Response to Crime and Drug Problems

Several respondents stated that one of the most important benefits of CPOP was that it provided a heightened and *visible* police presence in both the commercial and the residential areas. By walking the beat, the CPO has both the opportunity and the responsibility to enforce regulations, deter potential criminals, and deal with problems that arise in his or her area. The president of a large and prestigious merchants' association described the situation as follows: "The police presence itself is a very important service. I don't have to call the precinct; I can stick my head out and find an officer. It's the old-fashioned closeness returned. They enforce peddler rules and deter pickpocketing and shoplifting." He continued, "CPOP has helped us with the parking problems on the boulevard. They've gone out and given summonses. They also hang out outside the large stores that have a pickpocketing problem and give it their attention. They caught a few people who were doing a lot in the area."

The president of a prominent merchants' association in an economically and racially mixed area stated that CPOP had addressed certain street conditions, and to some extent allayed the citizens' fears:

> The public is concerned about robberies, because they are a direct threat to one's life. Concern fluctuates and is usually at a high point after a prominent person has been mugged. The general perception is that the streets are safer, but not safe. In the past you would have to weave your way through 400 junkies.

Although few of the survey respondents representing white, affluent residential areas expressed concerns about robbery or burglary, one prosperous neighborhood had experienced a rash of garage burglaries that had upset the residents. The CPO discussed this problem and possible solutions with members of various homeowner and community organizations, and they decided that a civilian patrol might ameliorate the problem. The CPO then went to the director of a federally funded, community-based crime prevention program to discuss the feasibility of the civilian patrol project. The director of that organization stated:

> The CPO came to me with an idea for a civilian patrol in one of the residential areas. He wanted to know if my organization would fund the car and the radio for the people to use. And of course we did, and it was a great success. The civilian patrol had caught several people and called about many others.

As described earlier in this chapter, many respondents were concerned about the problems posed by street-level trafficking in drugs. The following comment was made by the president of a homeowners' association in a predominantly white, working-class to middle-class community that had a condition involving the street-level sale of marijuana. The dealers and customers were local teenagers and young adults, and the exchange took place at traffic intersections. This respondent believed that, because the parties involved were white and the substance in question was marijuana, neither the precinct nor the patrol borough took the problem seriously. However, with the implementation of the CPOP, this interviewee found a police resource that was willing to address the problem:

> I'm pleased to say the drug problem has been significantly reduced—it's not as blatant and has been removed from the street. CPO "X" met with me. I identified problems to him and gave him information he confirmed as a police officer. The sergeant also lobbied for us at the [borough] Narcotics level. He was able to convince the captain that "Yeah, there really is a drug problem," and it wasn't just some fringe, lunatic civilians saying there was a problem. We got rapidly expanded uniform presence.

Or as an interviewee in an affluent area stated:

> There has been more effort in recent years to address the drug problem and prostitution. But again there does not seem to have been any systematic attempt to assign the number of police that are needed to be effective for long-term changes. CPOP has at least consistently addressed locations where this activity occurs. I think that constantly moving and arresting these people has forced some to go elsewhere. Also, CPOP has been an avenue for residents to use in bringing the police into the community.

According to other respondents, CPOs also tackled successfully the more difficult drug problems in marginal neighborhoods. The following statement was made by the president of a block association in an area that was becoming destabilized as a result of crack trafficking:

> For example, someone had the nerve to start a crack house right here on this block, which was insulting to me. And I saw the CPOP officer. I didn't call in the regular police. I didn't have to, like we did before. Because in the past you felt the guy in the field didn't care. Now we have a CPOP officer who works in the area and can go directly to that problem, and he can identify what you're talking about. If you call in a person's name, the CPOP officer sometimes will know who those people are. He can identify cars, and houses, and who the people in the community are.

CPOs were commended by the respondents for having not only an in-depth knowledge of the dynamics of the drug problems and the people involved, but also the expertise to deal with these situations. The following comments were made by the president of a block association in a minority neighborhood notorious for trafficking in cocaine and crack. He explained in the interview that there were high rates of unemployment, single-parent families, and drug dependence, and that the conditions had worsened with the advent of crack:

> Conditions are much worse due to crack. There are so many people employed in the drug business—from little boys and girls who act as "spotters" to the others who sell it to the addicts. The money to be made in it is far greater than the dollars they could make doing something else. . . . All of the problems in our neighborhood relate in one way or another to drugs, whether it's addicts hanging out on the corners scaring everyone or the gangs of kids looking for work in front of one of the crack houses.

He described the police response to the problem a year before the interview as follows: "The police at that time did not appear serious about stopping drugs. They seemed to ignore us. When they did come by, they hassled people, but nothing ever seemed to stop the pushers. We rarely saw the police." However, regarding the six-month period prior to the survey interview, he stated: "The police are really trying to help us now. They are always here, and they make arrests. The sales aren't on the street anymore. The pushers are getting frustrated with the police attention. I feel something drastic may happen soon." He elaborated on CPOP's contribution to the effort as follows:

> We see the CPOP van here, and we know they are watching our street. We feel safer, and there is justice. The sellers aren't able to get away with it so freely anymore. . . . What CPOP does is remarkable. They patrol our street, and they freely stop and question all cars and people entering our block as to their whereabouts. This alone scares buyers off. They'd rather go somewhere else. Sometimes they search people and find drugs.

Quality-of-Life Problems and the Police Response

In addition to describing the crime and drug problems in their neighborhoods, the community leaders were asked to describe the current and past quality-of-life problems they experienced, to assess the response of the police in general, and that of the CPOP unit in particular, to those problems. This and the next section present the results of those inquiries.

Again, a rather sharp contrast is drawn between the leaders' assessment of the general police response and that of the CPOP units. The contrast is even sharper with respect to these quality-of-life problems than it is with respect to the crime and drug problems. This finding was not surprising to either the research staff or to the department officials. The aforementioned resource strains that the department experienced from the mid-1970s through the early 1980s imposed especially severe limitations on the department's ability to address quality-of-life concerns. Indeed, this was one of the reasons that CPOP was directed to give special attention to those problems and why the TOPAC units were created and deployed around the same time that CPOP expansion began. This is the context within which the data describing perceptions and assessments of the community leaders should be considered.

Overall the respondents believed that, given manpower limitations, the nature of these problems, and the unpredictability of the criminal justice system, the police were doing their best to deal with crime problems. In contrast, several interviewees indicated that they were troubled and annoyed, because they perceived the police generally to be unwilling or unable to address quality-of-life problems. This response was the same when residents were asked about the general police response to quality-of-life problems two years ago, and at the time of the interview.

In this context, "quality of life" problems refer to annoying behaviors or conditions that may or may not be criminal, but that affect the individual's sense of security and well-being. The interviewees identified a variety of problems that included derelicts and homeless people camping out on the street or in parks, commercial vehicles parked in residential neighborhoods, abandoned automobiles, loud radios, prostitution, and peddlers or vendors blocking sidewalks. These conditions are annoying and aggravating, and in the extreme, fear-provoking. When these problems are not addressed by the police and persist, the merchants and residents become frustrated and angry. As one community leader said, "If the police can't control minor things like double-parking, how are they going to take care of big things?" One of the themes in the comments was that the police *in general* gave and have given very low priority to quality-of-life problems, and this was reflected in long response times. Although the respondents were sophisticated enough to realize that raucous parties and barking dogs were not emergency situations, they still expected some response:

> There really wasn't much of a response, because they had higher priorities. If you called to report loud noises, they would say, "Well, we only have three cars and they're out doing this or out doing that. And if we can get somebody, we'll send somebody." There would be quite a lapse of time between the telephone call and the time they would show up.

Or, as a merchant stated:

> Well, first you have to call them. Honestly, many times the police—and I know they are very busy—don't show up for minor calls, which they are considered. When they do arrive, they chase people away but their hands are tied somewhat. Some of these kids need a good shot in the head.

An official in a precinct community council described the situation as follows: "I have heard a tremendous amount of complaints about noise. The community feels that the police should give out more summonses, and that they could better address this problem." He concluded:

> The police aren't prepared to deal with these problems. They don't have the mentality or the desire. Their attitude just isn't conducive to it. They don't know how to address these problems, and they don't want to enforce noise codes. It's not a priority for them. The community really resents this attitude. We live here and want a response from the police about this.

A similar statement was made by a former district manager of a community planning board: "I have serious reservations about the police. I am not happy with their performance. The police are not responsive to the community. In my opinion, quality-of-life problems are totally ignored and when you call they say, 'We haven't got the time.' That's baloney!"

CPOP and Response to Quality-of-Life Problems

CPOs deal with a wide range of quality-of-life problems, ranging from the trivial to the serious. A merchant in an area undergoing gentrification stated that CPOP had had little effect on crime, and that he had *not* expected much impact in that area. He explained:

> Not regarding the crime problems so much. The main effect that I see them having is on the quality-of-life issues. I like the idea of being able to call CPOP if we've got a neighbor whose dog is constantly barking. So the CPOP officer stops by once, says that he'll stop by again. So there's a follow-up to the effort rather than it being a single instant kind of visitation.

One block association president described the CPOP response to the homeless problem in Greenwich Village as follows: "I think that CPOP, if anything, attempts to maintain an acceptable outlook with regard to the homeless, because they are not viewing homeless people as violators of the law as much as attempting to minimize the problems they may be creating."

One of the main targets of CPOP intervention has been order-maintenance problems in the playgrounds, commercial districts, and residential neighborhoods surrounding schools. One respondent in an economically and racially mixed area described a problem at a local high school that had been annoying the neighboring residents for years and was inadequately addressed until CPOP intervened. Students and truants loitered in front of the houses surrounding the school, sitting on cars, playing loud music on radios, tossing empty food containers on the ground, and otherwise making nuisances of themselves:

We had a school problem, and we worked with CPOP. The kids were congregating on a residential street near the school. The residents called our office, and they had been complaining for years. I arranged a meeting with the CPOP sergeant, several residents, the school principal, and CPOP. CPOP has been able to control the kids and move them off the street, dispersing them. The problem has gotten better. I've gotten calls from homeowners who said, "Thanks. The problem is under control."

Many quality-of-life problems involving street conditions and parks are seasonal—as the weather becomes worse the problems disappear without police intervention. And as the weather improves, the problems return. Thus these problems are never resolved and must be continually addressed. One of the goals of CPOP has been to find creative ways to address chronic problems within the framework of traditional law-enforcement tactics. In the following example, the problem pertained to a very small park in the middle of a densely populated commercial and residential area. The park contained swing sets and picnic tables and would have been quite attractive to the local community, except that methadone users and derelicts congregated there. One community leader explained the CPOP strategy as follows:

The most clever thing. . . . We have an ongoing problem at the park which has been a hangout for drug addicts, primarily because the hospital runs a methadone clinic right on the other side of the avenue. And so the clients get off either the subway or buses, and they walk up to the hospital to get their methadone. Then they come back, and they hang out in the park, which is nice—it has some tables, etc. But with all of those addicts there, it's totally unusable by any community residents. Turns out that up on the wall of the park is a notice that says that no adult is permitted in the park unless accompanied by a child. And so the CPOP officers have been regularly visiting the park, giving out summonses to any addict who is not accompanied by a child. So the addicts have left the park. That is an example of clever police work. It did a really positive thing in terms of community spirit, and what the officers are all about.

Several of our respondents noted that CPOP patrol, unlike RMP, is not incident-based, and because officers do not labor under severe time constraints, they have the opportunity and responsibility to follow up on problems. The latitude provided by the program allows the officers to develop a fuller understanding of the conditions and to work for solutions rather than concentrating on a "quick fix." More-over several of our respondents commended CPOP for recognizing the necessity of organizing and involving the community in the problem-solving process. As one indicated, "The idea that the same officer can follow up on these quality-of-life problems is extremely good. Add to that the fact that they are trying to organize block associations and community activities and things that will bring people together is really a beneficial effort." Or as another interviewee stated:

> They have been very active in trying to come up with some long-term solutions. For example, one officer has been working on disorderly groups of adults in the major commercial area. The problem has been reduced drastically. Another officer took a different approach with the group and got them to clear up some of the areas that were littered (mostly by them). He explained to them that other people objected to the litter they caused more so than the group's presence. The officer was able to establish a good relationship with these people.

Community Indifference or Ambivalence Toward Certain Quality-of-Life Problems

One of the difficulties that police confront in addressing quality-of-life problems is that there is often a lack of consensus in a neighborhood regarding what is unacceptable behavior. For example, in densely populated, lower-income areas, the community is often willing to tolerate people fixing their automobiles in the street. It is not uncommon to see five men huddled over an engine, while the carburetor, battery, spark plugs, greasy rags, and tools are scattered about on the sidewalk and in the street. The residents accept the fact that the men cannot afford the services of a professional mechanic and that they do not have driveways or garages in which to dismantle the car. However, when this type of behavior occurs in higher-income neighborhoods (as it did in a few areas in the current study), the residents are often outraged. They believe that this activity is unsightly, impedes the flow of traffic, obstructs the sidewalks, and is unsafe. Repairing cars in the street is, in fact, a summonsable offense. However, the statute is seldom enforced unless there is a complaint. Thus what constitutes a quality-of-life problem is, in part, a matter of context and community standards.[2]

In addition, large segments of the population may not be aware that a problem exists. And, even if they are aware, they may not be concerned unless the activity affects them personally. As one respondent explained:

> There are the traffic problems caused by double-parking, livery cabs, and the growth in the population. But unless the problem directly affects the residents, they do not get too angry. When the problem interferes with their daily lives, however, then it becomes very much a vocalized concern.

Similarly, another leader stated: "They are very concerned about drugs, but the other problems like abandoned cars and traffic conditions generate concern from people on an individual basis." Thus, if a resident does not own a car, he or she may not care that parking spaces are scarce and double-parking is rampant. Similarly, abandoned automobiles and commercial vehicles parked in residential zones may become troublesome only if they are detracting from the appearance of the neighborhood and thereby lowering property values.

Several merchants and residents in the sample expressed concern about *unlicensed* peddlers selling on the sidewalks in commercial and semicommercial/residential areas. Typically, these peddlers operate out of vans and display their wares (jewelry, perfume, scarves, radios, umbrellas, etc.) on a card table or a blanket. The merchants object to this activity, because it draws the attention of pedestrians and encourages potential customers to purchase merchandise on the street rather than in the stores. In addition, these vendors obstruct store entrances and block the sidewalks. One block association president explained the ambivalence of the community toward this problem as follows:

> Part of the community views the vendors as cute and charming. Others view them as blocking traffic and sidewalks. The concern depends on who you talk to. It's not such a problem now because of the cold. It's a social and economic problem. It's not a high priority with the police department.

She continued: "The police helped clear up the vendors, but on a piecemeal basis. The vendors just move on and then come back."

In certain circumstances the community may agree that a serious order-maintenance problem exists and that it merits police attention; however, there may be no consensus as to the appropriate form of police intervention. An example of this situation can be seen in the conflict that the police experienced within a particular community regarding the ways in which the problems posed by the homeless should be addressed.

The community is a fairly affluent one with a long tradition of political liberalism and social tolerance. Nevertheless the merchants, restaurateurs, and other business people in the area derive a large percentage of their income not only from prosperous neighborhood residents, but also from the tourist trade. The business community is therefore very upset by street conditions—including homeless people and derelicts sleeping in doorways or sprawled on the sidewalks—that might offend, frighten, or otherwise discourage customers.

The residents also have been very disturbed by the continuing presence of homeless and other undesirable people. A number of small "pocket" parks are scattered throughout the residential and semicommercial neighborhoods, and these parks have become the campgrounds for homeless people and derelicts, some of whom are mentally ill. Innumerable complaints have been lodged with the police and community leaders about vagrants shouting obscenities at passersby, panhandling, urinating in public, and otherwise behaving in an offensive and at times menacing manner. Despite public protest, the atmosphere of the community has proved congenial to the homeless and others, because the residents, many of whom complain to the police about this problem, are compassionate people who offer the homeless food, money, and clothing. In addition, the streets are well-lighted and relatively free of street crime; therefore, the homeless are less vulnerable to assault or robbery than they are in other areas of the city. Although it is difficult to estimate the actual number of homeless people living on the streets and in the parks, the respondents in this survey believed that it was large and increasing. Several respondents attributed the persistence of this problem to the inadequacy of the police response:

> A problem that has increased community concern deals with the influx of vagrants in the park and transients gathering near the piers on the river. If I were to speculate as to why there has been an increase in the number of vagrants, I would attribute it to two reasons. First of all, the overall increase in the number of homeless people in New York City over the years. Basically, doors have been shut to these people and, as a result, they seek out areas where they may be more accepted and bothered the least. Secondly, the lack of police attention to areas where problems originate or occur with more frequency only serves to escalate the problem.

The ambivalence of the community is evident in the following comments from two other residents:

> The police did sweeps of the parks. They took the abusive homeless out of the community and just tried to move them on when the community complained. They brought them to shelters. The police were generally gentle with them. The parks in the area are safer than the shelters for the homeless.

> I know that primarily in the winter the police try to get the homeless to go to shelters, but I don't believe that the police should be used to try and solve or correct this type of problem. It is the responsibility of the city to provide for these people.

Perceived Effects of CPOP on Police/Community Relations

One of the dimensions of CPOP is to work with existing organizations to identify problems and develop strategies for resolving problems. Four of the research precincts were highly organized before CPOP was implemented. In these precincts, one of the functions that CPOP served was to publicize the meetings of local organizations and encourage uninvolved citizens to join these community groups and attend meetings. The president of a precinct community council stated, "One way that the sergeant and the CPOs have been helpful is in getting support in the community for meetings. They've gone out of their way to get folks to attend group meetings." Similarly, a respondent in another precinct stated:

They've started block associations. They get information about contacts on the street. They attend community meetings and encourage people to join. They've made an effort to reach out to the community. I've seen them attend block watchers meetings and take complaints. The sergeant is always available if we need him. The Radio Identification Program has been advertised.

CPOP efforts in the community organizing area are often met with apathy and resistance. This is particularly true in impoverished neighborhoods, where the residents have less experience in forming groups and participating in meetings, and generally question their potential usefulness. As a member of the Precinct Community Council representing a blighted, drug-infested area stated:

I think people are misinformed generally, and tend to feel that the police don't care. The real picture is that many people are afraid to be involved with the police for fear of retaliation. Many people don't understand that in order for anything to be accomplished, they must also take action by being vocal and calling 911.

In these situations, the officer has to start organizing building by building. However, once the residents are persuaded that a tenants' association provides a mechanism for addressing their problems, then they are willing to participate. A community leader in a crack-plagued neighborhood explained: "The CPO has organized a tenant's patrol to chase drug violators away in our buildings. You see, he recognizes what most don't—that our area is filled with poor people who do work for a living and want to be safe." He continued:

Now I recognize that he's only one person, and he's limited in terms of hours and how much time he can spend with us, but he's a focal point, because everyone respects a cop. The tenants' organization is a prime example. No one wanted to do it, but he went around and spoke to the leaders and soon we had it going.

Historically, one of the sources of mistrust between the community and the police has been the fact that the general public does not understand police priorities, constraints on resources, and the ways in which law-enforcement practices are restricted by law, policies, and procedures. As a result of a lack of information, the general public often entertains a number of misconceptions about the ability of the police to address crime and quality-of-life problems. Moreover, many people are disillusioned by the police, because they believe that the police have made promises that have not been kept. One of the primary objectives of CPOP was to dispel these misconceptions by providing information about the capabilities and limitations of the police. Judging by the comments obtained in this survey, the community leaders in the research precincts believe that CPOP has been successful in this regard. The president of a civilian patrol organization said, "The CPOs are responsive, honest, and straightforward. They tell what cops can and can't do. They remind you that people have rights, and you just can't force those that annoy you to move on. They've been informative." Or, as an interviewee from a middle-class area in a different research precinct explained:

> CPOs help the community develop realistic ideas of what the police department can and can't do. They'll tell us what the police can affect. They're honest with us. They explain how sector cars work, [and the] priority ranking of 911 calls. They try to put aside people's fears—explain what crime is about, and at the same time the CPO tries to get people to join our organization. It is also a great time to get block watchers' groups going.

A community leader from a transitional area in Brooklyn commended the CPOs for their honesty in answering questions and stated, "These guys don't try to tell us just any old thing. They try to answer the questions, and when they don't know, they will say, 'I'll find out,' or 'I don't know.' You have to respect that." He also noted that by having the same officer assigned to the same beat, there is familiarity, continuity, and a continuous sharing of information:

> They know what our problems are, because they are around, because we discuss the community continuously. Before, we discussed our community problems intermittently with one officer here, one officer there. Now we have a pool of information that is held in place—that's a great thing. Nothing is lost. You don't have to start all over again.

As the following comment indicates, information is shared both formally and informally: "The CPO has spoken to our group. He shows films and gives lectures about drugs to our young. He patrols the area and stops in every week for a few hours and chases druggies away. He's gotten other cops to come around more often."

According to the respondents, one of the most important outcomes of the program has been an improvement in police/community relations. This point was emphasized by most respondents, regardless of precinct, socioeconomic background, or race and ethnicity. To a great extent this change seems attributable to the heightened police presence, personal interaction with the CPO, and the exchange of information:

> The police had a bad reputation in the eyes of the community. Drugs were everywhere, and the residents could not understand why the police were not doing anything about them. However, the perceptions of the residents have also begun to change due to having a foot patrol officer and getting to know her. The same officer on a daily basis gives the residents a feeling of safety.

The president of a large, prestigious community organization, in a mixed neighborhood with a history of negative experiences with the police stated:

> People are less antagonistic toward the police than they were in the past. There is still a general feeling that the police goof-off and take bribes, but there is less of a feeling that the police are the enemy. CPOP has helped the situation a lot because people care about their local cop.

He continued:

> They have definitely helped to improve the situation. Even if they continue in only a medium effective way they will continue to improve things. People know the CPOs and they like to talk to them, and the CPOs make people feel better. CPOs are able to break down the barrier between the police and the community, whereas the cop in the car just hassles people. Also, CPOs can deter crime more effectively, because their presence is felt more than that of a car which whizzes by.

The following comment is from the president of a large home-owners' association in a white, middle-class residential area. His statements are particularly noteworthy, because they indicate that, even in these types of neighborhoods, which are historically well-disposed toward the police, an undercurrent of resentment exists, based on what the residents perceive to be a lack of attention from the police department and broken promises. Nevertheless he believed that the implementation of CPOP has done a great deal to restore the community's faith in the police department:

> People's attitudes toward the police dramatically improved—my own as well as everyone else's. When we see a cop walking in our area it's no longer "Is this guy lost?" We expect the CPOP officer to walk down the side streets, and we actually say hello and smile to cops now. There's something very positive about that—some cops even smile back. We let the cops in our neighborhood know we appreciate them—not, "What the hell is he doing here?"—or, "He's not going to do anything anyway, so who cares?"

His final statement is also interesting, because it reflects his belief that what may be termed the CPOP approach has spread to RMP officers: "The police in general are learning the 'CPOP lesson.' They're starting to ask, 'What are the problems? What should we be looking for?' "

It is virtually impossible to determine whether, in fact, the police in general are trying to develop a better understanding of the problems in the community or becoming friendlier as a result of exposure to CPOP and its philosophy. Nevertheless it is clear from our interviews that the community leaders' positive encounters with CPOs lead to positive perceptions of the program and often carry over to positive perceptions of the police in general. The following comment is from the president of a merchant's association in a changing area:

> Since CPOP came into existence, things have changed. First of all, the police are friendlier, and that's very important. No one wants to call someone to help them, and that someone who you called is hostile, and sometimes that's the case. Honestly, I haven't seen or heard of that lately. That's not to say that it doesn't exist. But this precinct is very congenial. You don't hear of the police beating up people in the streets or pulling their guns. You can talk to them.

He continued:

> You have a police officer you see continuously, and you can say "hello," call him by name, and talk with him. I even heard a teenager say that the CPOP officer was responsible for getting him a job. This wasn't before. Before, the police wouldn't have known the kid. I could just go on. It's a wonderful program.

Summary

While the community leaders interviewed for this research evinced a reasonably good understanding of CPOP's purpose, the level of awareness of the program varied. Some showed an in-depth awareness of the program's operations and of the personnel who made up the unit. Those expressing this level of awareness were generally merchants, local office holders, and civic activists. They welcomed the introduction of this form of policing, and they believed it contributed to the economic and social vitality of the community.

A somewhat lower level of awareness was expressed by those who, though unfamiliar with the details of the program, knew that it existed and that the police were doing something special and positive in the neighborhood. This level of awareness was expressed by those who might be described as the "informed public" who read local papers and occasionally attended community meetings. A third level of awareness was expressed by those who perceived a change in the extent and nature of police presence in the neighborhood, but were unsure of the name of the program or the details of its operation. Finally, a few people interviewed as community leaders evinced no awareness of the program, or of any special police efforts in the community. They attributed their lack of awareness to insufficient efforts by the police to publicize the program.

The community leaders interviewed in the research precincts were not especially concerned with conventional street crime problems, but, in some precincts, they were very disturbed by the prevalence of street narcotics dealing. In general, they believed that the CPO program might be of some help with respect to street crimes, but could be especially useful in relation to drugs. They claimed that CPOs frequently took initiative in attacking drug locations and that their regular presence in the same neighborhoods made it easier for them to observe the drug trade and to receive information concerning it from members of the community. The leaders also believed that the persistent presence of the same officer encouraged dealers to move to other locations and gave residents and merchants a measure of safety and a feeling of confidence in the determination of the police to fight the drug problem.

The respondents claimed that the observable and potential effects of CPOP were greater on quality-of-life problems than they were on street-crime problems. Many of those interviewed expressed the belief that, prior to the arrival of CPOP, the police paid little attention to quality-of-life problems. The problems most often identified as matters of concern to the respondents were concentrations of derelicts and homeless people in the parks and other public places, the proliferation of illegal vendors on the sidewalks of commercial streets, the prevalence and aggressiveness of prostitutes in specific locations, noise violations, and various traffic and parking problems in the neighborhoods. The respondents were disturbed by the difficulties they experienced before CPOP in getting the police to recognize these problems and to take quick and persistent actions against them.

They indicated that this situation changed when the CPO program began in their precincts. They welcomed the presence of the same police officer in the neighborhood and applauded his or her efforts to listen to the people's definition of the major problems in the community. They believed that CPOs accumulated knowledge about specific problems and provided continuity for the residents who were concerned with those problems. They noted also that the CPOs were sometimes quite creative in bringing other resources to bear on the problems, including the organized activity of residents and merchants.

The interviewed leaders were unanimous in their belief that the CPOP units contributed significantly to improved relations between the police and the community. They believed that these effects flowed from the efforts of the officers to reach out to the people, to chat with them informally, to attend meetings of neighborhood organizations, to encourage residents to join such organizations, and to provide accurate information about what can and cannot be done about crime and quality-of-life problems in the community. The willingness of some of the CPOs to admit ignorance about a problem or the resources that might be used to address it, and then to look for that information and bring it back to the community meetings, strengthened the credibility of the police in the neighborhood.

Finally, the respondents said that the people appreciated the opportunity to know the CPO personally, and that positive encounters with the officers produced positive impressions of the program and of the police in general.

Notes   1. This decision represented a change from the original design, which envisioned conducting random citizen surveys of 50 respondents in each of the research beats (estimated at 50) at the start and at the end of the data collection period. Such a survey had been conducted in each beat at the end of the research period in the pilot project in Brooklyn's 72 Precinct. The survey revealed that approximately 30% of the respondents evinced at least a general awareness of the program, or the special efforts being made by the CPOs. However, very few had knowledge that was specific enough to shed much light on various aspects of the program's design or operation. Moreover, the sample size was not large enough to permit analyses aimed at determining whether there were meaningful differences between the perceptions and attitudes of those who were and those who were not aware of the program, much less to analyze such differences by levels of awareness. The number of knowledgeable citizens might have been increased by selecting samples from among those living or working in immediate proximity to the priority problems on which the CPOs were concentrating. However, that strategy would have required a much larger sample than the 5,000 originally envisioned, and a great deal more effort to establish sampling frames in 100 to 200 "problem areas." Thus the survey of leaders was considered a more productive and cost-effective strategy for describing how the program was perceived in the community and its strengths and weaknesses in the eyes of knowledgeable people in the community. The project's Advisory Committee concurred in this judgment.

2. This reality is a basic tenet of the CPOP philosophy. This is precisely why CPOs are encouraged to solicit community input into the problem definition and strategy development process. In addition, normative differences *between* communities regarding quality-of-life problems were anticipated in the program design. The CPO, in his or her planning and problem-solving efforts, is expected to address the concerns of the community in a manner that is both lawful and, to the extent possible, consistent with the wishes of the community. Nevertheless, differences in perceptions *within* a beat pose a substantial challenge to the CPO and the CPOP supervisor, because they must resolve the conflict without threatening the rights and interests of the parties involved.

Recommendations and Reflections

- Recommendations for Improving CPOP
- Reflections on Some Broader Questions

Our assessment of CPOP revealed many reasons for satisfaction with what had been accomplished and optimism for the future of the program. It also revealed shortcomings in implementation, community involvement, and command support. The recommendations of the research team for addressing these shortcomings and building on the strengths of the program are set forth below for the reader's consideration, along with a summary description of how some of the department's recent initiatives, under Commissioner Brown, embody the spirit of those recommendations. Of course, we are not in a position to assess the effects of these initiatives, but it is reasonable to expect the department to report on them in the future.

The second half of this concluding chapter was written some time after the rest of the book. In the interim, as authors we stepped back a bit to look again at some of the important questions regarding community policing and to consider what we can say about them, based on our experience with the program in New York. We agree with many of the authors cited in Chapter 1 who contend that community policing represents a potential paradigm shift in the organization and delivery of police services in urban America. The transformation will take time, perhaps decades, if it is to be realized at all. But it is clear, even now, that the transformation will require some dramatic changes in the basic organization and management of police agencies, in the relationship between the police and the citizenry and in the latter's capacity to collaborate with the police and other public agencies in neighborhood-based problem solving, and in the kinds of performance that local governments expect from their police and the ways in which they monitor actual performance. Our attention is focused on these matters in the last part of the chapter.

Recommendations for Improving CPOP

The core of the CPO role is the application of the problem-solving process in the context of a local community. When done well, it produces palpable and significant benefits for the people in the neighborhoods, greater empathy and mutual respect between the people and the police, feelings of personal and professional satisfaction in the police personnel involved, and impressive and hope-filled stories of cooperation and ingenuity resulting in greater control over the conditions that inspire fear, frustration, and fury in the city's neighborhoods. That it can be done well is clear from the stories presented in *CPOP: Community Policing in Practice* (see Appendix A). That it can and often does realize its basic problem-solving intentions is the first, and perhaps most important, judgment to be made about CPOP. It is an innovation, therefore, that should be continued by the NYPD, and the research reported here identifies ways in which to improve the modal level of performance by CPOs and to strengthen the influence of and the support given to the program. These include the observations and recommendations discussed in the following sections.

Intensify Training for CPOs and CPOP Sergeants

As reported above, the insufficiency and inadequacy of the problem-solving training provided to CPOs and sergeants was recognized some time ago by the program managers at Vera and in the department. In response, a manual has been developed on the problem-solving process (see Appendix B), and an intensive training program is being delivered to each precinct unit separately. Sergeants have been provided with a separate training program specifically focusing on the role of the supervisor in the problem-solving process. In addition, each sergeant participates in the training delivered to his or her unit. It is important that this be continued and, in fact, accelerated to complete this training in all 75 precincts as soon as possible.

When this objective is accomplished, arrangements should be made to provide the same training, or a modified version thereof, to all new CPOs within the first 6 months of their serving in the role. (At present, new CPOs go through the orientation training, but do not receive the intensive training in problem solving if the unit in which they serve has already received it.) In addition, a single-day refresher training should be provided to each unit, as a unit, at least once each year.

Similarly, arrangements should be made for providing new CPOP sergeants with special training in problem solving, and with a day's refresher training in the full scope of the supervisor's role, at least once a year. This training should focus especially on the responsibilities of the supervisor as leader and guide (see Chapter 5), including techniques for representing the unit within the precinct, representing it to the community, and assisting individual CPOs in the performance of their role.

Finally, regular meetings of CPOP sergeants with representatives of the CPOP Coordinator's Office should be reinstituted, at least on a quarterly basis. Meetings of this sort are a useful mechanism for surfacing issues regarding program operations, for providing training on specific aspects of the program, and for sharing experiences with one's peers.

Disseminate Information About Successful Problem-Solving Strategies

Effective problem solving on the neighborhood level cannot be performed from a recipe book; the strategies must be fashioned to the peculiarities of each problem and the community context in which the problem exists. Nevertheless CPOs can and should learn from the experience of others, both within and outside the NYPD. To some extent, that objective is served by the *CPO Newsletter*, which is assembled and published every 2 or 3 months. As valuable as that medium is, it is limited in the details that it can provide and in its capacity to display a variety of apparently successful approaches to similar types of problems.

A descriptive document should be developed for each of the major types of problems with which CPOP units deal frequently. Such a document would describe various ways in which a problem is manifested in the city, show what officers have done to learn more about that problem as it exists in their beats, describe the major elements of the corrective strategies developed by the officers, and show how those elements correspond to dimensions of the problem revealed through the problem analysis. In addition, it would provide some description of the process used by the officer to develop the strategy, especially how he or she involved representatives of the community in the process; highlight the obstacles to implementation that officers are most likely to encounter, and describe how they have been handled; identify the indicators used by the officers to monitor the implementation and effects of these strategies; and describe the processes that they used to review the implementation and effects with representatives of the community.

Documents of this sort are desired by the officers, who are looking for help with respect to both the process and the substance of problem solving. Effective supervision and regular dialogue with representatives of the community can check the tendency to use them as canned programs.

Encourage the Involvement of a Representative Body of Citizens in Each Beat

CPOs are good at meeting and talking with residents, merchants, and organization leaders in the community and taking note of the problems that concern them. This, in itself, is an important form of outreach that provides the police with information they often would not get otherwise and that signals police willingness to respond to community needs. In itself, however, this process of talking to individuals in the community is not sufficient for CPOP to realize either its community-oriented or problem-solving objectives.

The program design called for involving the community in the problem-solving process from start to finish, but did not offer any models for how this can or should be done. The research results reported here make it clear that, in each beat, the creation of a body of residents, merchants, and members of local organizations with whom the CPO could meet on a regular basis would strengthen the program in a variety of ways.

It would provide the continuity of membership that is necessary for effective citizen participation in the problem-solving process. It would assist the CPO in sorting out priorities among the problems and conditions brought to his or her attention, and, in this regard, it would help to check those officers who may be focusing their limited resources on one or more conditions that are relatively unimportant in the neighborhood. This stable body of citizens would help expand the officer's vision in developing the component elements of a problem-solving strategy and expand his or her reach in securing the commitment of local individuals and organizations in carrying out the strategy. In the same way, this body of people could help to monitor implementation and impact, help to understand and accept the fact that a strategy attempted in good faith may fail to alleviate the problem, and help to modify the strategy and motivate the people to try again. Finally, by arranging for the active involvement of such a stable body of citizens in the problem-solving process, the CPO greatly increases the likelihood that the community will take its proper share of responsibility for improving the quality of its daily life.

There are risks for the department in following this course. No single model describes how this can be done well. The composition of such a body and the process by which it is established will have to differ some from one community to the next. The possibility will always exist that its representative character will be challenged by residents in the neighborhood. It takes specific skills to work effectively with a group of people, in contrast to a number of individuals. The department probably does not have a cadre of people with sufficient skills in this form of community organizing to provide the CPOs with the hands-on, practical assistance they are likely to need from time to time. And, finally, in each beat, such a body of citizens could constrain police discretion in deploying resources and directing them to undertake specific activities.

Nonetheless, in the absence of such working groups on the beat level, CPOP performance in problem solving will suffer, and the opportunities that the program offers for creating a much more productive relationship between the police and the community will not be realized. The risks mentioned above are simply that. They can be lowered and controlled by identifying them forthrightly and bringing some of the skills of community organization to bear on their resolution. Because the potential gains are substantial, the risks are well worth taking.

Finally, in this regard, the CPOP Coordinator's Office should have the capacity, perhaps through contract services, to document successful processes used by CPOP units to establish and work with such bodies and to provide units with technical assistance to do so.

Help Strengthen the Capacity of the Community to Participate Actively

It is also important that attention be given by some agency other than the police department to assisting people in the neighborhoods to form such bodies and to participate actively and effectively in the problem-solving process. Often the community-organizing initiatives of the CPO die out because the people do not know how to organize themselves, or how to go about understanding the problems that concern them, or how to participate cooperatively in such a process with the police, or any other public agency.

The police department is not the appropriate agency to take on the general function of supporting local groups to organize themselves for problem solving. Other agencies, public and private, have more of the appropriate skills and more initial credibility in some neighborhoods than the department. Moreover, the skills developed by the citizenry in organizing and problem solving are transferable to more areas of public service than simply the police. It is important, however, for the department to recognize the benefit it can reap from the availability of such assistance and to press for its wider recognition in the halls of city government.

Strengthen the Integration of CPOP in the Precincts

As indicated in Chapter 6, the key to effective integration of CPOP with other police resources is the precinct commanding officer. And the key to the CO's effectiveness in this regard is his or her serious involvement with the problem-solving performance of the CPOs in each beat.

Involvement means ensuring that the officers understand what they are expected to do and that they develop increased skill in doing it. Involvement means that the CO periodically reviews with each CPO, in a constructively critical manner, the problems identified as priorities in the beat and the corrective strategies that the officer is developing and implementing. It means that the CO insists that indicators be developed to assess progress on each priority problem, and that he or she be informed regularly about what those indicators are showing. Involvement means that the CO responds to the CPO when suggestions are made regarding the commitment of other precinct resources in correcting a problem in the CPO's beat. Involvement means that the CO will take seriously these problems and resource demands when he or she makes long- and short-term decisions about resource deployment and issues tactical orders to subordinates. Finally, commanding officer involvement means that he or

180 COMMUNITY POLICING

she takes a hand in explaining the objectives and procedures of the CPOP unit to other personnel in the precinct, that he or she indicates to others just how important the problem-solving process is, and lets both CPOP and non-CPOP personnel see how that process influences his or her decisions as precinct commander.

More active support from the commanding officer in the work of the CPOP units is important because it will encourage the CPOs to perform better and will enable the CO to use his or her resources more effectively and in a manner that is more clearly responsive to the concerns of the community. It appears that this recognition has been growing among COs as they have accumulated more experience with CPOP. The department should encourage that trend by providing for information exchange among COs, ensuring that a new commanding officer is given at least a few hours of training regarding CPOP and the specifics of integrating it within his or her command, and ensuring that the COs understand that their work will be examined in the department's review of the commander's performance.

Ensure That the Principles of Community-Oriented, Problem-Solving Policing Are Made a Prominent Part of Training, Testing, and Performance Assessments

In the last several years, the department has committed itself to these principles and operationalized them in CPOP and, in a somewhat less obvious way, in other initiatives such as Operation Pressure Point, TOPAC, and, perhaps, the Tactical Narcotics Team (TNT). But the principles have ramifications that go beyond the structure and operation of special programs. They suggest a different way of defining police roles at various levels, involving the community in the work of the police, and choosing the conditions against which police resources will be deployed and the strategies and tactics to be used in addressing those conditions. If the implications of these principles are to become operative throughout the department, they must be made available, and their importance must be stressed to police officials at all levels.

The department should reexamine its training curricula at all levels to ensure that they provide a prominent place for identifying the principles of community-oriented, problem-solving policing; for understanding their meaning, rationale, and evolution in the history of American policing; for describing and analyzing the forms that these principles take in police agencies around the country; and for understanding specifically the manner in which they are carried out in the CPO program. In addition, promotional tests and procedures for the positions of sergeant and above should require that candidates demonstrate increasingly sophisticated levels of mastery over these principles and their implications for the NYPD. Finally, performance evaluations for all command-level personnel should be required to assess the individual's familiarity with the principles and the commander's facility in making them operational in his or her command. These steps will ensure that future generations of police personnel will be adequately exposed to both the conceptual and the practical dimensions of community-oriented policing and problem-solving policing.

*Develop
Additional Ways
to Enact the
Principles
of Community-
Oriented and
Problem-Solving
Policing*

In addition to sustaining the operation of CPOP in the precincts, the department should continue its effort to develop ways in which the entire precinct-based patrol force can contribute to the realization of community-oriented, problem-solving goals. CPOP can continue as the problem identification, planning, and coordinating agent for problem-solving activities of many other police personnel on the neighborhood level. Defining ways in which RMP officers can participate in problem-solving activities presumes some continuity in tour and sector assignments and is facilitated greatly by continuity in supervision and command. Therefore, the further expansion of the fixed-tour, platoon-commander system of precinct management would advance the influence of community and problem-solving principles, despite the fact that the management system was not developed for that purpose.

*Protect Officers
Against
Malicious
Complaints*

A widespread belief among CPOs and CPOP sergeants, especially those working in precincts with substantial narcotics problems, is that they are particularly vulnerable to civilian complaints and complaints alleging corrupt behavior. For a few officers, this sense of vulnerability reflects nothing more than the general belief that the more contact an officer has with the public, the more likely he or she is to be the object of such complaints. That view cannot be tolerated, especially in a community-oriented policing program. In its more serious and threatening form, however, this sense of vulnerability emerges from the following set of assumptions and perceptions.

It is believed that an active officer, continuously attacking drug locations on the beat, disrupts the drug traffic, leading the dealer to seek ways to neutralize him or her. It is believed also that the dealers know that an officer's career can be adversely affected by complaints made to the CCRB and/or the IAD, regardless of the disposition reached on the complaints. (This view, in turn, reflects the very widespread belief among police officers throughout the department that the simple *number* of complaints against an officer, regardless of how they were disposed, weighs against him or her when that officer is being considered for a desirable assignment along the career path.) Moreover the dealers are thought to be aware of the fact that commanding officers are held accountable for the number of civilian complaints made against members of their commands. Police officers infer from these beliefs that dealers make, or encourage associates to make, frequent complaints against the active officer in the belief that these complaints will either lead the CO to move the officer to reduce the precinct's complaint total or lead the officer to lessen the intensity of his or her activity to avoid damage to future career opportunities.

This research cannot substantiate or reject this set of perceptions. The department does hold commanding officers accountable for the volume of civilian complaints received by their subordinates; it does maintain a record of all civilian complaints, whatever their disposition; and it does provide information about all complaints, including the nature of the allegations and the dispositions reached, to superior officers recruiting patrol officers for special assignments. On the other hand, there is no evidence that CPOs receive more civilian complaints than do non-CPOs; nor is there any evidence that would permit one to estimate the proportion of the complaints received that might be classified as malicious or tactical in the sense described above. However, it is clear from the research reported here that this set of perceptions and inferences is widely held by CPOs and CPOP sergeants, and that it is seen by them as discouraging some officers from attacking narcotics problems as actively as they might. Thus it is recommended that the department find ways to address the set of perceptions itself.

This suggests that the department should make a special effort to educate the patrol force on the connection between its information concerning civilian complaints, especially those that may be maliciously motivated, and an officer's movement along the career path. If the suspicion that a complaint is maliciously motivated triggers special efforts by those investigating the complaint, and the results of their special efforts are maintained in the investigative file, that fact ought to be explained to the force. If superior officers recruiting candidates for special assignments routinely consider the contexts and mitigating circumstances related to civilian complaints, that fact should be made clear to the officers. If the system for holding commanding officers accountable for civilian complaints does not focus exclusively on the raw numbers, but permits a CO to show how reasonable increases in the level of complaints flow from changes in street conditions and the implementation of new, legitimate enforcement initiatives, those facts should be explained to the patrol officers.

The officers are not expecting to be told that civilian complaints are acceptable or unimportant. They merely want assurance that their actions are understood and judged within the context and circumstances in which the incident actually occurred.

Current Efforts of the NYPD
As previously indicated, the department has intensified its interest in community policing since this research was completed. Commissioner Brown's current plan for the department goes beyond our recommendations for training. In addition, the Vera Institute is working with the department on the production of problem-solving manuals resembling those recommended here. While it is not clear that any systematic action has been taken to establish stable groups of residents, merchants, and organizational representatives to carry out the problem-solving process with the CPO in each beat, the commissioner's plan does call for the creation of Precinct Management Teams to perform this type of function with the command staff in each precinct (Brown, 1991).

In principle, our recommendation that the CPOP program be more fully integrated with all operations at the precinct level is precisely what the commissioner has called for and planned for.

Several actions that have been taken, and others that are currently under way, are intended to advance that objective. Virtually all patrol officers now work fixed tours, and much greater continuity of supervision and command occurs at the precinct level. Dispatching procedures are being studied to develop ways to ensure that RMPs will be able to spend substantial portions of each tour in the specific sectors to which they are assigned. A number of the special assignments and tactical units are being merged into one Special Operations unit that can respond with more flexibility to problem-solving strategies in different parts of the precinct. And experiments are under way to spell out concrete ways in which all members of a precinct command can play a role in the identification and analysis of neighborhood problems, and in the design and implementation of corrective strategies.

Thus it is clear that the NYPD is not content with its accomplishments in CPOP; it is seriously pursuing a range of strategies intended to infuse the principles of community policing into all of its operations. The organization's commitment is emphatic and considerable. The content and effects of its implementation efforts should be watched carefully in the years to come.

Reflections on Some Broader Questions

Organizational Demands of Community Policing

CPOP was initiated and spread through the NYPD as a special program in the Patrol Services Bureau—an add-on to existing operations at the precinct level. But that was never its intended destiny. Commissioner Ward saw it as a first step toward a different style of policing, and Commissioner Brown is attempting to implement an ambitious plan to accomplish the transformation to community policing. The New York experience suggests some general ways in which community policing initiatives are likely to affect the entire police organization.

Community policing broadens the role of police from an essentially reactive concern with controlling street crime and responding rapidly to calls-for-service to a proactive involvement in reducing fear and improving the quality of life at the neighborhood level. Our research indicates that this more comprehensive conception of mission proved immensely popular among public officials and community leaders in New York City. There is a widespread desire for a more visible, accessible, and responsive police presence in the neighborhoods, and for greater police assistance in dealing with problems of disorder.

But community policing requires a department to create structures and processes that offer real access to the public, that are genuinely open to the public's primary concerns and its views on what

should and should not be done to address them, and that require the
police to account to the public for its policies, strategies, programs,
and effects. The New York experience indicates that making such
structures and processes work is an uncertain and difficult task that
will require time and creativity. In some respects, the New York City
Police Department is more fully decentralized than most police agencies. It delivers most services to the public through a network of 75
police precincts, each of which serves an average of approximately
100,000 people, under the direction of a commanding officer. The
precinct structure does increase the department's physical accessibility to the public and does facilitate the acquisition of knowledge
regarding the problems and conditions peculiar to each precinct. But
genuine openness to public input requires active solicitation by the
police; a system for converting the information received into identified, analyzed problems and a set of strategies for addressing them;
and a system that reconciles the priorities named by the community
with those imposed by the departmental hierarchy.

The early CPOP experience suggests that actively soliciting
public input and identifying neighborhood problems can be done by
officers working in a special unit, but the development and implementation of effective strategies for correcting them is greatly enhanced
when they are made the concern of the entire command. Moreover,
according priority status among these problems, and between them
and the principal concerns of departmental·commanders, cannot be
accomplished without the active involvement of several levels of
middle management. Even when all the relevant actors are involved,
the criteria by which priorities can be reconciled must be articulated
and complied with at the highest levels of command. Otherwise, local
commanders, who must decide on how to allocate resources, for
example, between the order-maintenance concerns of four neighborhood groups and the demands of superior officers for large numbers
of robbery arrests, will quickly perceive that their personal interests
are best served by "stroking" the community while producing the
arrest numbers by which their performance will be assessed.

The idea that the police should welcome a form of accountability
that would have them openly describing their policies, strategies,
programs, achievements, and failures in addressing the major concerns of the public is revolutionary. Sparrow and his colleagues (1990)
see such accountability as a necessary and beneficial element in the
future of policing. They contend that, "rather than retreating into
their shell and guarding it at all costs, police have to emerge from it
fully with a policy of aggressive and deliberate openness" (p. 161).

Of course, they recognize that professional insulation from outside "pressures," along with secretiveness and defensiveness in responding to outside demands for information, are the traditional
strategies of American police agencies. And later they suggest that
middle management must assume a major share of responsibility for
changing this state of affairs:

> Middle managers should wherever possible interact as fully with the community as the most senior and most junior officers. . . . But it has been almost impossible for neighborhood groups, community groups, and community institutions of varying sizes to find appropriate police ears for their concerns. It is the ears of the middle managers that must become available if policing is to become truly flexible and responsive. (p. 171)

We agree with the prescription and with the emphasis on the importance of middle management in this regard, but precinct commanders are not inaccessible in the NYPD. In fact, every such commander must meet regularly with a precinct council, a community board, and various other citizens' organizations. Nonetheless, joint planning and problem solving, in contrast to question-and-answer sessions, are rare. Moreover it is the exceptional manager who will risk revealing information about policies, resources, or failed problem-solving efforts that his superiors might find embarrassing or that they have traditionally withheld from the public. Openness and accountability at any level of organization require clear, encouraging signals from the top and the assurance that police officials who attempt reasonable and innovative problem-solving strategies will not be punished if they fail to produce the desired results, or if the officials reveal and consider such failures with members of the community.

Decentralization, openness, and accountability in attempting to solve the principal problems troubling members of the community require, in turn, flexibility, responsiveness, and creativity at the point at which the agency's contact with the public is most frequent and intense; that is, at the level of the patrol officer in the street. Yet for decades police agencies have striven to reduce police officer discretion to a minimum in the hopes of controlling mistakes, corruption, and abuse of authority. The control mechanism has combined an elaborate set of rules and regulations with an inevitably arbitrary, punitive response to deviation. This system too often spawns the belief that the rules rarely provide the officer with useful substantive guidance, but invariably provide superiors with something to hide behind when a scapegoat is needed. In this context, the smart police officer is often seen as one who does as little as possible, rather than one who uses his or her ingenuity actually to alleviate the conditions that threaten the public's sense of security.

Obviously, such attitudes doom problem-solving and community policing initiatives, so it is necessary try to counter them from the outset. In New York, the CPOs were given a great deal more discretion in how they spent their time and in recommending problem-solving strategies than they had ever experienced before. In the beginning, many were cautious about using that discretion, but became more adventuresome as they came to realize that they would not be punished for making recommendations. For example, after awhile, some actually complained about departmental constraints on the strategies they were allowed to try in addressing drug trafficking conditions. In the end, we had the impression that many CPOs were ready to approach their local problems with ingenuity and creativity, but their willingness to do so was influenced significantly by what they read to be the expectations of supervision and command. Where the precinct commander and the supervisor took the program mission seriously, they imposed greater expectations on the CPOs and generally secured more productive responses. On the other hand, where the commander saw the program as a public relations gesture, or another headquarters fad, the signals called for a no-risk, trouble-free response. In these circumstances, the officers tended to show less initiative, less creativity, and more cynicism.

In sum, the New York experience tends to confirm the contention that community policing is inevitably a strategic rather than a program innovation (Sparrow et al., 1990, pp. 198-202). It may be introduced as simply a special way of relating to the community, but if it is implemented with even a modest level of integrity, it will soon force a reconsideration of virtually all departmental operations and structures: the nature of the agency's mission; the grounds on which it claims legitimacy; the nature of its relationship to the political and social environment; the services it offers; the delivery strategies it uses; the criteria and processes through which it allocates its resources; the roles it requires its members to perform; the coordinating and management processes it relies on; the methods it uses to assess, control, and reward performance; and the values, goals, objectives, and procedures in which it trains its people will all come under the microscope sooner or later.

Community policing, in our opinion, is the desired direction for urban police agencies, but police administrators embarking on this course should know that, however they enter the process, they will be forced to think through its impact on every element of the organization.

Expectations of the Community

Community policing makes several assumptions about local communities, their capacity to control problems of crime, fear, and disorder, and their willingness to cooperate with the police in ventures toward that end. It is important to identify some of those assumptions and to consider them against the CPOP experience in New York, and against the highlights of what is known about community efforts to cope with problems of crime and disorder.

Explicitly or implicitly, it is assumed that residents, merchants, and representatives of local organizations have a different view of neighborhood problems and their relative priority than the police, and that these people will communicate this view to the police and will welcome the opportunity to work with the police in fashioning solutions. It is also assumed that the social structures and cultural processes of the neighborhood (often referred to as the "informal structure") are a more effective source of social control, or at least potentially so, than the formal interventions of the criminal justice system, and that these communal resources can be mobilized to participate effectively in joint problem-solving ventures with the police. Finally, it is assumed that positive experiences of this sort will empower the community and enhance its ability to control crime, reduce fear, and maintain a desirable level of order in the neighborhood.

The proponents of community policing have been cautioned and criticized because of what some commentators see as carelessness or naïveté in their assumptions about community, and for what others see as a blindness to the potential disadvantages of broadening the order-maintenance mandate of the police. Greene and Taylor (1988) have pointed out that, in sociological theory, the concept "community" carries elements of common origins, traditions, values, myths, and social structures. Its power as a force for social control derives, in substantial part, from those shared elements. Because there is no reason to assume a common culture in an area with boundaries drawn for administrative convenience (precinct, sector, beat), there is no reason to assume that such a "community" is or can be a powerful mechanism for social control in that area. In a similar vein, Skogan (1990) finds little evidence that social organizational efforts have a meaningful impact on crime and disorder, except in relatively homogeneous neighborhoods that enjoy some level of economic comfort. Yet, even in these neighborhoods, evidence suggests that such citizen efforts may be somewhat more successful when they are linked to and supported by the local police.

These and other authors have indicated that, where consensus is lacking regarding those conditions that are deemed to be problematic, or with respect to the objectives and strategies to be pursued in correcting them, the police will either be prevented from taking any action or forced to choose among the conflicting positions. Such choices will be particularly difficult when the different positions are associated with racial, ethnic, and socioeconomic differences within the community. Under these circumstances, ethnic and economic minority groups are especially vulnerable (Mastrofski, 1988; Bayley, 1988; Greene, 1989; Williams & Murphy, 1990; Skogan, 1990). With reference to such circumstances, Skogan suggests, "The problem is how to turn consultation into representation, which has the advantage of cloaking the process with symbols of legitimacy. This would be one of the benefits if locally elected representatives to consultative bodies represented the interests of the community in policing" (Skogan, 1990, p. 168).

Some commentators have expressed concern that extending the reach of the police further into the social and cultural life of the community may give the police more power than is desirable in a democratic society (Bayley, 1988; Mastrofski, 1988; Skogan, 1990). Finally, we have been warned that community organizations initiated or sustained by the police may simply become a resource used by the police to develop political support for their own agendas (Bayley, 1988; Klockars, 1988; Manning, 1988).

In most instances, these authors raise these concerns, not in opposition to community policing but as cautious warnings against inflated expectations, implementation efforts that are insufficiently sensitive to the social and economic diversity of urban neighborhoods, and an excessive politicization of the police service. Most of these writers recommend means for guarding against these developments. Sparrow and his colleagues (1990) recognize all of these concerns as legitimate, but insist that they are merely evaded, rather than eliminated, by maintaining the current distance between the police and the community. Instead they recommend that these dangers be confronted directly by accentuating the centrality of democratic values in police management systems (pp. 135-149) and by actively pursuing policies and practices that expand the police agency's openness and accountability to all segments of the community (pp. 150-171).

These concerns are well taken, but perhaps premature. Ironically, if the outreach of the police to the community is merely rhetorical, or if the local communities are unable or unwilling to respond as hoped, neither the disadvantages nor the benefits of community policing are likely to be realized. Thus it is appropriate to consider what the New York experience suggests can be expected in this regard.

The early years of CPOP indicate that when the police actively seek community input, residents, merchants, and organizational representatives are, indeed, willing to identify problems and to provide the police with information and suggestions that are useful in addressing them. Also consistent with the assumptions of community policing is the fact that the things about which the residents and merchants in a neighborhood are genuinely concerned are often different from the problems that have traditionally preoccupied the police. As has been discovered elsewhere, quality-of-life problems are identified more often and pressed with more passion than virtually any of the conventional street crimes, except for neighborhood drug trafficking. Experience in New York also confirms the belief that many residents and community leaders will respond quite positively to outreach efforts by the police.

On the other hand, it is also clear that organizing community resources to focus in a systematic way on problems of crime and disorder and to participate actively in the design and implementation of corrective strategies is a difficult task for the police to perform, and one in which they were not notably successful during the research period. Indeed, the fact that we did not observe any significant conflicts regarding problem identification or strategy development between different groups of residents in a particular beat may be attributable to the rarity of systematic group involvement during the research period. Success in obtaining more systematic community involvement in the problem-solving process was realized more quickly in the more stable, less impoverished areas, and the majority of people who responded to the early overtures of the police appeared to be people who were already involved in neighborhood improvement efforts, including some that involved cooperative action with the police. Eliciting citizen involvement is especially difficult in poor neighborhoods in which drug dealing is flourishing. More often than not, the residents of these neighborhoods have little experience with collective problem solving, are fearful of reprisals from the dealers, and are pessimistic about the ultimate effects of a more active police presence in the neighborhood. These observations have been documented elsewhere, as Skogan's (1990) work shows.

Both the New York experience and the existing literature underscore the difficulties of organizing neighborhoods and focusing their attention on the control of street crime and disorder. The police are neither well-prepared nor well-situated politically to take on a large share of responsibility for such organizing tasks. But they can initiate the problem-solving process on the neighborhood level and actively solicit citizen involvement in that process. General local government can be of assistance by helping the citizenry to organize and obtain training and experience with the problem-solving process.

Once the process is initiated, it is important that it seek to involve public and private resources outside the criminal justice system to reduce reliance on arrest and punishment as problem-solving tactics. More extensive involvement of such resources (a politically challenging objective in itself) will also increase the chances of successful problem solving, while helping to connect the residents of the community to economic and political institutions that directly and profoundly influence the quality of life and the extent of disorder that they experience there. Efforts to affect such institutional change will be important to the eventual effectiveness of community policing, for as Skogan (1990) has said, "Americans are more dependent on large bureaucracies that regulate their health, welfare, education, employment, and retirement. These features of life lead Americans to rely on formal mechanisms for settling disputes, and on formal social-control institutions for protection" (p. 171).

The need to make the police more responsive to the needs of people in neighborhoods, the need to assist those people to solve their problems and exert some control over the quality of their collective life, and the need to grapple with our institutions to rekindle hope among the urban poor are not new needs. Each in its own right is extremely difficult to achieve. Yet they are all so interdependent that achieving success with one requires the simultaneous pursuit of the other two. Effective community policing requires the simultaneous contribution to all three goals. Clearly it is a complex and difficult set of challenges to take on, but only by doing so can the police hope to be part of the solution.

Assessing the Worth of Community Policing

Police departments embarking upon the road to community policing, and the local governments they serve, should think seriously about how they will determine what is accomplished by their efforts. Recognizing the importance and complexity of such an undertaking, the Public Safety Committee of the New York City Council recently held hearings to consider how they might go about it. One of the authors of this work testified at the hearings (McElroy, 1991). Although his suggestions were tied to the specific work under way in New York, they address a number of matters that would be issues in any municipality. They are presented in summary fashion here in the hope that they will prove useful to police administrators, chief executives, and local legislators wherever the community-policing corporate strategy is under consideration.

All of the desired effects of community policing are hypothesized as emanating from effective implementation of the community policing model and the gradual accumulation of experience by the police and the community with each other and with the problem-solving process. This suggests, in turn, that the immediate questions that should form the focus of an assessment effort have to do with the implementation process itself. With reference to the NYPD's model of community policing, there are several fairly specific implementation questions with which the department and the city council should be immediately concerned. These include:

1. The police are expected to engage local residents, merchants, and organizations in a problem-solving process. Is that actually happening in the hundreds of beats that have been formed across the city and in the 75 precincts that make up the department's Patrol Bureau?

2. Where neighborhood people have been contacted by the police, are they participating in a meaningful process of problem identification, analysis, and strategy planning, or simply exchanging general information with the police?

3. The police are actually expected to implement problem-solving strategies involving fairly specific roles for local groups and residents, as well as other roles to be performed by other public and private agencies in the community. Again, the question is, to what extent is this actually happening in the beats and in the precincts that make up the department?

4. The community-policing model expects that these working relationships between police and citizens will continue even into the review phase of what has and has not been accomplished by the problem-solving strategies that have been implemented. Is that actually happening, or is the review of strategies generally ignored by the local police officials?

5. The model assumes that problem-solving strategies, once decided upon, will actually be implemented, although no one is naive enough to expect implementation to be perfect. This leads to the question of whether or not the implementation of specific problem-solving strat-

egies is being monitored at all. If not, why not; if yes, what does the monitoring reveal about obstacles to effective problem solving, and what is it that the police department and or other public agencies ought to be doing to overcome those obstacles?

6. Are the problems, which are the objects of these problem- solving strategies, affected at all by those strategies? In other words, do the problem-solving strategies work; if not, why not; and what can be learned from the experience of strategy implementation, and how can it be corrected? This is a difficult matter, but some form of assessment and review should be going on, and it should be producing some insight at the precinct level as to what works and does not work, why that particular kind of strategy does not work, and what might be done by the police and by other agencies, including general city government, that would improve the likelihood of effectiveness in addressing some problems.

7. Even where specific problem-solving efforts have not been notably productive, effective engagement between the police and the community at that local level is still important. Assessing the extent to which it is happening can be pursued through a series of subquestions, such as: Do residents, merchants, and organizations on the local level see the police as accessible and responsive to their concerns? Do they have some understanding of what the police are doing in relation to the problems and conditions in the community that the residents consider to be pressing concerns? Are they themselves involved in efforts to correct the problems? Do they see local problems of importance to them that are not given adequate attention by the police?

Answers to questions of this sort will indicate how successfully the community policing process has been implemented. If implementation is not successful, there is no reason to expect that the goals of community policing will be realized. When and where it is successfully implemented, it is appropriate to expect change in some of the conventional or traditional indicators of police effectiveness. Thus while the department and the city should monitor these indicators at all times, they should not be expected to show dramatic changes until a sufficient amount of time has passed (three to five years seems appropriate) for significant implementation to have been achieved. At that time, changes should be noted in various indicators.

As time goes by, attention should be focused not only on changes in the volume of crime complaints, arrest statistics, and calls-for-service, but also on changes in the mix of the types complaints, arrests, and calls received from various neighborhoods and precincts in the city. Of course, community policing might actually result in an increase in the number of calls-for-service, if it encourages citizens to have greater trust and confidence that something will come of the call. However, even while the total number of calls might increase, if the problem-solving efforts are having some of the desired effects on a beat level, or a precinct level, the causes of a significant number of calls may change, so that a condition that produced 60 or 70 calls the previous month in one precinct may produce 10 or 12 calls the next month.

Another conventional indicator of some interest is the clearance rate for various types of complaints. Theoretically it is reasonable to expect that as the people in the neighborhood communicate more frequently and intensely with each other and with the police, as they become more attentive to specific problems of crime and disorder, and as they become more actively involved in attempting to implement corrective strategies, they will also become better able to identify people in the community who are likely perpetrators of some of these crimes. They may also become more willing to communicate that information to the police. If all of that happens, then the clearance rates, at least for certain kinds of crimes, could go up. With that hypothesis in mind, looking at clearance rates would be useful.

Other indicators, which are also subject to some ambiguous interpretation, are citizen complaints and corruption complaints. Some people have been resistant to the community-policing style because they believe that the familiarity with the community that it breeds will result in dramatic increases in both civilian and corruption complaints. Vera's research on CPOP found no evidence of an increase in either type of complaint in the precincts studied. Indeed, a counterargument suggests that the more widely police officers become known in the community, and the more trust that is developed between the police and the community, the more likely it is that a corrupt police officer will become known both to the police and to the community, and the more likely his or her corruption will be reported. These are useful indicators to be monitored, but care is needed in drawing inferences from the changes observed, if any.

Eventually this assessment effort should look carefully at correlations, if any, between these conventional outcome measurements and the levels of progress achieved in implementing community policing. The capacity of the community-policing strategy to deliver the benefits it seeks would be attested to if the desired changes in outcome measures are observed in those precincts in which actual implementation of the strategy has been most successful. This would be especially strong evidence if the outcome indicators remain essentially unchanged, or continue to change in undesirable directions in those precincts in which implementation has been least successful.

It is important to emphasize again that this is all likely to take time, if it is going to happen at all. In the early stages of implementation, it is not logical to assume that the outcome indicators mentioned above are going to change radically, or that, if they do change, the change is attributable to community policing. To make that claim, it must first be established that community policing has, in fact, been implemented. That is why the focus of an assessment process should continue to be on the implementation issues. Simultaneously, measurements of these outcome indicators should be taken, but one should not necessarily expect to see appreciable changes occurring in them. At some point in time, after we are satisfied that community policing has been successfully implemented, at least in a critical mass of precincts, we should expect that the changes we had hoped for are observable there.

Community policing offers the hope of producing several internal benefits for a police department, such as increases in productivity, improvements in morale, improved police perceptions and attitudes toward the communities in which they are working, heightened effectiveness in supervision and command, and improved relationships between the police and other city agencies. Ideally, an effort to assess the effects of community policing would be capable of measuring some or all of these internal outcome measures. Obviously they are no easier to measure than some of the external outcome measures that have already been discussed. The perceptions and attitudes of police officers and supervisors toward the communities they are policing are important, in and of themselves, and may be a particularly important indicator of the impact of effective community policing. Clearly, community policing suggests that attitudes of this sort will change for the better as the model is more completely implemented. Vera's research on CPOP confirmed that expectation. For that reason, and because it is generally important in the governance of the city, change in this variable should be monitored regularly.

It seems fitting to conclude by expressing the hope that the current interest in community-oriented policing not reinforce the widespread tendency to see problems of crime and disorder simply as law-enforcement problems. While community policing can help to realize the contribution of the police and the criminal justice system to peace and order, that contribution is clearly not sufficient for realizing the goal. The police can help to contain problems and even to focus attention on their alleviation. But a significant impact on the problems of drugs, violence, and the destruction of property will require a rebirth of hope, especially in the neighborhoods of the poor. Such a collective sense of hope can arise only if some degree of trust exists in our determination to make employment, education, housing, health care, and participation in governance effective at all socioeconomic levels. It is crucial that government be seen as striving to achieve some level of improvement in all of these areas simultaneously. For, if all of our discretionary resources are committed to the criminal justice system, the peace and order that we seek will never be realized.

Appendix A

CPOP: Community Policing in Practice

In 1984, the New York City Police Department was still feeling the after-shocks of the city's fiscal crisis and had not fully recovered from the manpower cuts of the late 1970s. The massive volume of calls-for-service in New York City, numbering some 7.5 million calls annually by 1984, resulted in the vast bulk of the department's patrol force being assigned to emergency response cars on the 911 queue. While this strategy had allowed the police department to maintain a viable response to calls-for-service during the lean years, it did not permit the department to devote resources to dealing with low-level crime and disorderly conditions. As a result, local communities as well as the police department were struggling to devise ways to deal effectively with order-maintenance conditions and improve the quality of life at the neighborhood level.

Against this backdrop, the New York City Police Department implemented a pilot community-policing program in Brooklyn's 72 Precinct in July 1984. Named the Community Patrol Officer Program, or CPOP, the pilot sought to determine the feasibility of permanently assigning police officers to foot patrol in fairly large neighborhood beat areas and requiring them to perform a variety of nontraditional tasks in addition to their normal law enforcement duties. Police officers assigned as Community Patrol Officers, or CPOs, were expected to be full service police officers, and to serve as community resources, helping to organize community groups, attending community meetings, making service referrals, and helping to devise strategies to deal not only with local crime and order-maintenance problems, but also with social needs.

The Community Patrol Officer Program differed in significant ways from traditional patrol deployment strategies. All of the police officers assigned to CPOP were volunteers, which permitted the department to authorize wide flexibility in patrol hours. CPOs were recruited on their agreement to work those hours that permitted them to focus on the problems peculiar to their beat areas and to change those hours on a daily basis if need be. The officers were encouraged to solicit input from the residents and merchants on their beats in setting their patrol priorities rather than being guided solely by crime incidence, and to involve the community in formulating solutions to neighborhood problems where possible.

Of all of the ways in which CPOP differed from conventional patrol, the most notable was that the CPOs were given the responsibility to work on problems over time. Working in a police radio car is analogous to being a paramedic in an ambulance. Just as a paramedic's principal function is to stabilize the patient until he can be delivered to a hospital for appropriate medical treatment, the principal function of a police officer responding to an emergency call is to stabilize the situation, to prevent further harm or violation of the law, to make an arrest or issue a summons, to take a report of a past crime, or to make a referral for some follow-up action. That being done, the police officer must make her or himself available for the next emergency call. The police department is not at all like a hospital, however, and is largely unable to provide follow-up services, except where serious, unsolved crimes require investigation by detectives. CPOP sought to fill this gap by making the CPO available to follow up on community problems and by allowing the officer sufficient time to deal with them effectively.

The pilot CPOP project was judged to be a success, both by department officials and by community representatives. The CPOs demonstrated their ability to perform the wide range of duties assigned to them and expressed much satisfaction with their new role. The residents and merchants of Sunset Park voiced overwhelming support of the program, and other communities began to lobby for its implementation in their areas.

Based on these early results, the department began a careful expansion of the program in January 1985, when CPOP was implemented in six additional precincts. Usually, a precinct CPOP unit requires nine police officers assigned to individual beats and one assigned as unit coordinator, a supervisory sergeant, and a police administrative aide. Because CPOP represented a substantial investment of personnel, the pace of program expansion was constrained somewhat by the department's authority to recruit and hire new police officers. As budgetary increases allowed the hiring of new officers, new CPOP units were created until finally, in September 1988, CPOP had been instituted in each of New York City's 75 patrol precincts. Today, the program involves over 800 police officers (including trained alternates), 75 sergeants, and 75 administrative aides. Fortunately, the moderate pace of expansion helped preserve the pilot program design as more personnel were assigned.

This appendix presents brief accounts of effective problem-solving work by CPOs attempting to address crime or order-maintenance problems arising on their beats. Each account describes an undertaking that effectively embodies one of the program's stated goals or objectives. It is hoped that these illustrations will be useful in the CPOP training programs and to community groups anxious to understand what can be expected of their police force, operating in this mode.

These stories are not evidence that the design and implementation of the CPO program are without shortcomings. Nor are they intended to suggest that the structure and operations of CPOP are a model for all police agencies working to enact the principles of community and problem-solving policing. They do show, however, that a structure that frees a police officer to focus consistent attention on neighborhood problems and provides him or her with the tools to do so can produce genuine benefits for both the community and the department.

Mission of the Community Patrol Officer Program

The mission of the New York City Police Department Community Patrol Officer Program is to enhance the quality of life in the many neighborhoods that make up the City of New York.

Specifically, the primary objectives of the Community Patrol Officer Program are:

- To prevent and control conduct threatening to life and property, particularly that which affects neighborhoods as a whole
- To create and maintain a feeling of security in the community by reducing disorder and the fear of crime in neighborhoods
- To identify and address community problems that are potentially serious law enforcement or governmental problems

In order to achieve these objectives, the Community Patrol Officer Program is committed to:

- Involving the community in identifying its own public safety concerns and setting the department's priorities for addressing those concerns
- Increasing community participation in policing activities and community-based public safety programs
- Exchanging information with the community on a regular basis
- Using a problem-solving approach to developing strategies for police operations that respond to specific community problems, including nontraditional tactics and strategies
- Coordinating strategies for addressing communities' problems with other police personnel, other government agencies, and private organizations.
- Assigning Community Patrol Officers to permanent neighborhood beats.

Increasing Community Participation in Policing Activities and Community-Based Public Safety Programs

In May 1986, Police Officer Vincent Esposito joined the Community Patrol Officer Program in the 72 Precinct. Officer Esposito had been a member of the Transit Police, but had changed to the NYPD with the hope of being able to work more directly with people in communities. When the opportunity to join CPOP arose, he volunteered. One of the locations on Officer Esposito's beat was a neighborhood playground on 5th Avenue between 49th and 50th Streets in the Sunset Park section of Brooklyn. Typical of many of the vest-pocket parks in New York City, there are handball courts, basketball courts, a sandbox, swings and seesaws for small children, and benches to lure the senior citizens to come in and sit in the sun. At least, that was the intention. What Vinny found when he began patrolling the area was that there were no children in the park and no seniors sunning themselves. Instead the park was overrun with drug users and dealers.

Officer Esposito could, and did, observe these conditions, but he also heard about them from the residents of this neighborhood. He was repeatedly told that they had been unable to use the park for several years and that, although police officers in radio cars frequently caused the loiterers to disappear, they would return as soon as the police left the scene.

CPO Esposito began to spend as much time as possible in the vicinity of the park. He disbursed the loiterers; when he observed drug transactions, he made arrests. However, he knew that these tactics were not alleviating the problem. Officer Esposito's beat area was fairly large, and he had other community problems to deal with in other areas. This limited the amount of time he could spend at the park. Even more troublesome was the fact that every time he made an arrest he effectively removed himself from the area (and from the rest of his beat) for the balance of his tour, while he processed the defendant in the criminal justice system. When he was gone, the park reverted to the junkies.

Officer Esposito decided to take a different approach to dealing with the problem. He held meetings of the tenants in the apartment buildings that overlooked the park. At these meetings he told the residents he needed their help in dealing with the problems in the park. Through these meetings he recruited a number of homebound residents who agreed to watch the drug dealing from their windows and observe where the dealers hid their drug stashes. He instructed them to then call the CPOP office and leave anonymous messages telling him where the stashes were located. When such messages came in, the officer or police administrative aide receiving them would relay the information to Officer Esposito. He would then go to the park and confiscate the stash, taking it to the precinct and vouchering it as found property. This tactic only took Officer Esposito off patrol for 15 or 20 minutes.

The community cooperated with Officer Esposito, and on some days he went to the park and confiscated drug stashes as many as five or six times. In effect, he made it economically unbearable for the dealers to continue to use the park as their base of operations and placed some in the uncomfortable position of having to explain to their suppliers why they lost the drugs without being arrested. Some dealers began to hold their stashes on their person, and when this information was relayed to CPO Esposito, he arrested them. Within one month of initiating these tactics, the drug dealers left the park.

To Officer Esposito, the victory belonged to the residents of the community. He believes that the drug dealers knew that it was the community residents who were responsible for providing the information to the police that led to the seizures, and faced with this organized resistance to their activities, they chose to leave the area.

Today, more than 2 years after the community reclaimed their park, children play on the swings, teens use the basketball and handball courts, and seniors sun themselves. There are still drugs in the Sunset Park area, but not in that playground.

Involving the Community in Identifying Its Own Public Safety Concerns and Setting the Department's Priorities for Addressing These Concerns

A small apartment building, 239 Elizabeth Street is situated in the Little Italy section of Lower Manhattan. This area is primarily residential, with an ethnic mix of Italian and Spanish people. The economic status of most residents ranges from lower to middle income. This location had a long history of disputes between the tenants and the landlord, and police officers from the 5 Precinct had responded to 911 calls at the building at all hours. However, the real sources of these disputes were never clear; most often, incidents would end with referral of the complainants to the summons part of the lower court, for private prosecution.

CPO DeFazio first became interested in the problems at 239 Elizabeth Street in 1986, when an elderly woman, a tenant in the building, was standing outside as the officer patrolled the area. This woman approached the CPO to explain that she and other tenants were being harassed by the landlord, who lived on the first floor. The woman went on to explain that the landlord owned four pitt bull terriers, which he had stationed in the lobby of the building. Two of the dogs were always in the lobby, while the other two were held in cages in the back. The landlord had rigged the cages so that all he had to do was push a button to release the cage door and the dogs could be summoned. Late at night, the dogs would run up and down the hallways, barking and scratching on people's doors; on occasion, she said, the landlord rubbed dog feces on the tenants' doors. He had turned their electricity off, with the result that people were afraid to leave their apartments or ask for help from the police, fearing further retaliation by the landlord. This woman believed that these tactics were used to terrorize tenants whom the landlord wanted to move out, since he could raise the rent 10% when a new tenant moved in.

CPO DeFazio went to the building to verify the stories. He also wanted to speak with the landlord, to get his version; but when the officer went to the landlord's apartment to ask if there were any problems in the buildings, the door was slammed in his face. CPO DeFazio then went from door to door in the building and got the names and phone numbers of all the tenants. He felt that, if he could get all of the tenants together at a meeting, they could discuss the problems they were having with the landlord and perhaps work together to solve them. At first many of the tenants were unwilling to talk, fearing the landlord would find out, get angry, and harass them further.

However, with the officer's continued persistence and his patrol of the building, the tenants began to see that he was at least sincere in wanting to help them.

In due course, a tenants association was formed and CPO DeFazio encouraged the residents to make complaints against the landlord by calling the 5 Precinct station house. Over a short period of time, approximately 100 calls were received, which helped to document the problems in the building. CPO DeFazio got in touch with the Department of Housing Preservation and Development, which referred him to the chief prosecutor for the State Division of Housing and Commercial Renewal (DHCR). He also contacted the ASPCA, hoping that they could do something about the pitt bulls; the ASPCA, however, was unable to remove the dogs without documentation of violations.

CPO DeFazio began issuing summonses to the landlord for not having the dogs on a leash, for excessive noise, and other violations. He then learned that one of these pitt bulls had attacked a child in a nearby park and that an off-duty police officer had also been bitten. He referred this information, along with the information he had received from the tenants, to the ASPCA. He also referred the people hurt by the dogs to the Summons Part at the Manhattan Criminal Court. The criminal court judge ordered that the pitt bulls be removed from the building and secured in a holding pen until it could be determined whether the dogs were so dangerous that they should be put to sleep. (Two of the pitt bulls were eventually put to sleep and the other two were sent to a kennel.)

During the time that CPO DeFazio worked on getting the dogs removed from the building, the DHCR prosecutor had been filing lawsuits against the landlord for numerous building violations and for tax evasion. The prosecutor asked CPO DeFazio to serve the landlord with the summonses he had been able to obtain from the court, but the CPO's attempts to serve the landlord proved futile. The landlord refused to answer the door or to leave his apartment. Officer DeFazio also stood outside the building for hours on several days, waiting for the landlord to leave. He had the tenants watching for the landlord when he could not be there and asked that they contact him the minute anyone saw the landlord in the area. He also arranged with the tenants of another building owned by this landlord to contact him if any of them saw the landlord. Eventually the summonses, which covered both the landlord's buildings, were served. According to a *New York Post* article on the April 14, 1988, a total of 130 violations were filed against this particular landlord.

Several months later, the landlord had been found to owe so much in back taxes for these buildings that 239 Elizabeth Street was turned over to the city. Although the landlord was allowed to remain in the building, the president of the tenants' association was appointed by Housing Preservation and Development to serve as their agent in collecting the rent and maintaining the conditions in the building. Four months after the city gained possession of this building, the problems seemed to have been alleviated. CPO DeFazio visited the building periodically and found it clean and in good order. There were no complaints from the tenants who had originally complained about the problem. However, one Saturday afternoon CPO DeFazio received a call from two tenants who lived in the apartment above that of the previous landlord. They were having repair work done on their floor and because some of the floorboards were missing, could hear the landlord and his wife discussing a plan to blow the building up. Apparently, he had set up acetylene gas tanks with which to set the building on fire and kill everyone in the building, with the exception of a few tenants who had testified on his behalf in court.

Although CPO DeFazio felt the information from the tenants could very well be valid, he could do nothing without additional evidence. He advised tenants to be alert to the possible threat and, if they smelled gas, to get out of the building and call fire and police departments immediately. After speaking with the tenants, CPO DeFazio telephoned the landlord. He did not discuss the reported threat and said that he was calling to see if there had been any further problems in the building; he hoped thereby to test the validity of the threats he had heard about. The landlord's wife told Officer DeFazio that he was not to call them at all anymore and that if he did, they would register a harassment complaint against him.

The next week, when CPO DeFazio returned to work, he found a message to contact the tenants who had reported the landlord's arson plan to him previously. The message indicated that the officer should not come around the area or into the building because they had information, a taped conversation between the landlord and his wife, that the landlord was going to blow DeFazio's brains out. The taped conversation between the landlord and his wife indicated that they felt that DeFazio was up to something because he had telephoned them the week before. The landlord could be heard saying that if DeFazio came into the building he would shoot him. Also on the tape was a clicking sound, which CPO DeFazio believed to be the noise made by pulling the slide on a .45 automatic. At another point on the tape, during a fight between the landlord and his wife, the wife could be heard saying not to point that gun at her.

The taped conversation was taken to the 5 Precinct Detectives Unit to see what could be done. CPO DeFazio and one of the detectives went to the Manhattan District Attorney's office and obtained a search warrant for the .45 automatic weapon. The judge who issued the warrant requested to speak with CPO DeFazio and have him explain how he knew about the .45. CPO DeFazio convinced the judge that he was confident that the sound he heard on the tape was from a .45 automatic slide, and that he felt that the lives of the tenants, and perhaps others, were in jeopardy.

After obtaining the warrant, CPO DeFazio and the detective returned to the station house and met with the precinct commanding officer. The captain telephoned Emergency Service Division and, due to the possibility of there being gas in the apartment, the bomb squad was also contacted. The search ultimately involved as many as 50 police personnel, including the patrol and detective borough commanders; the commander of Emergency Services Unit 8; a detective from Terrorist Task Force; an agent from Federal Alcohol, Tobacco, and Firearms; the assistant district attorney, CPO DeFazio; and several other precinct personnel.

The raid was conducted at 12:30 p.m. The Emergency Service Unit had two unmarked cars parked outside the building, and the entire building was surrounded. Members of the EMS entered the building and knocked on the landlord's door. The landlord refused to open the door. EMS officers then attempted to break down the door, but were unsuccessful because the landlord had welded about five inches of steel to the door. Eventually, the officers were able to get inside. Both the landlord and his wife were arrested. The loaded .45 automatic was found under a towel by the television set. Old engine parts as well as garbage and newspapers were lying around the apartment. Bins of guns and ammunition were found in the apartment, but since the original warrant was issued only for the .45 automatic, the police had to return to court to obtain a warrant for additional evidence.

Ultimately 49 handguns, 13 rifles, 14 boxes of ammunition, and 48 assorted swords and knives were recovered from this apartment. The landlord had also set up a bunkerlike barricade in his basement, surrounded by 50 bags of cement. According to a *Post* article, the landlord's collection included Civil War-era muskets, automatic pistols, and some antique swords. It was later learned that seven or eight of the guns had hits on them. In fact, one of the guns may have been used to kill a drug enforcement officer in Florida, a possibility that is still being investigated.

Sometime after the arrest, CPO DeFazio indicated that the landlord was still in jail awaiting trial. The tenants at 239 Elizabeth Street can now live in peace. However, CPO DeFazio commented that the elderly woman who had first brought the problem to the officer's attention was no longer living in the building. The woman had moved before the efforts of CPO DeFazio and the tenants were complete.

Using a Problem-Solving Approach to Developing Strategies for Police Operations That Respond to Specific Community Problems, Including Nontraditional Tactics and Strategies

The 79 Precinct, which covers the Bedford-Stuyvesant section of Brooklyn, is burdened by a large number of abandoned apartment houses and brownstones. Some of these abandoned buildings are privately owned, some have been seized by the city. The abandoned housing stock has become the source of a lot of community problems, including crime. The level of crime in the precinct, which has been high, has increased over the past few years due to the influx of drugs. The precinct residents are primarily black, middle- to lower-income working people. Although some higher-income gentrification is taking place on the outlying boundaries of the precinct, the area is generally depressed economically and without a vital commercial sector.

The precinct CPOP unit found the abandoned buildings to be a recurrent theme in the crime and other complaints heard from residents throughout the area. Junkies used the buildings, of course; but even when empty, the buildings were extremely dangerous for playing children. In response to these complaints, CPO Mazzone, Coordinator of the 79 CPOP unit, resolved to get the buildings sealed. Because many of the buildings also were adjacent to garbage-strewn lots, he wanted to get the lots cleaned too. CPO Mazzone developed programs that addressed both these conditions.

Operation Seal-Up aims to close off all access to abandoned buildings in the area. The unit's CPOs identify abandoned buildings on their beats and report them, with city lot number and location number, to CPO Mazzone. Officer Mazzone records the information in proper form, including whether the building is owned privately or city-owned, for action by the local Community Planning Board. If squatters are found in city-owned buildings, the Community Board contacts the buildings inspector and begins proceedings to have the squatters evicted. Once a building is cleared, the next step is to get it properly sealed. CPO Mazzone has discovered that, unless the proper materials are used (cinder blocks or concrete rather than tin), the buildings are easily broken into, and the problems start all over again.

If a building brought to their attention by CPOP is not owned by the city, the Community Board attempts to contact the private owner. For example, if the building is creating a health hazard because there is so much garbage inside, or if junkies tend to hang out inside, the Community Board will request that the landlord work with them (e.g., as complainant) to alleviate the condition or to seal the building. If the landlord is reluctant to become involved, the Community Board may take steps to have the improvements made at the location, or to have the building sealed, and then charge the landlord for services performed by the city.

Often these abandoned buildings are infested with drug dealers, who conduct their operations out of individual apartments. CPOP refers such locations to the Brooklyn North Narcotics Unit, through intelligence reports, until arrests are made. If the problem is limited to drug use and dealing in plain sight, the CPOs will make arrests themselves. CPO Mazzone keeps careful records of when buildings were referred either to Narcotics or to the Community Board, so that he can respond to residents who call about abandoned buildings in their neighborhoods.

In addition to sealing abandoned buildings, the CPOP unit has effectively organized area residents to clean their blocks. CPO Mazzone contacted Community Board #3 to find out what resources were available for block beautification and was referred to We Care About New York, an organization funded by private donations to supply equipment for block cleanups. As a general rule, CPO Mazzone contacts the presidents of the various block associations to see if they would like to participate in a block cleanup and a date is chosen for the effort. A few days before the cleanup, garbage bags are given to block residents so that they can remove the garbage from their homes. Fliers are distributed announcing the cleanup and No Parking signs are posted on the block. The CPOP officers close off the street and announce over a loudspeaker that the block is having a cleanup. The CPOP officers also go door to door to encourage residents to get involved.

Residents are given gloves and brooms, supplied by We Care About New York, and sweep the debris from abandoned lots into the street. Once all of the garbage is cleared, the Sanitation Department workers cart it away and clean the block with the street flusher. Operation Clean-Up has done more for the precinct's neighborhoods than cleaning the streets: Cakes and other goodies now routinely appear at these events (the Precinct supplies juice and soda), and all participants receive T-shirts with "We Care About New York" printed on them.

Between February and October 1988, 76 abandoned buildings were referred to the Community Board, properly entered in the queue for seal-up, and are getting the attention this process requires. (About 6 months are required to get a building sealed after the CPO first reports it.) More than 400 precinct residents have participated in Operation Clean-Up. Both programs have generated significant community support for a closer working relationship with the precinct. Block association presidents and precinct residents now call CPOP to provide specific information about abandoned buildings and conditions in them that deserve police attention.

Increasing Community Participation in Policing Activities and Community-Based Public Safety Programs

On April 16, 1987, Community Patrol Officer Michael Lamm of the 44 Precinct CPOP unit received a phone call from a representative of the tenant's association at 1200 Woodycrest Avenue, a large, city-owned building located in his beat area. The resident informed Officer Lamm of 10 separate drug-dealing locations in the apartment building, specifically naming dealers and the apartments in which they sold drugs. The informant complained that the building was inundated with dealers and purchasers who occupied apartments and loitered in the halls, making deals. The building's residents were frightened and frustrated, as were other members of the community who later asserted that the problem had existed for three years prior to being brought to the attention of the police department.

Officer Lamm's initial move was to call a meeting with the tenants' association. There was a good turnout of the residents, and Officer Lamm initiated a discussion in which the conditions in the building were described clearly. He insisted that no specific details be given or accusations be made, however, because some of the building's drug dealers were attending the meeting in order to observe and intimidate others, and to acquire information for themselves. The meeting showed clearly that most of the building's residents shared a common attitude toward the problem, but also had simplistic expectations about the solution. From their perspective it seemed obvious that, because drug dealing is illegal, it is the responsibility of the police department to eliminate it. Their demand was clear; they wanted the police to clean up the building by more frequent patrolling and evictions or arrests of the drug dealers.

Officer Lamm believed it essential that he convince the tenants that they could not wait passively for the problem to be solved for them, but had to become active participants in the solution. He argued that the police could not possibly devote to one building as much time and attention as these tenants were requesting. He explained that the building's residents needed to act not only as reporters of the problem, but also to take some responsibility for eliminating it. Officer Lamm suggested the formation of a tenant's patrol of the building to supplement police activity, and promised his support of the patrol. The tenants came around; they formed their own patrol unit.

Within 2 weeks the tenants' association had been transformed from a rather limited and fragmented organization to a far more cohesive and powerful group. The association established an around-the-clock patrol of the building that monitored and recorded the presence of every person who entered it. The tenants gave this information to Officer Lamm, who conducted vertical patrols of the building five or six times a day, every day. During this period, Officer Lamm regularly informed Bronx Narcotics and the Precinct's Street Narcotics Enforcement Unit (SNEU) about the situation. In addition, he met with representatives the Department of Housing Preservation and Development (which managed the building for the city), the local city councilman, representatives of the Bureau of Family Services, and implementers of the Human Resources Agency's Multi-Family Development Program, which had targeted 1200 Woodycrest as a location greatly needing help. These different resources collaborated in providing information to the tenants, worked on renovating apartments, and assisted in responsibly choosing future tenants in order to ensure that the problem would not simply begin again with new faces when the present dealers were evicted.

After a few weeks, the combined effort of CPO Lamm and the tenants' patrol started to pay off, and the building's hallways began to clear. After a month the hallways were empty. At this point, Officer Lamm, working with the building manager, the superintendent, and the information from the tenants' patrol, began to enforce the eviction notices for which he had helped to gather evidence and to collar people for illegal occupancy of apartments or illegal possession of weapons or drugs. CPO Lamm also spoke with Judge Trussell of the Bronx Housing Court, who provided him with signs in both English and Spanish that forbade loitering and warned of the consequences of so doing. With warnings like these available to the public, Officer Lamm was then allowed to levy misdemeanor charges, which carry heavier penalties then a mere summons, on anyone caught loitering. To prevent the return of evicted squatters, Officer Lamm turned to the HPD and requested that they seal the windows and put proper locks on the doors of several of the empty apartments. This kept dealers away and, after six months, the tenants' association decided that the situation had improved to the point where they could end their patrol.

For CPO Lamm, however, the problem was not over, for the dealers had moved their transactions to the corner of Anderson Avenue and 167th Street, an intersection within his beat. He again committed himself to patrolling the area frequently, giving summonses for disorderly conduct to those who behaved suspiciously and refused to follow his directions to clear the corner. Lamm had won solid support from the residents of the community, and persisted in paying active attention to the dealers until they finally left the neighborhood altogether. Drug sales in the location have completely ended. The tenants at 1200 Woodycrest still experience occasional problems, but the frequency has been reduced considerably.

Officer Lamm faced many difficult issues in solving the drug problem of this area. He encountered bureaucratic difficulties in his relationship with some city agencies and had to proceed carefully, so as not to misuse the laws regarding the different treatment of squatters and trespassers. He had to gather information from community residents intimidated by the power of the drug dealers, and he devoted a great deal of time and energy to a persistent and dedicated attack on the problem. By returning to 1200 Woodycrest time and again, Officer Lamm gained the respect of the building's residents and the law-abiding members of the community, who then joined his effort to combat the problem. By convincing the tenants of 1200 Woodycrest that their responsible participation was an essential ingredient in the

solution of this neighborhood problem, Officer Lamm established a prece-
dent that may inspire community residents to combat similar situations
should they arise in the future. And by devoting himself so thoroughly to
the problem, CPO Lamm has won the trust and friendship of the residents
of the 9th beat of the 44 Precinct.

To Create and
Maintain a Feeling
of Security in the
Community
by Reducing
Disorder and the
Fear of Crime in
Neighborhoods

Police Officer Ronald MacGregor was frequently assigned to Sector Boy
of the 26 Precinct and often responded to calls for assistance in a single-
room-occupancy hotel on West 112th Street. His recollections of the location
are that it was a filthy place, infested with rats, roaches, and lice. Like many
SRO hotels, its residents were mainly persons holding marginal jobs, the
elderly and mentally handicapped, drug addicts and former prostitutes,
many of whom were AIDS victims. Most often, when he responded to the
location, he was unable to find out who had requested the police. It seemed
to him, and to the officers who responded with him, that the residents of the
building were afraid to be seen talking to the police, although from the
frequency of calls it must have provided them with some relief just having
the police show up.

In April 1988, the Community Patrol Officer Program was introduced
into the 26 Precinct and CPO MacGregor was assigned to the beat area that
covered 112th Street. The general area houses a racially mixed, predomi-
nately upper-middle-class population, and the Columbia University student
dormitories are close by. As the Community Patrol Officer for this beat,
Officer MacGregor felt that the SRO hotel was a source of many of the
quality-of-life problems in the area and decided that additional information
was needed if such problems were to be alleviated. In order to get to know
the tenants of the hotel, Officer MacGregor patrolled the building on a
regular basis while on foot patrol. He went into the building and spoke to
many of the occupants. Initially, the residents, who had been told by the
landlord that the police could not be trusted, were unwilling to speak with
him. However, as time passed, they started to open up and told him about
the problems they had encountered.

The living conditions inside the building were extremely bad. Officer
MacGregor contracted lice twice from patrolling inside. He was told that the
landlord was harassing the tenants, throwing firecrackers in their rooms,
scaring them and withholding their mail, and that there were drug dealers
in the building who were also intimidating the tenants.

A lot of crime was going on, both inside and in the areas surrounding
the building. Officer MacGregor was told about a number of rapes in the
building, almost all of which had gone unreported. Women were afraid to
leave their apartments, as were the many elderly people in the building.
One of the tenants, a former prostitute who had hepatitis B, reported that
she was being pressured to give sexual favors to men in the building in
exchange for protection. He heard about a man, a former prostitute and now
an AIDS victim, who had raped several women in the building; only one of
the rapes had been reported. (Another CPO had arrested the rapist, who
was later released from jail and moved back into the building.)

The first thing that CPO MacGregor did was to get in touch with the
landlord and explain to him that complaints of harassment had been made

against him. The officer made a point of going to the building when the mail was dropped off and told the desk clerk that federal charges could be brought against him if the mail was not delivered. Eventually the landlord began to cooperate with CPO MacGregor, and the internal telephone system in the building, which was being used by the drug dealers to conduct business, was disconnected. In addition, Officer MacGregor contacted the phone company and had the phone in the lobby, which was also being used by the drug dealers to conduct their business, altered so that no incoming calls could be received.

In order to curtail some of the drug activity, the officer gave summonses to the dealers who had double-parked their vehicles outside the building. In addition to summonsing the drug dealers, Officer MacGregor met with tenants and formed what they call an "intelligence network." This enabled the tenants to set up a self-monitoring system in which several people were designated as floor leaders. They were responsible for recording all information that other tenants would give to them, anonymously, about unusual and suspicious activity in the building. The floor leaders then passed this information on to CPO MacGregor when he came to the building. This system became necessary because most of the tenants did not own telephones and could not relay such information directly to the officer. Officer MacGregor also escorted the elderly tenants to the supermarket to lessen the possibilities of being victimized. He also felt that there was a need to teach some of the tenants how to take care of themselves to reduce the possibilities of contracting the diseases that were fairly common in the building. To do this, he held a class on personal hygiene, based on the training he had received in the Marine Corps.

CPO MacGregor also got in touch with several organizations that could address the various needs of the tenants. Through his contact with a nurse at St. Luke's Hospital, he was able to refer several mentally handicapped people to their Psychological Services Emergency Room. Because of his experience in the 26 Precinct, he was aware of several social welfare resources in the area. He contacted the Social Services Program at St. John The Divine Church, which provided several residents with food and clothing; other, needier tenants were referred to the Broadway Presbyterian Church food line as well. Officer MacGregor also referred tenants to the Living World Christ Center for clothes, drug rehabilitation, and marriage counseling. The officer also contacted the Department of Health, hoping they would be able to do something.

The concerted efforts of Officer MacGregor and the help that he received from residents themselves have worked some dramatic changes in the building. For example, building residents were aware of eight alleged attacks on women in June 1988, although almost all of them went unreported. In July, no incidents of this kind were known to the CPO or his network. Furthermore, the landlord, who was responsible for creating some of the problems in the building, has become involved in the attempts to improve conditions. Drug activity has decreased due to the efforts of Officer MacGregor, and the tenants now know their neighbors and feel a sense of self-determination and control over what happens in the building. Although the problems in the building have not entirely disappeared, Officer MacGregor continues to work with the tenants to alleviate them. The proper city agencies have been notified about problems they need to address at the hotel, and Officer MacGregor intends to continue his daily patrols until the horrendous conditions that allowed the building to become so hazardous have been corrected.

Coordinating Strategies for Addressing Communities' Problems With Other Police Personnel, Other Government Agencies, and Private Organizations

The area around East 158th Street and Courtland Avenue consists primarily of tenement houses, interspersed with abandoned buildings and burned-out structures. Nearby are the Jackson and Melrose public housing projects, which extend from East 158th Street to East 153rd Street. No discernible industrial or commercial trade goes on in the area, although a public grammar school is nearby, on East 157th Street. This area, like others in the South Bronx, is physically deteriorated, overrun with drug dealers and junkies, and has experienced an increase in drug-related crime over the past few years. The area is part of CPO Beat Area 9 in the 40 Precinct and is patrolled by CPO Bob Addolorato.

In July 1987, CPO Addolorato, known as Officer Bob to the residents on his beat, began patrolling the area of East 158th and Courtland Avenue on a daily basis because of the heavy incidence of drug trafficking at that location. CPO Addolorato knew about this area before he joined CPOP; he had worked the area in a sector car while on regular motor patrol. He believed that this location was the focal point of the delivery and distribution of large quantities of heroin, which were cut and prepared for street sale. However, his knowledge regarding the key actors and the dynamics of the overall operation was limited.

In order to obtain additional information CPO Addolorato, along with other members of the CPOP unit, began making surreptitious observations of the area at various times during the day and night. This allowed the officers to observe the dealers and the buyers without being detected. Specific groups of individuals, some who served as steerers and lookouts, and others who were responsible for delivering and distributing the heroin, were identified. Based on these observations, CPO Addolorato and other CPOs were able to apprehend and arrest both the dealers and the buyers. While making these arrests, the CPOs began issuing disorderly conduct summonses to individuals who failed to obey to the officers' orders to disperse. One of these arrested was wanted by the 40 Precinct Detective Unit in connection with a recent homicide.

As a result of his arrest and summons activity, CPO Addolorato became familiar with the regulars on the block and was able to share information with other patrol officers and units of the 40 Precinct. Residents whom CPO Addolorato had come to recognize from patrolling the area on a regular basis, but who seemed to be somewhat apprehensive about talking with him, began to introduce themselves to the officer. After seeing the police efforts to address this long-term condition, they began providing CPO Addolorato with solid information about persons involved in the drug trade.

The assistant district manager of the local Community Planning Board also became a source of information on the problem, as did representatives from the South Bronx Council of Churches. Several meetings were held with these groups, in which the area around East 158th Street and Courtland Avenue was identified as a major problem and concern of community residents. At these meetings CPO Addolorato emphasized the need for the area residents to work together with the police and for them to become organized as a group. At one meeting a community resident approached CPO Addolorato about organizing a block association. With the help of CPO Addolorato, a block association was formed about a month later, and the residents became involved in cleaning up a few of the garbage-strewn lots in the area. With the help of the Department of General Services, the lots were then fenced.

CPO Addolorato contacted Bronx Narcotics and supplied them with specific information about dealers and locations. Within a couple of weeks of the initial contact with Bronx Narcotics, the CPOP Unit, other 40 Precinct personnel, and Narcotics coordinated efforts to conduct a sweep of this location. The sweep was successful, resulting in 20 felony, 5 misdemeanor, and 42 violation arrests. One of those apprehended was in possession of $10,000 worth of heroin at the time of arrest. This particular arrest led the CPO to believe that the operation was much larger than he had originally suspected and was being run by a Cuban family consisting of several brothers who had been using abandoned apartments at the location to conduct their business.

CPO Addolorato continued to gather information and maintained steady contact with Bronx Narcotics. As a result, two officers from the 40 Precinct Street Conditions Unit were assigned permanently to the area, resulting in a series of additional arrests for possession of narcotics and weapons. Many of the arrests made at the locations targeted by CPO Addolorato led to the seizure of substantial quantities of heroin and currency. Many involved the arrest of illegal aliens. As a result, CPO Addolorato contacted the Federal Drug Enforcement Agency to request additional assistance. This resulted in the Drug Enforcement Agency (DEA) making arrests of some of the key dealers, and in other dealers moving out of the area. In a further attempt to stem drug trafficking in the area, CPO Addolorato contacted the city's Department of Housing Preservation and Development, which ultimately responded by vacating and sealing one of the most problem-prone buildings in the area.

In discussing the drug problem in his beat area, CPO Addolorato credits the information provided by community residents and leaders and the consistent support of both city and federal law-enforcement personnel with what has been accomplished to date. And while there are still drugs in 40 Precinct, community residents and the 40 CPOP Unit have learned that something can be done about them.

To Identify and Address Community Problems That Are Potentially Serious Law Enforcement or Governmental Problems

In East Brooklyn, 108 Siegal Street had been named by the city's Department of Housing Preservation and Development (HPD) as one of the 10 ten worst drug locations in New York. The building had also been targeted as a major community problem by the East Brooklyn Council of Churches. In 1986 alone, the 90 Precinct's Street Narcotics Enforcement Unit (SNEU) made 600 arrests at the location, working at the building one hour a day, one day a week. Originally, the primary drug was heroin, a brand called "homicide." Later both heroin and crack were being sold. The location was extremely active and often so many addicts were waiting to buy drugs that they formed a line outside the building. Drugs were not the only problem in the building; the CPOP unit was faced with robberies, burglaries, criminal mischief, and shootings there as well. All of this activity appeared to result from the overriding problem of drugs. The building itself was falling apart, and many of the apartments were vacant. To the neighborhood, it seemed that no one cared about the problems, which had existed for close to 10 years.

The CPOP unit was implemented in the 90 Precinct in March 1987. By January 1, 1988, the unit had an intensive effort under way to deal with the drug problem at 108 Siegal Street. As the building is city-owned, CPOP Unit Supervisor Sergeant Greenwood contacted HPD, which manages the building. Angelo Guzman, an area director for HPD, was assigned to work on the problem with the CPOP unit.

The people who lived in the building were potentially a valuable source of information, but they were clearly afraid to talk to the police. One of the first things the CPOP unit did was to hold a meeting with the tenants and Mr. Guzman. The CPOs distributed fliers announcing the meeting, which was held in the precinct station house to soothe tenants' fears. About 15 tenants, more than half of the building's residents, attended. The goal was to form a tenants' association that would work closely with CPOP. The tenants spent the first hour of the meeting, Sergeant Greenwood recalls, venting their anger and complaints, but in due course they were ready to tell the police what they knew. Many had very specific information about the dealers, the suppliers, and the buyers, having spent a lot of their time watching the activity. Sergeant Greenwood did not let anyone detail their information at the meeting, in case some of the dealers were present. He told them to call the CPOP unit and talk to him or another CPO, or to leave a message on the unit's answering machine, either giving their name or remaining anonymous.

A crucial next step in attacking the building was enforcing the Criminal Trespass Program. Angelo Guzman signed a statement on behalf of HPD that allowed the CPOs to act as complainants against building trespassers. With this power the CPOs could conduct vertical patrols to clear out the building. The steerers and spotters—the people who control the buyers and watch for the cops—are important people in this sort of drug operation. They are also extremely difficult to arrest, as they are never in possession of anything illegal. The Criminal Trespass Program gave the officers a way to arrest them.

At 108 Siegal, the CPOP sergeant was always present during vertical patrols. He and a few other CPOs would go from the roof to the basement, asking the people found in the hallways why they were in the building. Often people claimed to be visiting a friend. The CPO would then ask for a name and an apartment number and would accompany the person to the apartment to verify the story. Other times the trespassers admitted to being in the building to buy drugs.

On one of these patrols two women were arrested. One was in possession of 50 glassine envelopes containing drugs, and the other had twice that number. This arrest turned out to be a major breaking point, because the woman in possession of the 100 glassines wanted to help herself by helping the police. She told them the name of one of the guys running the drug operation, who went by the street name "Cracko." The sergeant took the woman with him to Manhattan Court (they had to go to Manhattan because it was midnight and the courts in Brooklyn were closed). There they were given a No Knock Warrant. At 1:00 a.m. the sergeant, the precinct's commanding officer, the CPOP unit, and 10 Emergency Services personnel raided the building. During the raid they got several of the main dealers, including Cracko, and a large quantity of drugs. The early morning raid was a big step, but it did not end the drug activity entirely.

Throughout the time the CPOP unit was working on the drug problem at 108 Siegal Street, they were sending complaint reports and intelligence reports to the Brooklyn North Narcotics Unit. Information was also referred to the precinct's anti-crime unit. This information led to additional arrests by these units as well as by CPOP and the precinct SNEU.

Shortly after the raid, the commissioner of Housing Preservation and Development came to see the building, and major renovation work began. HPD agreed to work on the building only if CPOP would continue to patrol the location. The presence of CPOP was needed both for the safety of the construction workers and to keep new fixtures from getting stolen. Sergeant Greenwood viewed the presence of the HPD renovators as psychologically helpful, providing residents with evidence that conditions were changing. The work crews also seemed to make the drug dealers uncomfortable. The CPOs made frequent visits to the building for HPD. They also continued to conduct vertical patrols.

Soon the drug trade was confined to the evening hours, and, after several months of continued attention from CPOP and HPD, the dealers moved out entirely. The building is now virtually drug-free. Sergeant Greenwood continues to hold informal meetings with the tenants and has several people in the building with whom he stays in close contact. They keep him informed of activities in the building. A CPO continues to patrol the building to make sure that the dealers do not return. The CPOP unit is using this same general strategy for cleaning up other drug locations in the precinct.

To Prevent and Control Conduct Threatening to Life and Property, Particularly That Which Affects Neighborhoods as a Whole

Typical of the melting-pot character of the area, Henry Street on Manhattan's lower east side has served as home to wave after wave of new immigrant groups. The Irish came in the latter half of the 19th century, followed by the Italians and the Germans. Today, Henry Street's tenements are home to a large Asian population, many of whom work either in the nearby Chinatown restaurant industry or in the numerous garment sweatshops that abound in the area.

Henry Street is also home to Police Officer Thomas McLaughlin, who patrols the area as a member of the 7 Precinct's Community Patrol Officer unit. Officer McLaughlin has been a police officer for four years, and a member of the CPOP unit for the last nine months. Before coming into CPOP, he frequently rode in the radio car that covered Henry Street, and his early recollections of the block are that there was always a problem with people frequenting the area in large numbers searching for drugs. He used to chase the loiterers off, as did the other officers who rode the sector, but could never spend enough time on the block to really deal with the problem.

Shortly after he joined the CPOP Unit in March of 1988, CPO McLaughlin began to spend time on a two-block stretch of Henry Street between Pitt and Jefferson Streets. These two blocks are primarily of four- and five-story tenement buildings, with a small playground in the middle of one block and a Catholic church on the corner of the other. During his patrols he observed what he believed to be a flourishing street drug trade, and by varying his tours, he learned that it operated 24 hours a day. As the residents of these blocks were almost exclusively Asian, he was able to see that both the drug dealers and the buyers were from outside the neighborhood. Tom began to talk to the residents of the block with the hope of enlisting their aid in dealing with the problem. He did not get far at first. The neighborhood residents were clearly afraid of the drug dealers and the junkies, but they seemed most afraid of being seen voicing their concerns to the police. For the most part, they just went to work, often for 16 hours a day, and they locked themselves into their apartments at night. The playground, intended to be a haven in the midst of tenement life, was relegated to being one of the focal points for the drug trade.

On the beat for about 2 months, CPO McLaughlin was finally approached by the president of the Henry Street Block Association, who asked the officer for help in dealing with the drug problems on Henry Street. The CPO was told that, while the block association was small in terms of numbers, they were very concerned. Parents were afraid to let their children play on the street, let alone use the park, and the noise made by drug dealers hawking their wares during the night prevented them from sleeping. Officer McLaughlin listened to more residents' complaints, which began to flow to him, and promised that he would try to do something to alleviate the problem.

CPO McLaughlin discussed the problem with his supervisor and arranged for a meeting between the members of the block association and a number of police department personnel. Using the community room of St. Theresa's Church, the meeting was held the following week. In addition to CPO McLaughlin and his supervising sergeant, the meeting was attended by the supervisor of the 7 Precinct's Street Narcotics Enforcement Unit (SNEU), a member of the department's Narcotics Division, and the director of Manhattan District Attorney's Community Affairs Office. Each promised to do whatever they could to help deal with the problem.

After the meeting, CPO McLaughlin began to spend a lot of time on Henry Street, doing what he could to interrupt the drug trafficking. He talked to the blocks' residents, and through information given by them and his own observations, began to pass on intelligence reports to the Narcotics Division and the precinct SNEU. He was given keys to the front doors of many of the tenement buildings, which were alleged to be used by the drug users as shooting galleries, and with the assistance of other CPOs, began doing vertical patrols in them.

Both the Narcotics Division and the SNEU responded to the information given them, and over the next several months made over 100 arrests on the two-block stretch. The Manhattan District Attorney's Office, alerted to the problem by CPO McLaughlin and the area's residents, began to press for higher bail for those persons arrested on Henry Street, and when convictions were obtained, sought jail sentences. Throughout the period, Tom and the other members of the CPOP unit held monthly meetings with the block association members, telling them what was being done and soliciting additional information.

All of these efforts, coordinated by CPO McLaughlin, have begun to have their effect. For the most part, the two blocks of Henry Street are clear of drugs, and the playground is again being used by neighborhood children. The drug trade has been pushed to one corner location and now operates almost exclusively during the midnight hours. While the residents of Henry Street are delighted with what has been done, the CPOs, the members of the SNEU and Narcotics units, and the Manhattan District Attorney's Office are intent on entirely ridding the area of drugs.

Assigning Community Patrol Officers to Permanent Neighborhood Beats

At 649 East 138th Street is an abandoned building, next to the St. Luke's grammar school in the 40 Precinct in the South Bronx. For several years it was also a shooting gallery for the junkies of the area who would buy their drugs and needles elsewhere in the neighborhood and then get high in the building and in the empty lots behind it, all of which adjoined the playground of St. Luke's. The playground had become a nighttime hangout for the junkies. During recesses, many of the school's students spent their time picking up used needles to show to each other and to their teachers.

Police Officer Eamon Donohoe is the Community Patrol Officer for the beat that covers this location, and he became aware of the problem both through personal observation and through complaints from parents of students and from the school's principal. Not only was the playground littered with used needles, he learned, but also cars parked on the block were being broken into with increasing frequency. Officer Donohoe visited the principal of St. Luke's and went to a meeting of the local Community Planning Board to learn more about the concerns of the area's residents. Within a week, feeling that he sufficiently understood the problem, CPO Donohoe contacted the Department of Housing Preservation and Development and recommended that the building be sealed to keep the junkies out. Two weeks later, HPD sealed the building. Officer Donohoe also involved the Sanitation Department, which removed the derelict cars from the street so that the ones belonging to residents could be watched more carefully. He increased his own patrol hours on the block and arranged with the police officers assigned to Radio Motor Patrol in the area to cruise the neighborhood as often as possible during their tours. These efforts produced results almost immediately. Deprived of their shooting galleries, the drug users moved elsewhere, and larcenies from autos began to decline.

CPO Donohoe continues to patrol the block carefully, making sure that the junkies do not try to unseal the building or somehow sneak into the lots behind St. Luke's. The building has remained sealed for 9 months, the junkies have not returned, and the number of auto burglaries has decreased substantially. The students of St. Luke's grammar school are no longer playing with used needles.

Appendix B

The Community Patrol Officer Program:
Problem-Solving Guide

Office of the Chief of Patrol
New York City Police Department
One Police Plaza
New York, NY 10038

Office of Management, Analysis, and Planning
New York City Police Department
One Police Plaza
New York, NY 10038

The Vera Institute of Justice
377 Broadway
New York, NY 10013

SEPTEMBER 1990

Acknowledgments

This guide was designed as a training and field aid for personnel assigned to the New York City Police Department's Community Patrol Officer Program. Material contained in the guide was drawn from a variety of sources, and its authors benefited from the work of a large number of people. Examples of problem-solving processes may be found in the fields of management, systems theory, and operations research, as well as in the currently emerging focus on problem solving as a tactical police strategy. All were of considerable help in the preparation of this guide. We wish to acknowledge especially the assistance received from the staff of the Police Executive Research Forum, who shared with us the training materials developed by PERF, and the Problem Solving Task Force of the Newport News Police Department, in connection with the introduction of a system of problem-oriented policing in that agency. In addition, Herman Goldstein, whose published work first provoked interest in the adaptation of problem-solving methods to policing, has been generous in the interest he has expressed and the recommendations he has offered concerning the program. Our work with the police department on this program has received additional support from the Chase Manhattan Bank, the Daniel and Florence Guggenheim Foundation, the Norman Foundation, and the Philip Morris Companies.

The Vera Institute of Justice

214

Contents

Problem Solving and the Community Patrol Officer Program

Introduction

The Community Patrol Officer Program is an effort by the New York City Police Department to assist local communities to deal more effectively with the problems of disorder and crime that adversely affect the quality of life experienced at the neighborhood level. As such, it is both a practical response to the needs of the people and a vehicle for adopting and spreading the principles of community and problem-solving policing throughout the agency.

For some, community policing is best understood as a set of philosophical principles that should inform the content and structure of policing. The proponents of the community policing philosophy recognize the importance of law and procedure in defining what the police should do and how they should do it. But they insist that the distinctive experiences, needs, and norms of local communities should also influence the goals of policing, the conditions that it addresses, the services it delivers, the means used to deliver them, and the assessment of the adequacy of police service.

For others, the term *community policing* identifies a wide range of programs being implemented by major police departments throughout the country. Although these efforts differ from each other in major respects, the following operational and organizational principles appear to be more or less common to all:

- Continuous assignment of police units to specific neighborhoods or beats

216

- Insistence that the unit develop and maintain a knowledge base regarding the problems, cultural characteristics, and resources of the neighborhood
- Emphasis on the importance of the unit's reaching out to neighborhood residents and business people to assure them of the presence and concern of the police
- Use of formal or informal mechanisms to involve community people in identifying, analyzing, and establishing priorities among local problems and in developing and implementing action plans for ameliorating them
- Delegation to the community police unit of responsibility for fashioning solutions to the crime and order-maintenance problems of the neighborhood, and for encouraging the commitment of a variety of police and nonpolice resources to those solutions
- Emphasis on increasing information flow from the community to the police and on the use of that information by various elements of the police agency to make important arrests and to develop intelligence on illegal enterprises in the community
- Sharing with representatives of the community accurate information on local crime problems and the results of ongoing efforts to address them.

These principles are not new to American policing or to the New York City Police Department. Some of them have long been part of policing operations in small towns throughout the country and some were prevalent among major urban departments a couple of generations ago. These principles will be recognized, as well, by those familiar with the Neighborhood Police Team (NPT) programs in the NYPD and other large agencies during the early seventies. While those particular programs faded away for a variety of reasons, the principles of community policing have persisted and are more influential among police administrators and scholars today than ever before. There are several important reasons for this influence.

Research and reflection on the focus, organization, and operations of urban policing during the sixties and seventies have yielded some useful lessons. Clearly, the police have a contribution to make toward the control of crime in the streets, but that contribution cannot be realized without the involvement of the people and other public and private agencies at the neighborhood level. While traditional forms of random preventive patrol have little impact on the volume of street crime, special patrol efforts targeted at particular crime problems occurring under specific conditions within confined neighborhoods can be quite productive. The flexible resources needed to implement such specially designed, local problem-solving strategies have been largely consumed by the apparent need to respond rapidly to the millions of calls-for-service received by the police annually. Yet we have only recently recognized that rapid response is necessary only with respect to genuine emergencies such as personal injuries, crimes in progress, and officers in need of assistance. And it appears that a thoroughly mobilized patrol force moving rapidly from one call to the next loses contact with street conditions and with the concerns of the people they are to serve.

The 911 system, central dispatching, rapid response, and the commitment of an ever-increasing proportion of the patrol force to the calls-for-service function were all intended to help in the fight against street crime. Yet we now realize that the vast majority of the calls received are not related to conventional forms of street crime and do not require a rapid response. In fact, although the power of the police to intervene in various situations is usually clear in law or regulation, the bulk of police activity involves the provision of information and referral services, mediating disputes and preventing them from escalating into serious violence, and helping to maintain some semblance of order in the streets. Moreover, the people who are most dependent on the police for such services are poor people living in neighborhoods that are often lacking in service resources and the organizations they need to improve the quality of life in the community.

Recent research shows clearly that the levels of fear and insecurity experienced by the people are influenced primarily by their perceptions of quality-of-life problems and general disorder in their immediate environs, rather than by the actual volume of street crimes occurring there. Moreover, as Wilson and Kelling (1990) have argued in their now-famous *Atlantic Monthly* article entitled, "Broken Windows," alleviating quality-of-life problems at the neighborhood level will not only reduce citizen fear but also may reduce the actual volume of crime in the streets.

Given the personnel shortages of the last decade,, and the enormous volume of calls received over the 911 system, the response to those calls consumed our patrol resources and left precinct commanders without the people and tools they need to address the street conditions that so aggravate the people they serve. CPOP is a reflection of the department's determination to reverse those developments and to assist people actively on the neighborhood level to maintain order and improve the quality of life on their streets.

In pursuit of that goal, CPOP gives the precinct commander a flexible resource for solving community problems. The program does not require a large commitment of resources or a significant restructuring of patrol operations. Instead, it relies on individual police officers assigned permanently to specific beats to function as planners, problem solvers, community organizers, and information links between the police and the residents of the beat. The officers assigned to each unit work with the assistance of and under the close supervision of a CPOP sergeant. Yet CPOP can help precinct commanders to make deployment decisions regarding all of the resources under their command. For those reasons, the commanders who have the program have welcomed enthusiastically the CPOs, and the CPOs themselves experience a great deal of job satisfaction. In addition, the program has proved to be enormously popular with local officials, community organizations, and neighborhood residents throughout the city.

Without Problem Solving as Its Foundation, CPOP Makes Little Sense

Intensive involvement with the residents and organizations in the beat, a proactive, problem-solving approach to the priority problems found there, and an effective integration of the CPOP operation with other units at the precinct and borough levels are the keys to a successful unit. This means, among other things, that the officers must operate with more discretion and under a more flexible, but probably more intensive, form of supervision than do RMP officers. It also means that some of the conventional indicators of productivity such as runs per tour, arrests made, and summons issued are not particularly good measures of either officer or unit productivity. The number and kinds of arrests made and summonses issued should be dictated by the strategies that the CPO and his or her supervisor undertake to address the priority problems in the officer's beat. Moreover, the level of interaction between the officer and the residents of the beat, the organizational meetings attended, the assistance rendered to block associations, youth groups, and self-help organizations, the utility of the information secured and passed on, and the reactions of the community to the officer's efforts, must become meaningful criteria in evaluating the performance of the CPO and the CPOP unit.

In short, CPOP differs from conventional patrol both conceptually and operationally. Those differences require adjustments in the department's procedures for supervising and assessing the work of patrol officers. Experience to date indicates that such adjustments are being made in dozens of precincts across the city. The benefits are substantial—CPOP helps make the department a partner with the community in improving the quality of neighborhood life and can be used to inform and supplement the entire patrol operation.

CPOP and Problem Solving

Police agencies throughout the United States are becoming increasingly aware of the value of developing a problem-solving approach to policing. Why this interest? Why has the New York City Police Department established the Community Patrol Officer Program and designed it to provide police officers with the time to identify and work on solving community problems? There are a number of reasons for this trend. Traditional patrol practices are reactive and incident driven. Routine patrol focuses on responding to calls-for-service and maximizing unit availability by closely monitoring response times. As a result, officers responding to 911 calls have little time to do other than make an arrest, take a report, or refer a complainant. This reactive, after-the-fact response does nothing to identify the underlying problems that cause the incidents. As a result, the same situation may recur again and again. This is one reason 911 calls have been growing at the rate of 10% annually. Problem-solving policing tries to look beyond the incident in an attempt to discover and correct the underlying problem that caused it. It allows the officer to design a corrective action that is tailored to the specific problem. If successful, problem-solving policing can reduce the overall work load of the police department.

Another reason for the increasing interest in problem-oriented policing is the growth of research that demonstrates that a relationship exists between crime and quality-of-life conditions and the level of fear in a community. In addition, other research suggests that there are links between quality-of-life conditions and the level of crime in a community. If problem-solving policing can identify and resolve the problems that underlie quality-of-life conditions in a community, it may impact significantly on both the level of crime and the fear of crime in that community.

Of all the functions of Community Patrol Officers, the most important one, and the one that makes CPOP different from other dpartment deployment strategies, is problem solving. Without problem solving as its foundation, CPOP makes little sense. Police officers assigned to RMP cars can cover more territory than those on foot, can respond to calls for service faster, and are more easily supervised. What makes CPOP important to the department and justifies the assignment of so many police officers to this form of patrol is the ability of a CPO to identify and correct problems at the community level. CPOP's continuing utility to the police department is dependent on the degree to which CPOs continue to identify and resolve these problems effectively.

As with other skills, some people seem to be better problem solvers than others. They seem to have an innate ability to get to the root of the problem and work out an effective solution. However, problem solvers are not born that way, they have learned either through experience or education how to attack a problem. Problem-solving skills can be learned. There is a problem solving process that, if followed, can assist anyone in coming up with better solutions to the problems they face. The steps in this process are:

1. Discovering and Identifying the Problem

2. Analyzing the Problem

3. Designing a Tailored Response

4. Gaining Concurrences for the Response

5. Implementing the Response

6. Evaluating the Effectiveness of the Response

7. Going Through the Process Again, If Necessary

Discovering and Identifying Problems

Sometimes problems come right up and bite you. Other times you have to sneak up on them before you can realize that it is a real problem that you are dealing with. In the simplest terms, a problem is anything that can have a negative effect on the community you are working in—something that causes harm to members of the community or is a potential source of disorder. Problems are generally a source of great concern to residents of the community, and they are not likely to go away unless something is done to correct them.

1. Learning About Problems

There are a wide variety of ways in which Community Patrol Officers can learn about problems in the community. Some of these are:

a. Personal observation while on patrol.

b. Talking to other police officers who work in the area and to members of the precinct staff.

c. Reviewing police department records; not just 61s, but any record that can be used to identify or shed light on a problem. Communications (citizen complaints) received either directly at the precinct or referred through channels are a good source of information on matters which are perceived by the public as being important enough to write the police department about.

d. Reading the local press. Local newspapers are major sources of information about problems in the community. Every CPOP unit should subscribe to local newspapers, and all members of the unit should be given a chance to read them, and not just for the "police" stories.

e. Conducting crime analysis. Look for similarities in crime patterns, time distribution of crimes, locations, and so forth.

f. Talking to representatives of other government agencies, particularly members of the local Community Planning Board and the district manager.

g. Talking to representatives of local merchants' and civic organizations (Block Associations, Tenant Organizations, Churches, Synagogues, etc.)

h. And perhaps the most important source of all, talking to the people who live and work in your beat area.

2. Learn More About the Problem

Okay, so something has come to your attention; you saw something, someone told you something, or you read something. But is it really a problem? Some things are, and some are not. A good deal of the time things will be fairly clear. The condition, incident, crime, whatever, will be significant enough to tell you right out, this is a problem, or at least the symptom of a problem. But other times you have to dig a bit to really make sure that it is a problem you are dealing with, and not just a random incident. And then you have to dig to make sure that it is the problem you are working on and not just one of its symptoms. What are some of the ways in which you can go about this? Let's take a look at a few.

a. **Using Police Records:** Among the principal sources of information about problems in a beat area are the Complaint Reports. Each CPO receives a copy of each 61 reported in his or her beat area and should review these on a daily basis. In addition to the information regarding the specific crime reported, 61s should be reviewed in an effort to determine crime patterns. What is important? Consider the following:

In the general scheme of things, 61s regarding lost property are not very informative or important. However, when CPO Joseph Alanga of the 114 CPOP unit began to get a large number of lost property reports concerning wallets lost from women's purses in the main shopping district of his beat, he began to doubt that that many careless women were walking around. Alanga began to call the complainants and question them about their activities on the days when they lost their wallets. Putting together the bits and pieces of information obtained from the complainants, Alanga began to suspect that there was a pickpocket ring operating in the area. The following Saturday, he staked out the location where the majority of women remembered last having their wallets and—you guessed it, made a grand larceny collar, breaking up a pickpocket ring that had been operating in the area for some time.

b. **An Incident or a Problem?** Every incident that is reported to you, either through a 61 or by way of a citizen's complaint, should be thoroughly reviewed. One of the first questions you have to ask is whether or not it is just an incident or a symptom of a problem. An incident is not necessarily a problem. It may be a one-time thing arising from circumstances not likely to recur. On the other hand, the incident, like the tip of the iceberg, may be symptomatic of a larger problem. What is important is that you begin to look for other incidents that may be similar to or connected to the current one, and that may indicate an underlying problem.

3. Verify the Problem

You have learned something about the problem, now what do you do? One thing you should consider before setting about analyzing it is to attempt to verify what you have learned from other sources. What is the community perception of the problem? Do a lot of people view it as a problem, or are you dealing with someone's pet peeve? Who else can contribute to what you have learned already? What other records can you go to for more information? Has the precinct ever dealt with this problem before? If so, how? Check all of your sources for additional information and verification.

While we are mentioning pet peeves, we should note that there is nothing wrong with trying to help one citizen deal with something that is a problem to him or her, even though it seems that no one else is concerned about it. The important thing is to make sure that you are not getting involved with some kind of a personal feud and that you not commit the bulk of your time to unrelated conditions of concern to only one or a few residents in your beat.

4. Make Sure You Have Identified "The" Problem

Analysis will sometimes reveal that what appears to be a single big problem is really a mixture of smaller, discrete problems, each of which may demand its own response. In analyzing information, you should attempt to capture both the big and the small pictures, and then decide how to proceed.

Sometimes it is difficult to determine exactly what is the real problem. Very often we deal with results of a problem and have to dig deeper to find out what caused these results. In private industry, correct and specific problem identification is regarded as essential to effective solution development. It is no different in police work; if we develop a solution to a symptom, the real problem may never be dealt with. Consider the following:

CPO Vinny Esposito reviewed a 61 for a shooting that took place in his Beat Area. It occurred on a commercial strip that, over the past several years, has seen a large increase in the number of Asian-American businesses. From the details in the 61, Vinny learned that the shooter was a member of an Asian youth gang and the victim was a member of a white youth gang known to be active in local narcotics trafficking.

From these details, it was possible that the problem stemmed from:

    a. A turf battle between two rival youth gangs

    b. An attempt by the Asian youth gang to take over drug trafficking in the area

    c. A private grudge between the shooter and the victim

    d. A move by the Asians to drive drugs out of the neighborhood

    e. None of the above

The answer, it turned out, was none of the above. It took Vinny some time to get to the bottom of things and find out the real problem (we will talk about that later), but when he did, he discovered that the problem was the emergence of a protection racket in which the members of the Asian youth gang were extorting protection payments from the Asian merchants. Once he discovered what the real problem was, Vinny began to do something about it. We will talk about that later too.

5. Take Interim Action   When an incident or problem is brought to your attention, you should take some immediate interim action, if this is appropriate. This could involve enforcement, issuing warnings, referral, or other short-term response. And then—go on to Problem Analysis.

Summary: Before going on to Problem Analysis, let's do a quick review of Problem Identification:

    1. Discover the problem

        a. Personal observation

        b. Information from other police officers

        c. Review department records

        d. Conduct crime analysis

e. Read the local newspapers

f. Information from other government agencies

g. Information from citizens' organizations

h. Information from the people who live and work in the beat area

2. Learn as much as you can about the problem. Use all of the sources available to you.

3. Verify the problem. Talk to other community residents, police officers, agency representatives. Get a broader perspective.

4. Make sure you have identified "the" problem.

5. Take interim action where appropriate.

AND THEN
Begin Problem Analysis.

Problem Analysis

Problem analysis is simply finding out what the problem is all about. It is important because problems differ in important details, and these must be fully understood if a workable, tailored solution is to be found.

Analysis is aimed at identifying and understanding the factors that give rise to the problem, contribute to its persistence, or prevent its correction. Once identified, all of these factors become potential targets for change as part of a strategy designed to correct the problem.

Beginning the Problem Analysis Process: Problems generally arise from the interaction of people. Someone does something that causes fear or actual harm to someone else. Sometimes the initial action causes a reaction from the person(s) affected by it. To begin to understand a problem, we must begin looking at who the actors are, what they do, how they react, and what the effects of these actions are.

1. Actors

Some problems may only involve a few persons; others may involve whole communities. It is important to identify who is involved in a problem, and in what way.

a. **Offenders:** While a problem may result from a physical condition (e.g., garbage accumulation), there is generally an offender, the person whose actions cause the harm or fear. Who is it? What are his or her primary characteristics? Why does he or she act in a given way?

b. **Victims:** Victims are the persons who are harmed by the actions of the offender. Who are they? What are their characteristics? Do they do anything that contributes to their vulnerability?

c. **Third Parties:** In many situations other people are involved. Some of them may be likely witnesses, supports for the victims, or supports for the offender. Who are they? How are they involved? What are their interests?

2. Actions   Looking at what took place involves more than just focusing on what each of the actors did; it involves looking at the whole physical and social context of the incident or incidents.

a. **Physical Settings:** What is the physical setting in which the incident or incidents took place? Are there environmental hazards that contribute to the problem (e.g., absence of street lighting, obstacles obstructing pedestrian visibility, abandoned buildings, etc.)? Where do the incidents take place? Is there something connected to the locations that contributes to the incidents (environmental hazards, focal points of community activity, e.g., subway entrances, etc.)?

b. **Social Context:** To what groups do the offenders and victims belong? Are they in conflict? What interests motivate the offenders? What actions of the victims contribute to their vulnerability?

c. **Sequence of Events:** What actions constitute the problem: What do the offenders do? To whom? How? When? Why? Where? What is the sequence of events that produces the problem?

d. **Results of Events:** What are the effects of the action? On whom? How do they react? Who else witnesses the action? How do the witnesses react?

3. Responses or   How do persons or institutions react to the actions or problem?
Reactions

a. **Institutions:** How do public and private agencies (including the police) view the problem? What have they done about it? With what results? What might they be interested in doing now?

b. **Communities:** How do the residents of the neighborhood view the problem? What have they done about it? With what results? What might they be willing to do now?

4. How Serious Is   Is this a serious problem requiring a serious response? If not, why not?
the Problem?   If it is serious, how can the community and relevant institutions be made to see its seriousness? If it is not a serious problem, what should be done about it? Is anyone aware of the "total cost" of the problem to society? Concern and cooperation can sometimes be gained if people are made aware of what the problem really costs them, both monetarily and in indirect nonmonetary terms.

Summary: 1. Problems are generally caused by people's actions affecting other people. (Although problems can result from, or be contributed to, by environmental hazards.)

2. There are generally three kinds of actors involved in a problem: the offenders, the victims, and third parties.

3. Problems take place in physical and social settings that may contribute to them and that may be possible points of intervention in resolving them.

4. Problems generally result from a specific sequence of events that cause harm or fear in a community.

5. People and institutions respond to problems. Their responses may either contribute to the problem or be useful in solving it.

6. And do not forget, get as much information as you can from a variety of sources. Do not be limited by traditional (canned) responses or traditional information sources. One source of valuable information that is often overlooked is offenders themselves. Consider interviewing offenders about why they do what they do. You may need some nonpolice help in doing this, but then again, you may not.

With all of this in mind, let's take another look at the problem that Vinny Esposito tackled in his beat area.

1. Who were the **actors**?

    a. **The Offenders:** Members of an Asian youth gang who were extorting money from Asian merchants

    b. **The Victims:** Asian merchants

    c. **Third Parties:** Other merchants in the area, patrons of the affected businesses, neighborhood residents

2. What were the **actions**?

    a. **Physical Settings:** All of the extortion threats and the actions that accompanied them took place inside the affected business premises.

    b. **Social Context:** The extortion of Asian merchants by Asian gangs is a cultural problem of long standing in Asian communities throughout the country. It relies on the reluctance of Asians to trust or confide in law-enforcement agencies.

    c. **Sequence of Events:** A group of youths enter a restaurant or other business establishment and cause a disturbance. The owner is approached by a gang member who informs him that he will have to pay for protection against such occurrences. Any reluctance is met with threats of continued disturbances or violence against the store owner or his family.

3. What were the **responses** to the problem by:

    a. **Persons:** The merchants' response was to pay the gang members and remain quiet.

    b. **Institutions:** Despite the fact that the racket had been operating for some time, no complaints were made to the police, and there was no governmental response.

    c. **Community:** Although knowledge of the racket was widespread throughout the merchants' community, fear of reprisal and a lack of faith in the ability of the police to protect complainants resulted in their not making any formal complaints to the police department.

How did Vinny find out all of the information necessary to do the problem analysis? Remember in the previous section [Discovering and Identifying Problems], you were told to learn more about the problem. That is just what Vinny did. After the shooting (remember, that is what this all started with), Vinny began to spend a lot of time in the area, basically trying to find out who was who, and what was what. He took license plate numbers and ran DMV checks on them. He gave out summonses and made a few low-level collars to address conditions on the beat, and in doing so learned the identity and criminal histories of some of the youth in the area. And he began an intensive effort to get to know the merchants.

Vinny's persistence began to pay off. He broke through with one merchant who told him what was going on in the area, and who introduced him to other merchants who were also experiencing the problem. Vinny began to attend meetings of the Asian merchants' association and to ask for their cooperation in dealing with the problem.

Through these contacts he was featured in several articles in the Chinese press that told of his efforts to rid the area of the protection racket and urged affected merchants to cooperate with him.

And that is how Vinny found out what the problem was. Officially, without complaints to alert it, the police department did not know that the problem existed. It took a lot of digging on Vinny's part to uncover it.

Besides illustrating what problem identification is all about, this story also points out some of the limitations in relying solely on crime statistics to identify problems.

Designing Responses

1. Objectives

In designing a response to a community problem, several objectives must be kept in mind:

a. The strategy chosen must go beyond the incident and address the underlying problem. Interim actions address incidents, solutions address problems.

b. The strategy should be aimed at providing a long-lasting solution to the problem.

c. The solution should provide a substantial improvement for the residents of the community, reducing both harm to them and fear of future harm.

d. The strategy should also be aimed at reducing police work load by eliminating the problem.

2. Types of Solutions

a. Eliminate the Problem—the best solution, but not always possible.

b. Reduce the frequency of incidents arising from the problem.

c. Reduce the harm to the public from such incidents.

d. Improve the public's perception of police handling of the problem. This is not an invitation to do a "P.R." job. Be honest with the people and let them know what the department is trying to do about the problem. And remember, if you do not know the answer, do not make one up. Promise to get back to them, find out the answer, and get back to them.

e. Clarify responsibility for the problem and advise the public.

3. Developing a Strategy to Solve the Problem

In the sections on identifying and analyzing problems, you were told to gather information on a number of factors—identity of actors, physical settings, social context, sequence of events, results of events, responses to events, etc.—as possible intervention points in designing a solution for the problem. Each should now be considered in developing a strategy to deal with the problem.

a. **Altering the Behavior of the Actors:**

(1) **Offenders:** If you can get the offender to stop doing what he is doing, you have solved the problem. How you go about that depends upon whether or not you are dealing with a serious criminal matter or an order-maintenance problem. There are a wide range of options that can be tried. Among these are:

   (a) Enforcement: Very often the most effective means for changing the behavior of an offender is through enforcement—arrest or summons.

   (b) Request for Compliance: For less serious problems, requests for compliance may be all that is necessary to solve the problem.

   (c) Education: Where the offender's actions are the result of a lack of understanding of the effect of his actions on the community, education may be the answer.

   (d) Providing Alternatives to Harmful Behavior: CPOs throughout the city have recognized the importance of attempting to provide meaningful alternatives to youth as a means of channeling their activity in positive directions. They have done this through the creation of recreational, educational, and counseling programs designed to deal with specific problems and needs in the communities they serve.

(2) **Victims:** Altering victim behavior can be an effective way of reducing the harm caused by offenders' actions and may reduce future victimization. Consideration should be given to:

   (a) Determining if the victim is doing something that contributes to his victimization—failing to take reasonable steps to protect himself or his possessions.

   (b) Encouraging the victim to become involved in community programs aimed at improving neighborhood conditions.

   (c) Encouraging the victim to adopt reasonable crime prevention measures: become a Block Watcher, enroll in Operation ID, secure a premises protection survey, furnish information to the police to assist in improving neighborhood conditions, and so forth.

(3) **Third Parties:** Attempts at altering the behavior of third parties depend upon whether those persons may be viewed as potential allies of the persons affected by the harmful behavior, or supporters (directly or indirectly) of the offender.

(a) Where third parties are witnesses to criminal activities, their cooperation and assistance as witnesses should be encouraged.

(b) Third parties who are indirectly affected by harmful behavior should be encouraged to take prudent steps to avoid future victimization in much the same manner as victims. (See (2) (a) and (b), above.)

(c) In some instances, third parties may be helpful in controlling the behavior of offenders because of either their personal or their legal relationship. If you can identify a person who exerts influence over the offender, such as a parent, spouse, clergyman, counselor, athletic coach, landlord, and so on, that person may be able to assist in working with the offender to curb his harmful behavior.

b. **Change Other Dimensions of the Problem:**

(1) **Alter the Physical Setting:** Some problems can be corrected by changing physical settings. One common example of this is to improve the crime resistance of homes and businesses through the installation of effective locks and alarm systems, improved lighting, and so on (target hardening). Consider the following:

> When CPO Fred Dwyer was first assigned to his beat in the 49 Precinct he discovered that the nurses who worked evenings and nights in Calvary Hospital were very afraid of walking to public transportation because they had to walk through an unlit railroad underpass. He was told by the hospital administration that they had tried, without success, to have something done about it. Fred began to check it out. The underpass was part of the Conrail system, and when Fred approached them, he was told that it was not their responsibility. So Fred dug a little and discovered a city agency called the Bureau of Public Lighting. It took a few phone calls and a lot of perseverance, but finally the city responded and better than adequate lighting was installed, much to the delight of the nurses.

(2) **Change the Social Context:** Problems can sometimes be addressed by changing the social context in which they take place. In our example of the Asian extortion racket, part of Vinny's initial approach to the problem was to make protection payoffs unacceptable to the merchants, despite both a cultural and a historical acceptance of the practice. You can also see this approach in the efforts of some CPOP units to create sports leagues to bring together youth from rival groups within the same precinct.

(3) **Change the Sequence of Events:** Some problems can be eliminated or lessened by changing the sequence of the events that which create the problem.

> In one of the CPOP units a three- to four-block area in the vicinity of three different schools became a major order maintenance problem for the CPO assigned to the beat. Each day, as the three schools were simultaneously dismissed, the streets were flooded with hundreds of children causing chaos. Residents complained about the noise and the pushing and shoving of the youth. Store owners complained of shoplifting. What to do? The CPO met with the principals of the three schools and arranged to stagger dismissal times. The problem was substantially lessened.

(4) **Change the Results of Events:** Problems can also be addressed by changing or altering the result of the events that cause them. Examples of this can be seen in the efforts being made by many CPOs to reduce drug trafficking by taking the profit out of it. More than one CPO has arranged with citizens to inform him or her of the locations where the street dealers hide their stashes. Instead of attempting to make an arrest and be lost to the beat for the rest of the tour, these officers use the information to seize and voucher the stashes, thereby increasing the cost of doing business on that block.

4. What Kinds of Solutions Can You Try to Develop?

The Community Patrol Officer Program is only as limited as the imagination of the sergeants and police officers in it. You are only limited by your imagination, department policy, and law. And remember, both policy and law can be changed if approached in a proper manner.

There are, however, types or categories of solutions that have been used in the past, both in New York and elsewhere, that may be considered when trying to formulate a plan of action. Some of these are listed below. This list is not exhaustive and is provided only to acquaint you with some possible approaches to think about when trying to solve a problem.

Before we look at these categories, there is one more thing to remember. Most problems respond to a combination of solutions. Do not limit your approach to any single tactic. Try to see how a number of different approaches can be combined to have a long-lasting effect on the problem.

With all of that said, let's take a look at some types or categories of plans that you can consider when designing responses:

a. **Identifying high-risk offenders, locations, or victims and targeting them for special attention.** This should look familiar to you, as it is the strategy employed in some of the department's

---

Note: The material presented in the next three pages is paraphrased from an unpublished paper by Michael Scott, Legal Assistant to the Police Commissioner, City of New York, when he was engaged in providing research support to professor Herman Goldstein. This material, more fully developed, will appear in a book being written by Professor Goldstein, with support from the Police Executive Research Forum.

citywide efforts to deal with significant problems. The targeting of career criminals by the Career Criminal Investigating Units and the use of Case Enhancement techniques on persons arrested for serious crimes are both examples of this tactic.

Where problem analysis discloses that there are specific individuals are responsible for creating a disproportionate amount of problems in the community, or that some locations are the focus of activity that causes harm or disorder in the community, efforts targeted at incapacitating these individuals or at improving conditions at these locations might be part of the answer.

Part of the answer might also be to mobilize the community in support of your efforts. This might take the form of having community residents correspond with the District Attorney's Office or actually come to court in support of vigorous prosecution of local offenders. In the case of problem locations, community support might be effective in getting other city agencies involved in dealing with the problem through Code enforcement, and so forth.

b. **Supporting existing relationships of social control as a means of influencing and controlling the behavior of persons responsible for creating problems.** Some persons may be in a strong position to influence the behavior of offenders. If the police can identify such persons, they may be able to shift the primary responsibility for the control of the problem away from the criminal justice system and back to those who have a longer-lasting, more powerful relationship with those who are creating the problems.

c. **Organizing and assisting the community to get directly involved in solving their problems.** The solutions to some problems are within the capacity of the community to carry out themselves. CPOs can play a critical role in helping citizens join together to work on a problem and in guiding them through the necessary steps.

d. **Addressing directly social and economic conditions that may be contributing to problem behavior.** If the police can identify certain conditions in a neighborhood that seem to be precipitating problems to which the police will ultimately be called upon to respond, then perhaps the police themselves can head off future problems by working to change those conditions. This approach is reflected in the efforts of a number of CPOP units that have instituted a wide variety of efforts to provide constructive activities for neighborhood youth.

e. **Coordinating the police response with responses of other governmental agencies or encouraging other agencies to alter their responses.** Many problems that police confront are also partly the responsibility of several other governmental agencies.

Schools, courts, prosecutors, health officials, corrections agencies, welfare bureaus, social service agencies, traffic engineering departments, and other governmental and quasi-governmental bodies share responsibilities for controlling antisocial behavior or at least have the capacity to help alleviate problems that come to the attention of the police.

With respect to some problems, it may be sufficient merely to inform the citizens of the availability of the services of other agencies. With others, however, the officer may want to go beyond merely providing information to citizens by making specific referrals to appropriate agencies.

Many of the CPOP units have adopted this approach by working closely with other agencies on a variety of problems. In a number of units, CPOs are coordinating their drug enforcement activities with Housing Preservation and Development, seeking to have drug dealers evicted from city-owned buildings, and in addition, are utilizing their network of contacts to help drug users get into treatment.

f. **Communicating with the public.** The police can sometimes be effective in bringing a problem under control simply by conveying accurate information to the public about the nature of the problem or about ways in which the public can protect itself from the negative effects of the problem. This category of response encompasses at least five specific purposes for conveying information:

   (1) **Educating the public about the seriousness of a problem.** The public is not aware of every problem in their community that they should be. Some widespread but discreet problems have gone unacknowledged for many years. Such was true of the problems of child abuse, spousal abuse, and drunk driving until the relatively recent past. Other more localized problems can also go undetected by the majority of citizens, but call for greater attention.

   Before the police can take action to deal with problems of these sorts, they first need to convince the citizenry that a problem does in fact exist. This must be accomplished by being specific about the consequences of the behavior or condition in question and not by sounding a general alarm that may later prove to be unsupported by any tangible evidence.

   (2) **Reducing exaggerated fears about perceived problems.** The reverse of the above situation is one in which the public overreacts to what it perceives is a serious threat to its safety or welfare. In this case, where analysis of the perceived problem discloses that no real problem exists, or that the public's

perception of the problem is distorted, the police can effectively deal with the problem by informing the community of the reality of the situation.

(3) **Conveying accurate information to the public to help them comply with the law or to resolve problems themselves.** At times the public, or more likely certain segments of the public, either do not know what the law expects of them or, knowing what the law says, do not know precisely how to comply with it. This can result in the police spending inordinate amounts of time in enforcing minor regulations, an activity that might be prevented by the police educating citizens about specific regulations.

(4) **Warning potential victims about their vulnerability and advising them about ways to protect themselves.** Educational campaigns, aimed at informing citizens about potential hazards, are an effective means of reducing victimization, particularly with respect to local problems. Such campaigns can take the form of posting warning signs in local businesses (as did the 5 Precinct CPOP unit in warning shoppers in the Canal Street area about the sale of bogus gold jewelry by street hawkers), addressing community meetings, or seeking the co-operation of the local press (as did the 114 CPOP unit in seeking to reduce the theft of expensive radios from parked cars).

(5) **Warning potential offenders that their behavior will be monitored and warning them about the consequences of that behavior.** This response seeks to enhance whatever general deterrence effects flow from enforcement efforts. It is only effective, however, if the warnings can be backed up by an enforcement capability that makes apprehension sufficiently certain.

g. **Enforcing relevant laws intensively to address a particular problem.** Investigation, arrest, and prosecution can be directed either toward a single offender or toward a larger population of offenders. While strict enforcement seldom eradicates entire broad problems, that need not be the goal of police in every case. Depending on how a problem gets analyzed, the enforcement response may adequately correct part of the problem.

h. **Increasing rates of police intervention short of arrest or prosecution.** If the problem is such that many easily deterrable people are causing it, significant increases in police efforts to stop, educate, or warn offenders may significantly reduce the problem.

i. **Altering the physical environment to reduce the likelihood that problems will occur.** Strategies within this category may include making likely targets of crime less vulnerable; seeking to control behavior that, while not criminal, is nonetheless dangerous or disturbing; or attempting to enhance a sense of security by correcting conditions that either make people less safe or make them feel less safe.

5. Get Help in Developing a Solution

Problem solving is not a one-person operation. Seek and get all the help you can. Among those who can be helpful are:

a. **Other CPOP Unit Members:** CPOs should discuss the problems they are working on with the CPOP supervisor and the other CPOs. Brainstorming sessions should be held on a regular basis.

Brainstorming: A discussion among team members working on a particular problem—helps sharpen good ideas and rejects bad ones. Initially, the search for new responses should be uninhibited—nothing is silly, and everyone should feel free to suggest anything that could remotely impact on the problem. Some of the best solutions have emerged from what was initially a whimsical suggestion. Brainstorming should neither be confined to nor rule out the traditional police responses of criminal investigation and the enforcement of relevant laws.

b. **Other Police Personnel:** Other members of the command and specialized units can contribute both to the understanding of a problem and to its solution. Reach out and tap them. Among these are: RMP crews, community affairs officers, crime prevention officers, anti-crime personnel, and so forth.

c. **Public and Private Agencies:** Persons working in other public or private agencies can contribute to the development of a strategy to deal with a problem. Reach out and network. And above all, do not forget to touch base with the Community Planning Board. District managers are, first and foremost, problem solvers. Work with them.

d. **Community Organization:** Members of community organizations, civic organization, block associations, tenant organizations, merchants groups, and so forth can all be of assistance in both developing and contributing to the solution of a problem.

e. **Individual Citizens:** Discuss the problem with local residents, both those directly concerned and those who may be helpful in developing a solution.

6. Determine What Obstacles Must Be Overcome

What are the barriers to effecting a solution to the problem? Who will be against it? How do we get their cooperation? Are there legal barriers or policy considerations that must be overcome? What is the cost of correcting the problem? Can the necessary resources be obtained?

7. Develop a Plan
of Action

a. **Establish Goals and Define Objectives:** Determine exactly what the ultimate changes in the problem are that you want to accomplish (the Goal) and the changes in behavior of the citizens, the police, and/or other interested agencies that must be brought about in order to achieve the goal (the Objectives). Objectives should be as specific as possible. They should set a standard or set of standards by which success can be measured.

b. **Specify the Steps to Accomplish the Goals:** Determine what must be done, by whom, and when, to make the plan work.

c. **Identify the Resources Needed to Make the Plan Work:** Get all the help that you can. There are a number of resources that a CPO should always consider in developing a problem-solving strategy. Sometimes all will not be available to him or her, but they should always be considered.

   (1) The most available resource is, of course, the CPO himself or herself. What is your role in implementing the strategy?

   (2) The next most available resource is the rest of the CPOP team. What help is required from other CPOs in implementing the strategy?

   (3) Precinct Resources: How can other precinct personnel—RMP units, Anti-Crime, and so forth—assist in implementing the strategy?

   (4) Other Department Resources: What other department units can be of help in dealing with the problem? Can their help be obtained? Who will coordinate?

   (5) Other City or Private Agencies.

   (6) Community Organizations.

   (7) Individual Citizens.

d. **Develop a Timetable:** Determine how the plan is to be carried out—the order in which the activities need to be performed—and establish a timetable for its implementation.

8. Consider
Alternate Plans

Consider different ways of approaching the problem. Review each of these tentative plans in terms of its benefits and liabilities. Sometimes the best plan cannot be implemented either because it is not possible to get the resources necessary to carry it out, or because of some other reason. Consider each, and then select the best option available to you.

9. Implement the
Plan

10. Think Big   Do not be limited by traditional police responses. There is nothing wrong with enforcement as a tactic, but it has its limitations, and on some problems it just does not work. Be creative and go at the problem from several different directions.

Do not limit your response to one tactic. Think in the long term; if the initial strategy is successful in eliminating or reducing the problem, what else is necessary to keep from losing the benefits that you have attained? How do you keep it from recurring?

Summary:

1. Set realistic goals and then objectives to get you to those goals.

2. Get help in developing a solution.

3. Develop a strategy to address the problem.

    a. Alter the behavior of the actors

    b. Change other dimensions of the problem
   - Alter the physical setting
   - Change the social context
   - Change the sequence of events
   - Change the results of events

4. Consider alternate plans and then select the most feasible.

5. Develop a timetable for implementing the plan.

6. Implement the plan.

Gaining Concurrences for the Response

Designing a response is one thing, getting people to do what is necessary to carry it out is something different. If a plan of action to address a specific problem requires the assistance of resources not under your direct control, it is essential to gain the concurrence of the persons who are in a position to commit these resources. Even when there are no resources involved, it is sometimes important to gain concurrences for a plan of action for other reasons. Understanding is one reason: It is important for people who will be affected by a plan of action to understand what is going on, even if they do not have a direct role in its implementation. Feedback is another reason: It is important for you to get feedback from relevant sources (community, other police officers, etc.) as you implement your plan of action. Unless these sources are aware of what you are doing, you will not get the feedback necessary to evaluate your efforts and possibly make modifications to the plan as you go along.

1. Who Do You Go to?

Where you go to get agreement on participating in the plan of action depends on what resources you need to carry it out. Let's go down the resource list again and suggest who may be in a position to agree to your plan.

a. **The CPO:** Where the plan of action depends solely on the CPO concerned, only the agreement of the CPOP supervisor is required. In gaining this, you should make sure that the supervisor fully understands what it is you want to do, what the commitment of your time is, and what actions you wish to carry out. In doing this, you not only get his input and approval, but also you lay the groundwork for your selection of tours, and his possibly running interference for you to prevent you from being diverted to some less important function.

b. **Other Members of the CPOP team:** Where the plan calls for assistance from other members of the CPOP team, the CPOP supervisor is, again, the man or woman to see. Make sure he or she understands exactly what resources are necessary, for what period of time, and for what purposes. If the unit van plays any part in the plan, make sure he or she knows that too.

c. **Other Precinct Resources:** Yes, you guessed it—the CPOP supervisor again. If the plan calls for the assistance of other precinct resources—anti-crime personnel, TOPAC, conditions, community affairs, crime prevention, and so forth, the CPOP supervisor is in the best position to get the commanding officer's approval and commitment and the cooperation of the other supervisors concerned. If the plan merely calls for the RMPs or foot patrol officers giving some extra attention to a location, you might speak to them yourself. However, even in this case if you really want the plan to work, talk to the supervisor and see if he will carry the ball with the other supervisors and perhaps even get the location listed on the roll calls for special attention.

d. **Other Department Resources:** By now you should be getting the idea—it's the CPOP supervisor again. Nothing prevents you from reaching out and talking to personnel or supervisors from other department units, but as far as formally getting their assistance, it is better left up to the supervisor and the precinct commander. Your role is important enough: You have to lay out the plan in detail, specify what assistance is needed, when, how, and with what end in mind. If you do that well, you enhance your chances of getting the help you need.

e. **Other City or Private Agencies:** Here is where networking comes in—reaching out to find out who does what, and how, and if they do not, who you can call next. Do not be afraid of calling another agency. Begin at the level of execution (the workers) or their supervisors, and work your way up. Find out if they can do what it is you need done. Whose approval do they need? What is the process? Who has to be asked? Does it have to be in writing? Who has to sign the request? After you find all of this out, run it past the CPOP supervisor for his or her approval.

One good place to start when you need help from other public or private agencies is with the district manager of the local Community Planning Board. District managers are problem solvers, and their knowledge of city government and the private resources available to help the community is probably as extensive as you are going to find. Get their input, and when possible, their assistance.

f. **Community Organizations:** The assistance of community organizations can be solicited in several ways. Community Patrol Officers should begin with those organizations with which they have had prior contact. Where the CPO knows one of the officers of the organization, that person should be approached. If no officers are known, the CPO should begin with whomever he has had prior contact with, and through that person, attempt to reach the organization's leadership.

Where a CPO is aware of the existence of a community organization that may be helpful in the implementation of a plan to deal with a community problem, but with which he has had no prior contact, the officer should determine if other members of the unit have established contacts with that organization. If not, the officer should determine if the precinct's community affairs officer or precinct commander has a contact in the organization, and if so, attempt to schedule an appointment with an officer of the organization through that person. If no one in the precinct has had prior contact with the organization, the CPO should attempt to schedule an appointment with one of its officers.

2. What to Get Agreement to

In attempting to gain concurrences for your plan of action, the persons or agencies approached should be fully briefed both on the general scope of the plan and on their role in its implementation. To do this, it is important to:

a. Review the objectives of the plan with them

b. Focus on the kind of solution you are seeking:

    (1) Eliminating the problem

    (2) Reducing the frequency of incidents

    (3) Reducing the harm from such incidents

c. Outline in detail their role in the implementation

d. Determine their ability and willingness to participate

e. Establish a timetable for implementation

f. Provide a mechanism for getting feedback as the plan is implemented

**Implementing the
Response**

If all of the steps leading up to implementation have been successfully completed, the plan should be implemented as scheduled. In doing this, several things should be kept in mind.

1. You should stick as closely as possible to the strategies that were agreed to in designing the plan and gaining concurrences for it.

2. Be flexible. If the initial strategies do not seem to be working, or if conditions change as a result of what you have done, do not be afraid to modify your response accordingly. However, keep in mind that if others are involved in the plan's implementation, keep them abreast of any changes in direction.

3. Provide for as much feedback as you can during the plan's implementation.

4. Keep records as you go along. Make entries in your Beat Book and activity log; keep a file of the 61s arising from the problem, and so forth.

**Evaluating the
Effectiveness of
the Response**

Evaluating the effectiveness of the response is an essential part of the problem-solving process. Without evaluation, we can never be sure if the strategy we have implemented is having the desired effect, or indeed any effect on the problem.

*1. What Are We
Looking For?*

Evaluation begins on the day that the strategy is implemented. Too soon for results? Perhaps so, but evaluation deals with more than just results. Information gathered for evaluation purposes can tell us:

a. Is the solution being implemented? This is the first thing that we should be looking at. Has the plan been implemented as designed? Are other people who have committed to participate in the strategy doing their part?

b. Do the initial results indicate a need to modify the plan of action?

c. Do the initial results indicate the need to look for an entirely new solution?

d. Does the plan appear to be working?

*2. Developing
Measures of
Effectiveness*

To determine if the plan of action is having any effect in dealing with the problem, we must develop measures that show if the strategy is working or not. These measures should be designed to show:

a. The effect of the strategy on the goals of the plan:

(1) Has the strategy eliminated the problem?

(2) Has the frequency of incidents been reduced?

(3) Has the harm from the incidents been reduced?

(4) Has the police handling of the problem been improved, and does the public perceive this?

b. The effect of the strategy on the dimensions of the problem:

(1) What was the effect of the strategy on the actors?

(a) How were the victims affected by the strategy?

(b) How were the offenders affected by the strategy?

(c) How were third parties affected by the strategy?

(2) What was the effect of the strategy on the other dimensions of the problem?

(a) If the strategy was designed to change the physical setting, did this occur? Was it effective in dealing with the problem?

(b) Was the social context changed? Was this effective in dealing with the problem?

(c) Did the sequence of events change? Was this effective in dealing with the problem?

(d) Did the result of the events change? Was this effective in dealing with the problem?

c. The effect of the strategy on the institutions and organizations involved or concerned:

(1) Did the resources committed to the implementation of the plan respond as required?

(2) How did the community respond to the implementation of the plan?

(3) How did institutions, public and private, respond to the implementation of the plan?

d. Was the plan sufficient to deal with the problem?

(1) Were sufficient resources devoted to the implementation of the plan?

(2) Were the components of the plan (the scheduled activities) done in the order needed for the plan to succeed?

(3) Was the plan really directed at the root problem (or problems) or just at the incidents produced by the problem?

3. What Are Appropriate Measures for Determining the Effectiveness of the Plan?

A number of techniques may be used to evaluate the effectiveness of a plan. All are designed to determine if the plan was effective in accomplishing its goals. Whichever method of evaluation is chosen, its underlying goal is to determine if anything has changed as a result of the implementation of the plan. Toward this end, you should gather and evaluate the same kinds of information that led to the identification of the plan in the first place.

a. Your personal observations while on patrol. Has anything changed? Does the strategy seem to have alleviated or eliminated the problem?

b. Talk to other police officers who work in the area and members of the precinct staff. Do they have any information on the problem? Do they observe any change in its magnitude?

c. Review police department records. Are there any changes in the number of incidents, their severity, their frequency, and so forth?

d. Conduct crime analysis. Has the crime pattern changed—hours of occurrence, location, and so forth?

e. Talk to representatives of other governmental agencies. Do they have new information on the problem? Has their perception of the problem changed?

f. Talk to representatives of local civic organizations (Block Associations, merchants' associations, etc.). Do they have new information on the problem? Has their perception of the problem changed?

g. Talk to the people who live and work on the beat. What can they contribute to your understanding of the success or failure of the strategy?

4. Keep in Mind That the Basic Purposes of Gathering This Information Are:

a. To determine the levels of success or failure of the plan.

b. To determine the reasons for the success or failure.

5. Draw Conclusions From the Data You Have Gathered

a. Did the plan succeed? If so:

(1) Make sure that the plan was implemented as designed. If it was, chances are that the solution worked, and you should continue monitoring the situation to prevent recurrence.

(2) If the problem was solved but you discover that the plan was not really implemented as designed, try to find out what really affected the problem so that you can use that information in the future for similar problems.

b. If the plan failed to impact on the problem, determine:

(1) Was the plan actually implemented as designed? If it was, it was not the answer, and you should go back to problem analysis to determine a new approach.

(2) If the plan was not implemented as designed, try to find out why. Can it be implemented? If not, go back to problem analysis and work on developing a new solution.

Summary: 1. Plans must be evaluated to determine if they are working.

2. To evaluate effectiveness, appropriate measures must be developed.

3. Information relative to the measures decided on must be gathered from a variety of sources.

4. The results must be interpreted.

Beginning Again Not every strategy designed to solve a problem will be successful. When evaluation discloses that the designed response was not totally successful in addressing the problem, the problem solving process should be begun anew.

1. Focus on what you have learned through experience and evaluation. Review what you did and what results those actions produced.

2. Is the original problem description valid? Did you identify the real problem or problems, or were you sidetracked by incidents resulting from the problem(s)? Would you still define the problem in the same terms, given what you have learned through attempting to deal with it? If not, how should the problem be redefined?

3. Go through problem analysis again. See if anything you learned changes the way in which you analyze the problem.

4. Design a new response. Review what you learned from the evaluation of your first plan and make necessary changes. If necessary, change your focus. If you cannot make the problem go away entirely, what can you do to mitigate it?

5. Gain necessary concurrences for the new response.

6. Implement the new response.

7. Evaluate the new plan's effectiveness.

8. Begin again if necessary. Some problems are tough, but if you stick with them long enough there is probably something you can do to alleviate them.

Problem Solving—The Long View . . . and the Longer View

Problem solving, by its very nature, is a long-range approach to dealing with the crime and order-maintenance conditions facing a community and the police who serve it. It seeks to go beyond incidents to identify and correct the problems that are their cause. It is a proactive approach to policing that holds great promise for improving the quality of general police services.

In subscribing to this philosophy, the New York City Police Department, through its Community Patrol Officer Program, has sought to identify and correct or ameliorate a wide range of problems. In carrying out this mandate, individual Community Patrol Officers and entire CPOP teams have developed a wide range of strategies designed to deal with specific community problems. The majority of these strategies have been narrowly directed at achieving specific goals—the elimination or reduction in severity of problems of concern to local communities. Other strategies have been developed, however, that take a longer view toward dealing with one of the most critical problems facing our communities—the care and nurturing of its youth.

CPOP units sponsor sports leagues, drug awareness programs, child safety programs, youth counseling, bicycle registration, rap sessions, scouting troops, and a number of other youth-oriented activities. Why this level of activity? Why are thousands of police hours being devoted to creating and maintaining programs for which there is no proven crime prevention payoff? Why do many CPOs and other police officers devote their own time to working with youth? One reason is because there is a need; a need caused by poverty, a genuine lack of opportunity, an absence of family stability, and a whole host of other socioeconomic factors. A need that exists in every community in our city. A need that has resulted in CPOs using portions of their time and energy in attempting to address it. A need that has also resulted in the police department devoting substantial resources in attempting to address portions of it (for example, SPECDA). There is, of course, a direct police objective for such activities, crime prevention. Regardless of the absence of scientific evidence to demonstrate that these various programs do indeed reduce delinquency, that is the hope. And after all, other kinds of evidence shows that these police efforts produce results. This is the evidence of personal experience and observation. CPOs throughout the city see much to encourage belief in the efficacy of these efforts. Minor miracles happen out there: Youthful drug addicts who, with the help and encouragement of a CPO, have entered rehabilitation programs for the first time. Neighborhood youth who have not dropped out of school because a CPO linked them to a counseling service or helped get them an after school job. And thousands of schoolchildren who never had the opportunity to know a police officer before and who now not only know their CPO, but also have begun to believe that cops really do care, and are there to help.

Some people question the police department's involvement in these activities. But you cannot tell that to CPOs, or to the personnel assigned to SPECDA (School Program to Educate and Control Drug Abuse), or to those other police officers who regularly give of their time and energy in attempting to help the youth in this city. You also cannot tell it to the police commissioner and the rest of his command staff, who not only encourage and support these activities, but who believe that they are the right thing to do even though they may not see any measurable results during their careers. It would be easy for a police commissioner, recognizing the relatively short tenure of a police chief in large American cities, to emphasize enforcement over prevention. To seize the immediate result rather than to invest in the future. It would be understandable for a CPO or any other police officer to want to advance his or her career by amassing an impressive arrest record rather than by diverting some energy to try to help some young person make a better life for himself or herself. Programs of this type may not produce immediate results for large numbers of people, but they often have demonstrable effects on individual lives and may provide long-term benefits for large numbers of people exposed to them as youths. That they exist reflects the vision and dedication of all involved. They are your, and the department's, investment in the future; in our greatest resource, our children. We cannot always prove that something we do really makes a difference, but sometimes you just have to believe.

References

Alpert, G., & Dunham, R. G. (1989). Community policing. In R. G. Dunham & G. P. Alpert (Eds.), *Critical issues in policing: Contemporary Readings* (pp. 406-424). Prospect Heights, IL: Waveland Press.

Barker, T., & Carter, D. L. (Eds.). (1986). *Police deviance*. Cincinnati, OH: Anderson.

Bayley, D. (1984). A world perspective on the role of the police in social control. In R. Donelan (Ed.), *The maintenance of order in society*. Toronto: Canadian Police College.

Bayley, D. H. (1988). Community policing: A report from the devil's advocate. In J. R. Greene & S. D. Mastrofski (Eds.), *Community policing: Rhetoric or reality* (pp. 225-238). New York: Praeger.

Behan, C. J. (1984, April). *The comprehensive robbery impact program of the Baltimore County Police Department*. Paper presented at the International Robbery Seminar.

Bittner, E. (1967). *The functions of police in modern society*. Washington, DC: Government Printing Office.

Bittner, E. (1983). Legality and workmanship: Introduction to control in the police organization. In M. Punch (Ed.), *Control in the police organization* (pp. 1-17). Cambridge: MIT Press.

Boydstun, J. E., & Sherry, M. E. (1975). *San Diego community profile: Final report*. Washington, DC: Police Foundation.

Brown, L. P. (1991). *Policing New York City in the 1990s: The strategy for community policing*. New York: New York City Police Department.

Brown, M. K. (1981). *Working the street*. New York: Russell Sage.

Chavis, D. M. (1987). *Evaluation of the police and community training program: Training, evaluation, and community needs.* Unpublished manuscript, Citizen's Committee for New York City.

Cosgrove, C. A., & McElroy, J. E. (1986). *The fixed tour experiment in the 115th precinct: Its effects on police officer stress, community perceptions, and precinct management.* New York: Vera Institute of Justice.

Eck, J. E., & Spelman, W. (1989). Problem-solving: Problem-oriented policing in Newport News. In R. G. Dunham & G. P. Alpert (Eds.), *Critical issues in policing: Contemporary readings* (pp. 425-550). Prospect Heights, IL: Waveland Press.

Farrell, M. J. (1988). The development of the community patrol officer program: Community-oriented policing in the New York City Police Department. In J. R. Greene & S. D. Mastrofski (Eds.), *Community policing: Rhetoric or reality* (pp. 73-88). New York: Praeger.

Fogelson, R. (1971). *Big city police.* Cambridge, MA: Urban Institute.

Goldstein, H. (1977). *Policing a free society.* Cambridge, MA: Ballinger.

Goldstein, H. (1979). Improving policing: A problem-oriented approach. *Crime and Delinquency 25*(2), 235-258.

Goldstein, H. (1990). *Problem-oriented policing.* New York: McGraw-Hill.

Goldstein, H., & Susmilch, C. E. (1981). *The problem-oriented approach to improving police service: A description of the project and an elaboration of the concept.* Madison: University of Wisconsin Law School.

Greene, J. R. (1989). Police and community relations: Where have we been and where are we going. In R. G. Dunham & G. P. Alpert (Eds.), *Critical issues in policing: Contemporary readings* (pp. 349-368). Prospect Heights, IL: Waveland Press.

Greene, J. R. (1991, November 14). *So what is community policing?* Testimony presented to the Public Safety Committee of the City Council of New York City.

Greene, J. R., & Taylor, R. B. (1988). Community-based policing and foot patrol: Issues of theory and evaluation. In J. R. Greene & S. D. Mastrofski (Eds.), *Community policing: Rhetoric or reality* (pp. 195-224). New York: Praeger.

Hartmann, F. X. (Ed.). (1988). Debating the evolution of American policing. *Perspectives on policing* (No. 5). Washington, DC: National Institute of Justice and Harvard University.

Kelling, G. L. (1988). Police and communities: The quiet revolution. *Perspectives on policing* (No. 1). Washington, DC: National Institute of Justice and Harvard University.

Kelling, G. L., & Moore, M. H. (1988). The evolving strategy of policing. *Perspectives on policing* (No. 4). Washington, DC: National Institute of Justice and Harvard University.

Kelling, G. L., & Stewart, J. K. (1989). Neighborhoods and police: The maintenance of civil authority. *Perspectives on policing* (No. 10). Washington, DC: National Institute of Justice and Harvard University.

Kelling, G. L., Wasserman, R., & Williams, H. (1988). Police accountability and community policing. *Perspectives on policing* (No.7). Washington, DC: National Institute of Justice and Harvard University.

Klockars, C. B. (1988). The rhetoric of community policing. In J. R. Greene & S. D. Mastrofski (Eds.), *Community policing: Rhetoric or reality* (pp. 239-258). New York: Praeger.

Manning, P. K. (1988). Community policing as a drama of control. In J. R. Greene & S. D. Mastrofski (Eds.), *Community policing: Rhetoric or reality* (pp. 27-46). New York: Praeger.

Manning, P. K. (1989). Community policing. In R. G. Dunham & G. P. Alpert (Eds.), *Critical issues in policing: Contemporary readings* (pp. 395-405). Prospect Heights, IL: Waveland Press.

Mastrofski, S. D. (1988). Community policing as reform: A cautionary tale. In J. R. Greene & S. D. Mastrofski (Eds.), *Community policing: Rhetoric or reality* (pp. 47-68). New York: Praeger.

McElroy, J. E. (1987). The police. In R. J. Janosik (Ed.), *The encyclopedia of the American judicial system: Studies of the principal institutions and processes of law* (Vol. 2, pp. 653-668). New York: Scribners.

McElroy, J. E. (1991, November 14). *Suggestions concerning city council oversight of community policing.* Testimony presented to the Public Safety Committee of the City Council of New York City.

Moore, M. H., & Kelling, G. L. (1983). To serve and protect: Learning from police history. *The Public Interest 70*, 22-48.

Moore, M. H., & Trojanowicz, R. C. (1988a). Corporate strategies for policing. *Perspectives on policing* (No. 6). Washington, DC: National Institute of Justice and Harvard University.

Moore, M. H., & Trojanowicz, R. C. (1988b). Policing and the fear of crime. *Perspectives on policing* (No. 3). Washington, DC: National Institute of Justice and Harvard University.

Moore, M. H., Trojanowicz, R. C., & Kelling, G. L. (1988). Crime and policing. *Perspectives on policing* (No. 2). Washington, DC: National Institute of Justice and Harvard University.

New York City Commission to Investigate Allegations of Police Corruption and the City's Anti-Corruption Procedures. (1972). *The Knapp commission report on police corruption.* New York: George Braziller.

New York City Police Department (NYPD). (1985, October). *The Community Patrol Officer Program: Implementation guide.* New York: Author.

New York City Police Department (NYPD). (1987). *The Community Patrol Officer Program: Orientation guide.* New York: Author.

New York City Police Department (NYPD). (1988, May). *The Community Patrol Officer Program: Supervisory guide*. New York: Author.

Police Foundation. (1981). *The Newark foot patrol experiment*. Washington, DC: Author.

Reiss, A. J. (1971). *The police and the public*. New Haven, CT: Yale University Press.

Rumbaut, R., & Bittner, E. (1979). Changing conceptions of the police role: A sociological review. In N. Morris & M. Tonry (Eds.), *Crime and justice: The annual review of research* (Vol. 1, pp. 239-288). Chicago: University of Chicago Press.

Sadd, S. (1989). *CPOP: Impacts on robberies, burglaries, and calls-for-service*. Unpublished manuscript.

Sherman, L. W. (1973). *Team policing: Seven case studies*. Washington, DC: Police Foundation.

Skogan, W. G. (1990). *Disorder and decline: Crime and the spiral of decay in American neighborhoods*. New York: Free Press.

Skogan, W. G., Lewis, D. A., Podelefsky, A., Dubow, F., & Gordon, M. T. (1982). *The reactions to the crime project* [Executive Summary]. Washington, DC: National Institute of Justice.

Skolnick, J. H., & Bayley, D. (1986). *The new blue line*. New York: Free Press.

Smith, D. C. (1991, November 14). *Measuring the success of community policing in New York City*. Testimony presented to the Public Safety Committee of the City Council of New York City.

Sparrow, M. K. (1988). Implementing community policing. *Perspectives on policing* (No. 9). Washington, DC: National Institute of Justice and Harvard University.

Sparrow, M. K., Moore, M. H., & Kennedy D. M. (1990). *Beyond 911: A new era for policing*. New York: Basic Books.

Trojanowicz, R. C. (1983). *An evaluation of the neighborhood foot patrol program in Flint, Michigan*. Lansing: Michigan State University.

Trojanowicz, R. C., & Bucqueroux, B. (1990). *Community policing: A contemporary perspective*. Cincinnati, OH: Anderson.

Uchida, C. D. (1989). The development of American police: An historical overview. In R. G. Dunham & G. P. Alpert (Eds.), *Critical issues in policing: Contemporary readings* (pp. 14-30. Prospect Heights, IL.: Waveland Press.

Wasserman, R., & Moore, M. H. (1988). Values in policing. *Perspectives on policing* (No. 8). Washington, DC: National Institute of Justice and Harvard University.

Weisburd, D., & McElroy, J. E. (1988). Enacting the CPO role: Findings from the New York City pilot program in community policing. In J. R. Greene & S. D. Mastrofski (Eds.), *Community policing: Rhetoric or reality* (pp. 89-102). New York: Praeger.

Weisburd, D., McElroy, J. E., & Hardyman, P. (1988). Challenges to supervision in community policing: Observations on a pilot project. *American Journal of Policing* 7(2), 29-50.

Williams, H., & Murphy, P. V. (1990). The evolving strategy of police: A minority view. *Perspectives on policing* (No. 13). Washington, DC: National Institute of Justice and Harvard University.

Wilson, J. Q., & Kelling, G. L. (1982, March). Broken windows. *The Atlantic Monthly*, pp. 29-38.

Wilson, J. Q., & Kelling, G. L. (1989, February). Making neighborhoods safe. *The Atlantic Monthly*, pp. 46-52.

Index

About the Authors

Jerome E. McElroy is Executive Director of the New York City Criminal Justice Agency, a nonprofit agency that provides pretrial services to the city's criminal courts. He was an Associate Director of the Vera Institute of Justice for a number of years, during which time he directed the research reported on here, as well as projects dealing with other police-related matters, including civilian complaints against the police, police officer stress and tour rotation, and the effects of postarrest investigations by police on dispositional outcomes in felony arrests. He was Deputy Administrator of the New York State Division of Criminal Justice Services when that agency served as the state planning agency under the LEAA program. He was a member of faculty at the John Jay College of Criminal Justice, Fordham College, and Fordham University Graduate School of Social Work, and serves as an adjunct faculty member to the New York City Police Academy. He is a member of the board of directors of the National Criminal Justice Association and has served on several advisory committees concerned with various criminal justice matters in his home state of New Jersey.

Colleen A. Cosgrove is Senior Research Associate at the New York City Criminal Justice Agency, where she directed an extensive study of criminal court case processing of misdemeanor arrests effected in New York City. Currently, she is directing various research projects pertaining to pretrial services. From 1979 to 1989, she was a Senior Research Associate at the Vera Institute of Justice where she collaborated with

258

Jerome McElroy on several studies on policing. She received her Ph.D. in criminal justice from the State University of New York at Albany. Her dissertation addressed the conceptual, legal, and policy issues involved in the formulation and implementation of sentencing and parole guidelines.

Susan Sadd received her Ph.D. in personality and social psychology from New York University. She is a Project Director at the Vera Institute of Justice in New York City and is currently directing a national evaluation of the Bureau of Justice Assistance's Innovative Neighborhood-Oriented Policing programs. Other Vera projects on which she has worked include the recently completed evaluation of the New York City Police Department's Tactical Narcotics Teams and the ongoing study of the Neighborhood Defender Service of Harlem.